Climbing and Screening Plants

This old-world cottage, with its Horsham stone roof, at Billingshurst, Sussex, is made all the more attractive by the clematis and wisteria covering its walls. A well-clipped hedge and screen of laburnum and conifer adds charm to the scene

Climbing and Screening Plants

Noël J. Prockter

With a chapter on *Pests and Diseases*
by Audrey V. Brooks, B.SC., M.I.BIOL.
and Joyce Maynard
and a chapter on
The Law Relating to Trees, Hedges,
Screens and Climbers
by Robert S. W. Pollard, L.A.M.T.P.I.

FABER & FABER
3 Queen Square London

First published in 1973
by Faber and Faber Limited
3 Queen Square London WC1
Printed in Great Britain by
Latimer Trend & Company Ltd Plymouth

ISBN 0 571 09786 3

To
my wife
SYBIL MARY
and in memory of my mother
ELIZABETH MARY

Contents

9

Illustrations

11

Preface

Good fences make good neighbours.
A hedge between keeps friends green.
18th-Century Country Proverb

Today, many owners of gardens have nothing like enough room to grow all the beautiful plants and shrubs which are now available. It may, therefore, be encouraging to know how wide a variety of plants, especially shrubs, can be grown successfully on a fence, wall or trellis. I am sure it is not widely appreciated that, by growing climbers and wall shrubs, the effective size of a small garden may be increased by as much as a quarter. Furthermore, it is not always realized how interesting and colourful shrubs can be when planted as a screen or hedge.

Even though modern planners have done their best to sweep away hedges there is still that inherent demand of the British people to achieve their privacy somehow. What could be better than an evergreen, flowering or mixed hedge? Then there are those who have plenty of room but may need a screen of broad leaved trees or conifers, or colourful climbing and twining plants.

It is for this reason that I feel there is a very real need for a book which caters for all such requirements, and describes the great variety of material available that will help to beautify the ugliest wall, shed, fence or building, or mask other features which may mar the landscape.

Crawley,   NOËL J. PROCKTER
Sussex

Acknowledgements

I am extremely grateful to Miss Audrey V. Brooks and Miss Joyce Maynard for Chapter 4 on *Pests and Diseases* and to Mr. Robert S. W. Pollard for Chapter 5 on *The Law Relating to Trees, Hedges, Screens and Climbers*. Their expert advice on their respective subjects is of great value to the book.

I am also grateful for the use of photographs from R. J. Corbin, Anthony Huxley, Christopher Lloyd, Alan Mitchell, A. and P. Oldale, Peter Wood and Harry Smith, who also supplied the colour photograph. And I much appreciate the help and co-operation given to me by the publishers.

16

Uses and Advantages

Twiners, climbers, trailers and screening plants have untold uses and advantages. Let me at once say that there are few gardens, even roof gardens in cities, which cannot accommodate a climber, such as a clematis, grown in a tub. Even in the smallest garden where room may be very limited, there is usually a wall which can take a climber like a rose, jasmine or honeysuckle.

Again, there are those who may be blessed with a larger garden, where perhaps there is an old apple tree, tree stump or something similar—such objects can be beautified by planting climbers and twiners to grow over them. Wisteria, clematis or Virginia creeper are very effective when used in this way.

All too frequently gardeners are faced with the task of covering or hiding an ugly building, and nothing is more suitable for this than a climbing plant or shrub. It may be that such a building is not in one's own garden, and when this is the case some other method will have to be adopted, for instance the use of a screen; in this sort of situation a hedge could be grown which would block out the offending building. Where room is not so precious, a screen of evergreen and/or deciduous trees can be planted. What is more, these can later act as supports for twiners and climbers. Or the problem may be a wall which is not high enough to screen the offending ugliness—here, then, provide a screen by pleaching (see page 293).

In coastal areas, hedges, walls, fences and belts of trees are almost essential to protect other plants against strong, drying winds and salt spray, in fact without such protection no other plants can be cultivated with any great success.

Then there are certain plants, particularly some shrubs, like passiflora and ceanothus, which need the protection of a wall or fence against the cold winds and frost.

B

Certain plants immediately spring to mind in connection with climbing and screening; one which is all too often maligned is the ivy; when grown against a wall or up a tree, or over an archway, ivy can look very charming. Equally, it can, and undoubtedly has, caused damage to walls and trees, though I must admit on an east wall of my childhood home at The Gables, Lingfield, ivy grew on a roughcast surface without apparent damage, where the rain never reached it—only the sparrows! I must, however, put in a plea for ivy as a good ground coverer, and also as a good fence coverer, especially *Hedera colchica* 'Dentata Variegata', with its large soft green leaves which are freely variegated with pale yellow. Ivy can also be used to make a fedge (see page 190).

Some plants are happier when they have a partner and where this is so, it is possible to have a longer season of beauty by planting two different kinds of plants together. A good example is a clematis planted along with a rose. A happy pair which I had in a previous garden was that beautiful early-flowering rambler rose 'Albertine', along with *Clematis jackmanii*. This meant that we started with 'Albertine' flowering in June, and followed with clematis from July to September, and frequently into early October.

Many shrubs which benefit from wall or fence cultivation have considerable merit in offering both flowers and berries, while others afford attractive autumn foliage; one which qualifies for both fruit and foliage is *Celastrus orbiculatus*.

It is not always possible or practicable to fix wires or trellis to a wall, but this can be overcome by planting climbers which are self-attaching like *Campsis radicans* and *Parthenocissus tricuspidata veitchii* which cling by their aerial roots.

When the planting area is small, this, too, can be overcome by choosing a shrub like *Cotoneaster horizontalis*, which appears to thrive in such situations. I know of a large house, now offices, which has several plants of *C. horizontalis* growing hard against the walls with a tarmac drive right up to the base of the stems—and they flourish.

In fact, today, with such a wealth of planting material, it is possible to find a climber or twiner, or hedge shrub, or screen tree, deciduous or evergreen, with interesting foliage, flowers or fruit to fit the requirements of the most fastidious of gardeners, and to provide the right setting to enhance every kind of garden.

Cultivation, Care and Maintenance

CULTIVATION

I find it a little difficult to decide which subject should be dealt with first
—rather like the question of the chicken or the egg—however, choice of
plants and their purchasing is, perhaps, all-important. After all, it is no
good going to a great deal of trouble in preparing the ground if, after it
is all done, you do not know what to grow or where you are going to
plant your climber, hedge or screen.

CHOICE OF PLANTS

As regards choice, this is in some ways just as difficult for the knowledgeable as the unknowledgeable. The first probably knows too much
and finds it hard to decide, the second knows nothing and does not
know where to start. Therefore, the second has to ask the first. There
are, however, various criteria upon which to base one's selection, and to
begin with, one should decide what is expected of the plant in relation to
the situation in which it is to be grown. One, is the plant to cover a wall,
a trellis, a fence or even climb or scramble up a tree? Two, is it to make
a hedge or a wind-break? Three, is it to block out an objectionable
neighbour, a factory or a power station? Four, is it wanted for its foliage,
flower, fruit or scent? Five, is the plant expected to grow fast or slowly?
Six, how many plants will be needed, how much will they cost, and
where can they be obtained? To the knowledgeable all such problems
should not really be a problem, but a pleasure, and that is the purpose of
this book, in which I have tried to provide sufficient information to help
the reader to beautify his or her garden according to pocket and
purpose.

So back to square one—what do we expect? Most people who ask me such posers as those I have enumerated have uppermost in their minds such points as, how soon will it flower and how quickly will it cover the wall, fence or trellis? If it is a climber or if it is to be a hedge, when will it reach a height of 5 or 6 feet? Does it need clipping at once, and so on.

Much the same applies to questions about screening trees, though pruning is not, as a rule, such a problem. Today, however, when screening trees are required, large or fairly large trees, in fact mature trees, can be purchased and planted—at a price. So when you hear your friends or would-be advisers tell you about 'instant' trees, remember that they are not as cheap as instant tea or coffee is to buy, or as easy to achieve. But such trees can be obtained, provided you deal with a firm that has properly prepared them some three to four years beforehand. No one in their right mind can expect a tree that has been growing in one place for a great number of years to be suddenly bulldozed up and replanted, and expect it to be just as it has been in the last 12 months—any more than human-beings can be transplanted when they have become set in their ways. Maybe I have laboured my point, but my task is to impart to my reader the pros and cons of this and many other points when dealing with climbing and hedge plants and screening trees.

Now, what about the choosing of the plants. First, decide where you want to plant your climber, hedge or screen, and what you expect it to do, when it is planted. Once these factors have been decided, the actual plants can be chosen with reference to the alphabetical lists which appear in Chapters 6 and 7.

Choosing climbing plants

If it is a climber, you must first decide where it is to be planted, and how much it can spread both in height and width. Is it to be deciduous or evergreen? Will it require some kind of support or will it attach itself, like ivy, by its aerial roots—or can it cling by its tendril-like leaves, such as clematis, or twist its stems like honeysuckle? Is it wanted for its flowers or for its foliage? If it is for flowers or autumn foliage, then the time of year when either is to be at its best must have a bearing on what is planted. It may flower, fruit and have fragrance. The last quality is, indeed, an added joy when planting on house walls, especially if they are near windows, or where there is a sitting-out place, for example, a patio.

Aspect must also be thought of—some climbers prefer full sun, while others are better in partial shade or even prefer or tolerate a northerly or easterly aspect. But, above everything else, all must have light—lack of this element can cause loss of vigour, poor flowering, and so on.

Choosing hedging and screening plants

When choosing a hedge, first decide whether it is to be evergreen or deciduous. Is it simply for a decorative purpose, perhaps to part one section of the garden from another, for example the flower garden from the vegetable or fruit plot? It may be required to disguise the coal bunker or dustbin. In such cases, an evergreen or at least a beech hedge, which retains its foliage through the winter, would be the choice. Suppose it is to be a hedge between garden and farmland, where livestock will be grazing, then make sure that what you plant is not poisonous or likely to harm the animals, for example *Taxus baccata* (yew), all parts of which are poisonous to both animals and man. Where a hedge or screen is required to surround a tennis court, then an evergreen will be the obvious choice, and something that will grow high enough to reach the normal height of a boundary fence. I have on more than one occasion seen *Thuja plicata* planted with success, for this purpose.

Soil and site must also be taken into account. Where the soil is chalk, avoid lime-hating plants, such as rhododendrons, azaleas and ericas. Then, again, do not plant hedges that prefer a well-drained soil in a situation where the soil is basically a heavy clay, where water is likely to be a nuisance, especially in winter. In a soil of this kind *Carpinus betulus* (hornbeam) or *Viburnum opulus* would be suitable.

Planting a hedge or screen in a coastal area has to have special consideration, salt spray and strong wind have to be contended with, together with chalky or dry sandy soil.

When thinking of screens, annoyance to neighbouring properties must not be overlooked, particularly when planting in industrial areas. So be careful to plant trees that can give the owner privacy without upsetting neighbours.

In choosing hedges or screening trees for industrial areas, special care must be taken, as some trees stand up better to dirt and grime than others; for instance limes (*Tilia*) and the evergreen oaks (*Quercus ilex*) are both suitable.

When a hedge or screen is to be planted near a public highway or footpath, endeavour to keep the hedge as far back from the public as possible. This has two advantages. First, there is less likelihood of overhanging branches being an annoyance to passers-by; secondly, if there is a wire fence already erected, it will make access easier between fence and hedge when trimming time comes round.

To some extent these remarks also apply to screen trees, though with these, there are other matters to consider. Avoid planting trees which bear edible fruits near a public highway, as boys will be boys, and after all who can blame them? Also avoid lime trees, unless *Tilia euchlora* is planted, as this species is practically free of aphid trouble, which can be so messy and tiresome. I remember walking along a pavement in Cambridge in 1964, or should I say trying to walk, where the pavement was just a black sticky mass of insect excreta deposited from aphids living on the lime leaves above. Also, when near a public highway, plant trees which need the minimum of pruning. This, of course, does not apply where room is unlimited.

A hazard which frequently bothers amateurs when planting screen trees is the effect their roots will have on drains and masonry. Poplar roots can play havoc with walls, and cracks will travel up from the ground to several storeys high. Poplar trees should be at least 50 to 60 ft. away from house walls and drains.

Conifers, on the other hand, are far less bother, as their root system is fibrous and not deep or tap-rooted like so many large-leaved deciduous trees.

PURCHASING

Having decided on your choice of hedging, screening or climbing plant, the next problem is what to purchase. How many times have I heard people say, 'You get what you pay for,' and to a great extent that is so, though not always. For example, you could purchase beech plants 5 to 6 ft. tall, pay a big price for them, and then find that an existing hedge started with plants 1½ to 2 ft. or 2 to 2½ ft. high would win hands down. I know, I have experienced such happenings. Equally so, a large plant of Ceanothus would not transplant anything like as satisfactorily as a smaller plant. Little or medium and good, is far better than a large one which may possibly have a lingering life.

Cost of plants depends sometimes on size, newness of one variety or species, sometimes on demand, but cheap goods rarely pay except when one buys small plants from a reliable source and is fully prepared to wait for them to grow larger.

Size

With screen trees, whether deciduous, evergreens or conifers, size is a relatively different matter, as such trees can be considerably larger, and often are. If mature trees are required for planting, do make certain that they have been properly transplanted, within the last five years—but not five months before they are bought.

Visiting nurseries

It will be well worth while to visit nurseries and flower shows, especially the larger ones like Chelsea, Southport, Shrewsbury, and also those held fortnightly by the Royal Horticultural Society in the Old and New Halls at Vincent Square, Greycoat Street, Westminster, London SW1. At such venues you will be able to see and talk to people who can explain the advantages and disadvantages of this or that plant. And in many nurseries you will be able to see mature specimens of climbing plants, hedges and screen trees.

Also, visit the gardens open to the public in aid of The Queen's District Nursing Association, The Royal Gardeners' Benevolent Society, and those gardens maintained by the National Trust. All such gardens have much to teach the would-be purchaser and many ideas can be obtained. At the same time one can see what to avoid. Always remember that gardeners are most friendly people and are always ready to help those who have little knowledge.

It will be found that certain firms specialize in particular plants, for example, clematis, roses, hedge plants, screening trees, conifers and so on, though most of the leading tree and shrub nurseries embrace all those plants I have mentioned.

Apart from everything else, go to a reputable nurseryman—but make it plain what you require by giving the correct name of the plant you want, its size, where the plant is to grow and on what soil and under what conditions. If you are not satisfied on receipt of goods inform the nurseryman at once, not weeks or months afterwards, for then the weather, the soil, or you yourself could be to blame. I had 20 years in the nursery trade and I have now had 26 years away from it, so I can see both sides of the nurseryman's fence.

If you are intending to collect your plants, be sure to inform the nurseryman of your plans, as during the busy lifting season, October to March, there is little time to break day-to-day routine.

23

Any particular points to look for when buying certain plants will be given individually in the alphabetical list.

PREPARATION OF GROUND

The initial preparation of the ground is vital, where a climber, hedge or screen tree is to be planted; it is not like an annual, here today and gone tomorrow, but will remain in the same position for many years. Therefore, thorough preparation is essential. I am still a great believer in double digging or bastard trenching. This does at least let you know what lies below the top spit of soil, most important where a new house has been built, for only too often the topsoil has been buried among the rubble and other rough unwanted material.

Let us first take the planting of a climber to grow against a wall, a position where the soil invariably becomes dry and is frequently starved and of poor quality. See to it that the ground is well prepared and enriched with humus, such as farmyard manure if it can be obtained, or peat, leafmould or well-rotted material from the compost heap, together with some bonemeal, two good handfuls to the square yard. Such advice is equally applicable whether a climber, a hedge or a screen tree is to be planted.

When planting hedges and screen trees, an even greater expanse of ground will need to be cultivated. For a hedge, a strip of ground at least 4 ft. wide should be thoroughly prepared. This will allow for a 1-ft. strip for the trench in which the hedge is to be planted with a 1½-ft. strip either side; these are necessary to facilitate weeding, watering and manuring or mulching in the early life of a successful hedge. Again, such advice applies to climbers and screen trees. Where large mature or semi-mature trees are to be planted, as a screen or windbreak or even as an isolated specimen or specimens, an area not less than a square 4 × 4 ft. should be cultivated, even 6 ft. or more should be allowed for large specimens. Here too, double digging should be practised.

The method is as follows. Mark out a strip of ground 4 ft. wide, then take out a 2-ft. wide trench across the strip at one end. Remove a spit depth of soil (10 in. or the height of a spade blade) and wheelbarrow this soil to the end of the strip where it will be needed to fill the very last trench. Now break up the bottom of the trench with a fork or spade, again to a depth of 10 in., but leave in its present position. On top of this place well-rotted compost, farmyard manure, leafmould, turf or weeds other than tap-rooted or pernicious weeds such as dandelion, couch grass, bell bine, ground elder, and so on. Then dig out the next 2 ft. width using the soil to fill the previously opened trench. This pattern is repeated until all the required area of ground has been dug.

PLANTING

Having selected, purchased and prepared, we now have to wait for the great day of the arrival of the plants.

If it is not possible to plant the newly-arrived plants from the nursery at once, dig a hole or short trench and line the plants out in this. The roots should be covered with soil which is trodden in firmly. This is known as heeling in, and is a good means of temporary storage. If weather conditions do not permit heeling in, then place them in a shed, preferably where they get plenty of light, and cover the roots with moist peat, leafmould, bracken or damp sacking; here they can remain for several days or a week or so if necessary. Do not plant when there is a deep frost in the ground or during heavy falls of snow, or very wet weather when the soil may become pugged and later hard and dry.

As I have already said, allow ample room in the hole or trench to give plenty of space in which the roots can spread themselves naturally and comfortably. In other words a pint pot into a gallon—but not vice versa. When planting a clematis, honeysuckle or wisteria for example, a hole 1×1 ft. will usually be ample, as such plants are mostly grown in pots or containers. But if planting a climbing rose, a larger hole will be required, $1\frac{1}{2} \times 1\frac{1}{2}$ ft. square. Hedges will need a trench 1 ft. wide, and as long as necessary. Screen trees require a space not less than 4×4 ft. square.

The depth of each hole can be predetermined in accordance with the size of the root ball; always place a root ball at the same depth as the plant was growing in the nursery before it was lifted. For pot-grown plants use as a guide the top of the ball of soil. For plants lifted from the open ground, look at the stems just above the ball of roots where a soil mark can be seen, indicating where the soil came to in the nursery bed. Re-plant so that this mark is just below the natural soil level.

With all climbers, once their roots have been spread out in the hole, give them a light covering of the following mixture: 2 good handfuls of meat and bonemeal added to 3 gallons of moist peat. Having spread the mixture over the roots, continue with finely broken up or sifted soil, firming it lightly as filling-in proceeds, and finally complete filling-in with the ordinary coarser soil, making it reasonably firm—not as hard as concrete—but, still, firm rather than loose.

25

Plants from pots are not disturbed by re-planting, or if they are, only very slightly. If the roots around the ball of soil are very thickly matted it may indicate that the plants have been in their pots for a very long time, and in such cases a slight easing of the roots will be advantageous.

Hedge plants, screen trees, deciduous trees and conifers will need firm planting, especially the screen trees, because of their greater weight of growth, stems and branches; evergreens, too, have more material to carry water in wet weather, and these can all help to cause movement around the base of the stem or trunk. Any such movement should be avoided, as damage can easily be caused to the roots. For this reason secure staking is necessary for all trees with stems and a head of branches. Always see that the stake holds the trees up. All too often one sees the tree holding up the stake! All stakes should be placed in position in the hole and driven into the ground before any soil is filled in. By this method it can be ensured that the roots will not be damaged.

With large trees and open ground plants not grown in pots trim all damaged roots with a pair of secateurs or a sharp pruning knife. In fact I usually give the roots of all climbers, including roses, that have been lifted from the open ground, a light pruning. When several plants are to be planted at one session, cover the roots of those waiting for their turn, with sacking, polythene, straw or bracken, or the wind will dry them.

In very wet soil it is an advantage to place the plants so that the finished planting level is a little higher than normal soil level, but it will be necessary to give an extra depth of soil over and around the roots. Such a practice is only required in very exceptional cases. Be sure to inspect newly installed plants after a frost as it will often be found that plants rise up out of the soil, and on inspection it will be noticed that cavities have formed around the base of the stems. If these are left, more frost and rain can seep down to the roots and should they become frozen damage will be caused. To prevent this, firm the soil again around the plants. Similar trouble can be caused by plants swaying in the wind. There, too, the soil must be refirmed to prevent further damage.

WATER AND MULCHING

Whether the plants are climbers growing beside a wall or fence, part of a hedge, or screen trees, attention must be paid to moisture at the roots. But let me at once say it is almost useless giving a climber a 3-gallon canful of water in very hot dry weather, as the soil will simply soak it up like blotting-paper. Such advice also applies to a hedge or screen tree, whether deciduous or evergreen. The answer is to give it a thorough soaking. On one occasion I had a tree of *Prunus serrula* which in one very hot summer was dropping its leaves by the barrow load, so I gave it 30 gallons of water. After this dose you could see the tree throwing up its branches—as a gesture of thanks—and the leaves taking up the moisture. Leaf dropping stopped and the tree continued to flourish. I know this is perhaps a drastic measure, but it surely illustrates that when you water you must give the plants a real drink.

Where evergreens are concerned, spray the foliage as well, for after all they have a very large surface of living material that has to be kept functioning. A good spraying with clean water in the evening after sunset will work wonders with a flagging 'panting' conifer or broad-leaved evergreen such as a laurel or rhododendron.

Another point to remember about newly-planted evergreens is that, if the foliage starts to fall off easily, this is an indication that the roots are making fresh growth. There is no need to be alarmed; on the contrary, it is when the foliage droops but remains on the plant that all is not well. I once had a laurel which was almost denuded of foliage, but by the treatment I have suggested it recovered and put forth a fresh batch of young green leaves.

Having given moisture at the roots, save yourself further work by applying a mulch of peat, leafmould, rotted manure, rotted garden compost, lawn mowings, sawdust or composted bracken, creating a blanket-like covering about 2 in. thick to retain the moisture in the ground.

AFTERCARE IN WINTER

This entails protection from frost and cold drying winds, and these, I may say, can be devastating—often disastrous—particularly with young conifers. Plants are like people, they need care and attention in their early days. Today we are more than fortunate in having polythene, which is so easily adaptable, even to the extent of possibly completely surrounding the plant with it. It is, however, very necessary to give protection to young conifers. One too often sees newly-planted conifers in late spring looking literally browned off, all due to lack of shelter from cold winds and frost. A few stakes driven in around a climber or young hedge plants, and a length or polythene or sacking erected on either the windward side or all around the plants in early autumn, will help to keep the foliage green and supple. Then in late spring or very early summer when the weather is more amiable, the covering can be removed. Another method of protection is to fix wattle hurdling, wire-netting interlaced with bracken, or with straw tied to it, or anything which will keep off the wind, close to the plant. This does not mean that the plants should be coddled.

FEEDING

It must be remembered that climbers, hedge plants and screen trees will probably be growing in the same ground for a very long time, therefore they will need some form of nourishment from time to time; though shrubs and trees, on the whole, do not require very rich soil or an abundance of artificial fertilizers as do many soft-wooded or herbaceous plants, such as dahlias, chrysanthemums, delphiniums and so on. As a general rule the most satisfactory food for hard-wooded plants, both deciduous and evergreen, is farmyard manure, when you can get it. Failing farmyard manure, then peat and bonemeal or dried blood or a mixture of the two will be satisfactory. Bonemeal contains valuable plant foods especially phosphorus and calcium, with small amounts of nitrogen; whereas dried blood is high in nitrogen. Bonemeal can be applied at the rate of 3 to 4 oz. per sq. yd., dried blood at 2 oz. per sq. yd., or in liquid form at 1 oz. per gallon of water; it is, however, best applied in a dry form. A mixture of dried blood and bonemeal, 50 per cent of each, can be applied at a rate of 3 to 6 oz. per sq. yd., using the larger quantity for established hedges or screens.

Where farmyard manure can be obtained, see that it is thoroughly rotted before it is used, either dug in or as a mulch. Leafmould is also more beneficial when well rotted. Peat should always be properly moistened before it is applied either as a mulch or when incorporating it at the time of digging or planting.

Hop manure or spent hops are excellent as a mulch and can be applied at the rate of one barrow load to 6 to 12 sq. yd.

PRUNING

The first essential in pruning is to have good tools with which to do the pruning and secondly, to have the right type of tool for the job. Today, there are several excellent makes of secateurs on the market, though often it is a matter of personal taste which one uses. Many prefer to use

28

the 'anvil' type, where the cutting blade presses down on to the 'anvil'. Others prefer the cutting blades curved like those of a parrot's bill, or the type like a guillotine where a sharp-edged cutting blade passes closely beside another blade. Then there are shears, the long-handled parrot-bill pruners, the long-arm pruners and, where large limbs or branches have to be cut off, plenty of good pruning saws are available.

The pruning of climbers in a good many cases simply entails tidying up and re-tying. Individual instructions will be given where it is necessary in the alphabetical list, Chapter 7.

One point to be remembered is always to make a clean cut, and not to leave snags, i.e. a piece of shoot or branch above a growth bud, which could rot and eventually cause decay further back in the plant. Always cut to a bud, whenever it is possible, and endeavour to cut to a bud which is pointing outwards.

Where plants have grown out of hand, most can stand hard pruning, and most will usually respond to drastic cutting back; needless to say in some cases this will cause loss of flower or berry for a season or two, but the eventual result will be worth while.

The amount of pruning necessary immediately after planting varies from plant to plant. Clematis for example, need to be cut back in March after planting, to within 12 in. of ground level. But such treatment would not be used on *Magnolia grandiflora*.

As for hedges, most will benefit from being cut back after planting, usually in March or early April. Though even here there are exceptions: beech and hornbeam do not require any pruning during the first two years after planting. Screen trees may or may not need any pruning, if well-grown specimens have been purchased. Overgrown hedges can be severely pruned and after such treatment even thicker hedges will result.

Sometimes hedges need to be 'laid', this entails cutting out all unwanted growths, down to ground level, the remainder being half-severed at the base. These growths are then bent over at an angle of 45° to the ground; they are kept in position by being interlaced between freshly cut or 'dead' stakes driven into the ground some 6–8in from the centre of the hedge and at the back of the cut-down stools. Stakes can be made of beech, hazel, thorn or sweet chestnut. All half-severed growths are laid in the same direction.

The time to prune, of course, varies very considerably, though with many climbers pruning is carried out immediately after flowering, but, again, be guided by the notes in Chapter 7. In most cases prunings are best destroyed by burning, though soft prunings can be composted.

In the pruning of established trees where large limbs have been cut off, all wounds should be carefully cleaned and treated with a bituminous tree dressing.

Hedge trimming the old-fashioned way with shears, secateurs or sickle has been largely superseded by mechanical hedge cutters except for the smallest hedges. There are machines which can be operated direct off the mains, but when using such a machine it is wise to have it operated through a transformer. Alternatively, there are machines which can be operated off a battery-powered electric motor mower or a knapsack battery. There are also petrol-driven machines. When there is not an undue amount of hedge trimming to be done, the most sensible machine to use would be one taking power from a knapsack battery type. With such machines there is only a minimum of cable to worry about, whereas with a machine direct off the mains, the length of cable can be considerable.

Each year manufacturers are improving on their designs and making them as safe to use as possible, but for obvious reasons they can be dangerous if not used correctly. Never allow children to use them, and keep them well away when a hedge cutter is in use. If the machine should fall out of your grip do not try to catch it—let it fall—always remembering that there is another hedge cutter but not another 'you'.

There are single- and double-bladed machines. The lengths of blade vary from 12, 15 to 18 in. In weight they vary from about 5 to 8 lb.

I would emphasize again, though, the importance of taking care when using powered hedge cutters. They are a boon to so many of us but they are not machines to be used by the careless.

PROPAGATION

It is not my intention to deal with the subject of propagation in too great a detail, but only to give enough information for an amateur to reproduce some of his favourite plants, either for his own use or to give away to friends.

There are five main methods of propagating plants: seed, division, layering, cuttings, and grafting (including budding, which is a form of grafting).

Seed

This is the method by which most flowering plants are spread and reproduced. Many plants come true from seed and are replicas of their parents, but not all, and, that is why we need to resort to other methods of propagation, which I will explain later.

If it is intended to collect seed from your own plants, see that it comes from healthy stock. Collect seed heads or pods on a dry day and afterwards place them in a dry, cool airy shed or room. There are many different forms and shapes of seeds. Some are almost dust-like, others are fleshy, oily, winged, plumed or hard-coated. With certain seeds special treatment is required to induce them to germinate. Such seed as that of holly, hawthorn and rose must be stratified, this is because the seed coats are very hard. To stratify seeds place the berries or rose hips in a mixture of half peat and half sand, and put this in a pot or box. These receptacles must then be left beside a north hedge or fence for 6 to 12 or 18 months (taking care to protect them from vermin), after which time the seed can be sown.

Seeds can either be sown out of doors, or in pots, pans or boxes, which can be placed in a frame or greenhouse. The basic needs for successful germination are moisture, air, warmth and, finally, light. The last is particularly necessary after germination.

With outdoor sowing, obtain a fine tilth on the seed bed, by raking and re-raking the soil until it is in a good crumbly condition.

When sowing in pots, pans or boxes, these should be clean and well crocked by putting some pieces of pot, placed with the convex curve upwards, or small pebbles at the bottom of the receptacle to aid good drainage.

Fill the containers with specially prepared seed compost such as John Innes Seed Compost, which can be purchased or made up as follows: 2 parts loam (sifted through $\frac{3}{8}$-in. sieve), 1 part moss peat (horticultural grade), 1 part coarse sand (grading evenly from dust to $\frac{1}{8}$-in. particles). Add to each bushel of the mixture: $1\frac{1}{2}$ oz. superphosphate and $\frac{3}{4}$ oz. chalk. Compost which is suitable for growing on is the John Innes Potting Compost, consisting of: 7 parts loam (sifted through $\frac{3}{8}$-in. sieve), 3 parts moss peat (horticultural grade), 2 parts coarse sand (graded evenly from dust to $\frac{1}{8}$-in. particles). Add to each bushel of the mixture: $\frac{3}{4}$ oz. chalk or ground limestone, 4 oz. of base fertilizer. The base fertilizer can be prepared by mixing equal parts by weight of hoof and horn and superphosphate of lime and half a part of sulphate of potash. 2 lb. hoof and horn meal, 2 lb. superphosphate of lime and 1 lb. sulphate of potash will make a convenient quantity which can be stored in a tin indefinitely.

Alternatives can be used, dried blood instead of hoof and horn meal,

31

at the same rate, and muriate of potash at $\frac{1}{2}$ oz. per bushel in place of sulphate of potash. As a substitute for peat, well rotted beech or oak leaves can be used. But good loam is essential.

One of the soilless composts can be used for seed sowing instead of John Innes Seed Compost. Always sow seed thinly, and see that the compost is nicely moist but never saturated. Cover the containers with a piece of glass or polythene and newspaper. These must be removed as soon as the seeds germinate. Prick off the seedlings when their seed leaves are formed and they are large enough to handle. Such seedlings are dibbled into boxes or pots of the growing-on compost.

Division

This is an easy and simple method of increasing plants vegetatively, which entails separating an old plant and either planting or potting up the divided pieces singly to grow into larger plants.

This method of propagation is not used much with climbers, though some smaller hedge plants can be increased in this way, for example, lavender and heathers (ericas).

Layering

This is one of nature's ways of reproduction, just as seed is. Take, for example, the blackberry, which roots at the tip of a shoot when it touches the ground. The propagator, on the other hand, prepares his layer by bending down a conveniently-placed shoot, and either giving it a twist or making a small cut in the under surface to form a tongue at the point where the shoot touches the soil. The cut or twisted part is then inserted and pegged in a V-shaped trench in the soil, to which should first be added some peat and sand to aid rooting. Once the layer has formed roots it can be separated from the parent plant. Ivies, wisteria and clematis are examples of plants which can be layered successfully.

Air layering

With some ornamental trees, such as cherries or magnolias, air layering can be used. This is usually undertaken in April. Choose a young healthy shoot of the previous season's growth (i.e. one-year-old wood) about pencil thickness or a little thicker, depending on the tree or shrub to be layered. At about 6 to 12 in. from the tip of the shoot, make a longitudinal cut $1\frac{1}{2}$ to 2 in. long in an upward direction. Start the incision

ABOVE LEFT: the flowers of *Carpentaria californica* are pure white
CENTRE LEFT: *Dendromecon rigida* has buttercup yellow flowers
LEFT: the lantern-like flowers of *Abutilon megapotamicum* are red and yellow
ABOVE: *Abutilon vitifolium* 'Album' has white flowers

ABOVE LEFT: *Choisya ternata* has almond scented, white blooms
ABOVE RIGHT: the white flowers of *Osmanthus delavayi* are sweetly scented
BELOW LEFT: Laurustinus, *Viburnum tinus*, produces white and pink blossoms
BELOW RIGHT: the fragrant white and pink flowers of *Viburnum burkwoodii*

below a leaf-stalk or joint and continue it through the joint so as to leave a tongue. Both surfaces of the cut should be treated with hormone rooting powder, and a wad of clean sphagnum moss can be placed in the cut to keep the tongue open. Now cover the partly severed portion with clean sphagnum moss, first soaked in rain water, and slip over this a polythene sleeve. Secure either end with adhesive tape, making sure the ends are air tight. It will be 8 to 12 weeks before rooting will be noticeable. When well rooted the young layer can be cut off and potted to grow on. The weaning of the rooted air layers is the most tricky part of the operation.

Cuttings

Like seeds, there are various types of cuttings, but the three which concern us most are soft-wood cuttings, half-ripe cuttings and hard-wood cuttings.

Soft-wood cuttings are prepared from young growth and are mostly taken in spring and early summer and rooted under glass, while cuttings taken earlier are given some heat. The cuttings are 2 to 3 in. long, and the leaves, together with the leaf stalk, are removed from the lower part of the cuttings. They are then put in a rooting medium consisting of sand, peat, vermiculite or similar materials, and the container covered with a sheet of glass or polythene, to prevent moisture loss while the cuttings are rooting.

Half-ripe cuttings are as the name implies—not soft, yet not hard; they are taken from older growth that is beginning to harden. These, too, are rooted under glass in the same way as soft cuttings, mostly without heat, though here again some require a little bottom heat. Today, with mist propagation—which I shall briefly describe later—almost any cutting can be rooted at almost any time of the year.

Hard-wood cuttings are taken from well-ripened (that is, woody) one-year-old shoots of such shrubs as kerria, forsythia and climbing roses. The cuttings are usually anything from 9 to 12 in. long, and taken in autumn or early winter. The leaves are trimmed from the lower half, and the cuttings are inserted out-of-doors in a sandy cuttings compost in open frames, or sheltered borders. Rooting of all these kinds of cuttings can be hastened if the base of the cutting is dipped into a hormone rooting powder.

Mist propagation

By this method the cuttings are regularly enveloped, at set intervals, with a very fine mist. The mist is regulated by the use of an artificial or 'electronic leaf', though in point of fact it neither resembles a leaf, nor is it electronic. What this instrument does is detect, by a controlling electrical circuit, the need for moisture, when it automatically turns on the water supply. The leaf or detector is placed in the centre of the cuttings, and all the time it is moist no water is ejected, but as soon as it becomes dry, the water is turned on for a predetermined period and applied through jets fixed above the cuttings to give a very fine mist. Today, there are several instruments on the market.

Composts for the cuttings
I recommend those used by the Royal Horticultural Society at their garden, Wisley.
   For most non-ericaceous plants:
      1 part fine Bedfordshire silver sand
      1 part sharp, gritty, river-washed sand.
   For acid-peat-loving plants:
      1 part fine Bedfordshire silver sand
      1 part sharp, gritty, river-washed sand
      1 part acid granulated peat.
   After rooting in this way it is important that the cuttings should not receive a check, and they must, therefore, be potted and grown on in the first place in a greenhouse.

Budding and grafting

This is far too wide a subject to try and explain in a few words, and probably only the most ambitious amateur will undertake the grafting or budding of ornamental trees.
   However, many amateurs bud their roses so, for those who wish to propagate climbing roses in this way, I will give very briefly the methods used for budding. First, you will need stocks of briar seedlings, or rooted cuttings of *Rosa canina*, or *R. rugosa*. If you are using cuttings these must be planted the previous autumn for budding-on the following July. Select the buds from shoots that have already flowered. Having cut off the shoot, remove all leaves, but leave a small portion of each leaf-stalk about $\frac{1}{2}$ in. long. This will act as a handle when inserting the bud in

34

the stock. To remove the bud, make a slanting cut, starting ½ to 1 in. below the bud and emerging the same distance above it. Now hold the bud in the left hand by the piece of leaf-stalk that remains, and with the right thumb and first finger grip the sliver of wood at the back of the bud and give it a sharp lift upwards, pulling backwards towards the base of the bud with a quick bending action. This will leave a little knob (the bud trace) in the shield.

Once the bud is ready, make a T-shaped cut in the stock, just above soil level. First make a horizontal cut, then a vertical cut to form the T. The two flaps or lips are then opened by the spatula end of the budding knife; the bud is inserted by pushing it into the T-shaped incision. Cut off any unwanted leaf-stalk level with the top of the T and bind in the bud with wide moist raffia or one of the special budding ties now on the market, which consist of a small piece of rubber and two little teeth to fix the ends together.

In the following February or early March the stock should be cut back carefully to just above the inserted bud. Suitable supports should be provided so that the new growth can be tied to them as they grow. Any suckers which may be produced must be removed at once.

Supporting Materials

This chapter deals with materials used to support climbing plants, in some instances because they have no natural method of attaching themselves, even when support is provided. It is, I think, generally accepted that the majority of climbing plants need some kind of artificial support unless it is intended that they should cover a man-made or natural bank.

WALLS, FENCES AND TREES

Undoubtedly the most common type of support is the garden or house wall or wooden fence. More natural support is found on trees alive or dead. The living trees can be either deciduous or evergreen. An example of the latter is *Tropaeolum speciosum*, the Scotch Flame Flower, which is sometimes seen growing on an old yew tree where its stems and 5- to 6-lobed leaves scramble through in search of the sun, rewarding its owner with pretty little scarlet-coloured nasturtium flowers. Roses, clematis, wisteria, honeysuckles, vines and many others look well when scrambling through the branches of large or medium-sized trees.

Support against walls

Walls and fences can support many climbers without any other additional form of support, at least those that have aerial roots which securely attach themselves to a wall or fence. Where climbers that do not have these natural forms of attachments are to be grown, additional support must be found. Wire netting, vine 'eyes' with galvanized or plastic-coated wires, and trellis made of wooden laths, are all well tried methods of support.

An excellent support which I have used in my own garden is a plastic-coated wire, coloured an attractive shade of green. It is made in two sizes: 6 × 3 ft., and 4 × 2 ft., in 6-in squares. And although modern, it looks very pleasing and in no way spoils the look even of older houses. It is easy to fix, and ideal for all kinds of climbing plants or shrubs.

Other materials of a similar kind which can also be used are chain link fencing and a square-meshed, rigid netting, in various sizes. I personally favour the 2-in. square for climbing plants. It can be obtained in various colours, green, white, black or yellow.

MATERIALS FOR FENCES AND WALLS

Fences can be oak palings, chestnut fencing, interwoven slats, slats which are well spaced, interwoven willow or hazel wattle hurdles. Not only are these useful for supporting climbers, but they will also act as protection against wind damage in an exposed garden; this is especially necessary in coastal areas. Hurdles are ideal as protection against drying winds when hedges are first planted, particularly so in the case of conifers, such as *Chamaecyparis lawsoniana*. More young plants are lost through wind damage, almost more than through frost damage, though hurdles help to protect newly-planted hedges against both wind and frost damage.

Trellis can be constructed from hard or soft woods, though the former will naturally last very much longer. For rustic work larch or chestnut is best, though if birch is used its life is not long. Rustic fencing can be bought ready for erection. Walls can be built of brick, sandstone or concrete, and today there are many attractive precast concrete bricks and slabs which can be readily used to act as a support for climbing plants.

PERGOLAS AND TRIPODS

Pergolas can be made of brick, stone or wood and joined by wooden beams, rope or chains, though today pergolas are not used as much as they were in the first half of the twentieth century. This is partly due to the cost of the materials and labour, and partly because gardens are smaller than they used to be. Wood pergolas can also be bought ready for erection.

Tripods of larch or chestnut poles are excellent, particularly for growing climbing roses, honeysuckles, wisteria, clematis and similar plants.

As wood rots in the ground it is essential to treat it chemically, at least the portion of each post which is to go in the ground. This can be achieved either by treating them with a copper naphthanate preparation, or with creosote, which is sometimes used, though I am always scared of it lest it should damage the roots of the climber. An even further precaution against rot is to insert the end of each post in a drainpipe sunk in the ground all but some 6 in. The post should be a little wider in diameter than the diameter of the drainpipe.

HEDGES AS SCREENS

Where hedges are planted it is not usually necessary to give them any form of support, unless large established hedge shrubs are being planted, such as yews, laurels or conifers. Where a screen of large conifers is being planted in a windswept place, then support of either individual stakes, or posts and wires, may sometimes be necessary. Such support will be required with deciduous screening trees like poplars, maples, limes, birch and so on.

Where any tying to trees has to be done, see that some form of buffer is made between the tree and the stake, by wrapping sacking or strips of rubber around the stem of the tree before it is tied to the stake. And always see that the stake holds the tree up, and not the tree the stake.

There are also rubber tree ties, though today toughened-plastic ties have taken their place.

Pests and Diseases

by AUDREY V. BROOKS, B.SC., M.I. BIOL.
and JOYCE MAYNARD.

It is not always readily appreciated by the amateur that an insecticide will not deal with a disease any more than a fungicide will kill a pest (insect), and in some cases neither an insecticide nor a fungicide will be the answer, for instance where the trouble is a physiological disorder. In many instances the attacks of pests and diseases can be greatly reduced by good cultivation; this is not always so, but it undoubtedly helps.

To make things easier for the reader we have indicated in each case whether the trouble in question is caused by an insect or a fungus.

ACER

Acer Gall-Mites, *Phyllocoptes acericola* (Mite)

Clusters of red pustules on leaves, caused by microscopic gall-mites. Not important.

CONTROL: If feasible, spraying with lime sulphur in spring when leaf buds are opening should be effective.

Root Rot, *see* Ligustrum

Scorch (Physiological disorder)

Leaves turn brown, particularly around the margins, and they then curl and shrivel, giving a scorched appearance. Cold winds or frost, or occasionally hot sun, cause this trouble on leaves of weak trees or those affected by too dry soil conditions.

39

CONTROL: Plant tree in sheltered spot. Mulch and water in dry periods.

Tar Spot, *Rhytisma acerinum* (Fungus)

Large black spots with a bright yellow edge develop on leaves during summer.

CONTROL: Rake up and burn affected leaves. Spray with a copper fungicide in the spring, soon after leaves unfold.

ARBUTUS

Leaf Spot, *Septoria unedonis* (Fungus)

Small brown spots are produced on the leaves.

CONTROL: Pick off affected leaves.

AZALEA, *see* Rhododendron

BAMBOO

Aphids (Insects)

CONTROL: Spray with malathion at first signs of attack.

BEECH, *see* Fagus

BERBERIS

Aphids (Insects)

CONTROL: Spray with malathion as necessary, except at flowering time.

BETULA

Aphids (Insects)

Infestations often lead to blackened foliage due to growth of sooty moulds on the honeydew secreted by the insects.

CONTROL: Spray with malathion in early summer, if feasible.

Rust, *Melampsoridium betulinum* (Fungus)

Bright reddish-yellow spots develop on the leaves and powdery masses of orange spores are released from raised spots on the undersurface. Premature defoliation may occur.

CONTROL: The disease is rarely serious enough to warrant special control measures.

BIRCH, *see* Betula

BOX, *see* Buxus

BUDDLEIA

Capsid Bugs, *Lygocoris pabulinus* (Insect)

Leaves perforated and shoots distorted.

CONTROL: Spray with trichlorphon or BHC as necessary except during flowering period.

Earwigs, *Forficula auricularia* (Insect)

These insects eat holes in the foliage at night.

CONTROL: Spray with trichlorphon but never during flowering period. Trap in rolls of corrugated cardboard fixed around stems.

BUXUS

Box Sucker, *Psylla buxi* (Insect)

Tips of shoots become cabbage-like due to tiny, crab-like sucker nymphs feeding inside.

CONTROL: Spray with malathion or BHC at 14-day intervals during June and July.

Leaf Spots, *Phyllosticta buxina* and other fungi (Fungus)

Pale brown spots develop on the leaves.

CONTROL: Pick off affected leaves and spray with a copper fungicide.

Mussel Scale, *Lepidosaphes ulmi* (Insects)

Stems encrusted with small, flat, mussel-shaped scales.

CONTROL: Spray with malathion whenever seen.

Rust, *Puccinia buxi* (Fungus)

Small dark brown powdery masses of spores are produced on both leaf surfaces.

CONTROL: Burn affected leaves.

CALLUNA

Wilt, *see* Erica

CAMELLIA

Bud drop (Physiological disorder)

Too dry soil conditions during period when buds are beginning to develop causes them to fall off just before flowering.

CONTROL: Mulch well and water in dry periods, especially in late August and September.

Vine Weevil, *Otiorrhynchus sulcatus* (Insect)

Wingless Weevils.

Clay-coloured Weevil, *O. singularis* (Insect)

Leaf margins notched by nocturnally feeding weevil adults.

CONTROL: Spray with BHC when fresh damage is seen from about late April until autumn.

42

CARPINUS

Leafhopper, *Typhlocyba douglasi* (Insect)

Pale yellow wedge-shaped insects; adults winged. Cause silver mottling on leaves.

CONTROL: Spray with BHC or malathion as necessary.

Root Rot, *see* Ligustrum

Winter Moth Caterpillar, *Operophtera brumata*, etc. (Insect)

'Looper' caterpillars, active in early spring, eating young foliage.

CONTROL: Spray with derris or trichlorphon at first signs of attack.

CEANOTHUS

Brown Scale, *Parthenolecanium corni* (Insect)

Young scales are small, flat oval creatures which move freely over the plant. Later, they settle in one spot on the stems and become glossy, chestnut-brown and dome-shaped. The females lay eggs and die, but the dome-shaped husks remain, protecting the eggs.

CONTROL: Spray with malathion when young scales are observed but never at flowering time.

CHAENOMELES

Fireblight, *see* Crataegus

CHAMAECYPARIS

Aphids (Insects)

CONTROL: Spray with malathion as necessary.

Conifer Spinning Mite, *see* Picea

43

Juniper Scale, *see* Juniperus

CHERRY AND CHERRY LAUREL, *see* Prunus

CLEMATIS

Earwigs, *see* Buddleia

Powdery Mildew, *Erysiphe ranunculi* (Fungus)

Leaves become covered with a white powdery coating.

CONTROL: Spray with dinocap.

Wilt, *Ascochyta clematidina* (Fungus)

One or more shoots wilt and die very rapidly, often right down to the base of the plant. New shoots usually develop in due course.

CONTROL: Cut out all dead parts back to living tissues and paint wounds, however small, with a fungicidal wound paint. Spray developing shoots with a copper fungicide.

Wingless Weevils, *see* Camellia

CORYLUS

Winter Moth Caterpillars, *see* Carpinus

COTONEASTER

Brown Scale, *see* Ceanothus

Fireblight, *see* Crataegus

Green Apple Aphid, *Aphis pomi* (Insect)

Shiny, black, oval eggs on shoots in winter, colonies of green aphids in spring.

CONTROL: Spray with malathion when aphids observed but never at flowering time.

Hawthorn Webber, *Scythropia crataegella* (Insect)

Very small plum-coloured caterpillars in gossamer web.

CONTROL: Spray with trichlorphon or dust with sevin, except at flowering time.

Lackey Moth, *Malacosoma neustria* (Insect)

Caterpillars, striped brick-red and slate-blue, live in webbing 'tents' on shoots.

CONTROL: Cut out affected twigs or spray with trichlorphon, except at flowering time.

Root Rot, *see* Ligustrum

Woolly Aphid, *Eriosoma lanigerum* (Insect)

Colonies conspicuous in spring and summer because of secretion of white, waxy 'wool'. Swellings form on the shoots where they feed.

CONTROL: Spray with malathion whenever insects are seen, except at flowering time.

CRATAEGUS

Aphids (Insects)

Several species attack crataegus.

CONTROL: Spray with malathion whenever seen, except during flowering period.

Brown Scale, *see* Ceanothus

Caterpillars

Several species attack crataegus.

CONTROL: Spray with derris or trichlorphon whenever seen, except during flowering period.

Fireblight, *Erwinia amylovora* (Bacterial)

This is a destructive disease of rosaceous plants, causing dieback of young shoots and limbs. Leaves on affected branches wither and turn brown so that they look as if burned, but they do not fall.

CONTROL: This is a notifiable disease and if the presence of Fireblight is suspected it *must* (under the Fireblight Orders) be reported as soon as possible to the local Plant Health Inspector or Divisional Office of the Ministry of Agriculture, Fisheries and Food.

Powdery Mildew, *Podosphaera oxyacanthae* (Fungus)

Leaves and shoots become covered by a powdery white coating and the disease can be very injurious to newly-planted hedges or young soft shoot growth.

CONTROL: Cut out badly affected shoots and spray with dinocap or sulphur. Late trimming will help check the disease by the removal of many buds in which the fungus overwinters.

Root Rot, *see* Ligustrum

Woolly Aphid, *see* Cotoneaster

CUPRESSUS, *see* Chamaecyparis

CYDONIA, *see* Chaenomeles

CYTISUS

Aphids (Insects)

CONTROL: Spray with malathion as necessary, except during flowering period.

DEUTZIA

Aphids (Insects)

CONTROL: Spray with malathion as necessary, except during flowering period.

ERICA

Wilt, *Phytophthora cinnamomi* (Fungus)

Affected plants first take on a greyish appearance followed by progressilve wilting of the branches until the whole plant is affected and eventually dies.

CONTROL: Burn affected plants and if possible sterilize the soil. See that cultural conditions are suitable for good growth of the plants and, in particular, see that waterlogging does not occur.

EUONYMUS

Aphids (Insects)

CONTROL: Spray with malathion as necessary.

Ermine Moths, *Yponomeuta spp.* (Insects)

Dark caterpillars form tents of webbing on shoots.

CONTROL: Cut out or spray with trichlorphon.

Leaf Spots, *Phyllosticta bolleana, P. subnervisequa* and *Septoria euonymi* (Fungi)

Whitish or pale yellowish-brown spots, sometimes angular in shape, develop on the leaves.

CONTROL: Spray with a copper fungicide.

Powdery Mildew, *Oidium euonymi-japonicae* (Fungus)

A common and often severe disease which shows as a whitish powdery deposit on leaves, often covering them completely.

CONTROL: Cut out badly affected shoots and spray with dinocap or a sulphur fungicide.

47

Root Rot, *see* Ligustrum

Scale Insects

Colonies of dirty white scales give stems a scurfy appearance.

CONTROL: Spray with malathion giving two or three applications at 14-day intervals.

FAGUS

Beech Aphid, *Phyllaphis fagi* (Insect)

Aphids on underside of the leaves, secreting trails of white waxy 'wool' and much sticky honeydew.

CONTROL: Spray with malathion as soon as colonies are observed.

Beech Scale, *Cryptococcus fagi* (Insects)
Colonies of scales on bark resembling cotton wool.

CONTROL: Spray with malathion whenever observed.

Root Rot, *see Ligustrum*

FIRETHORN, *see* Pyracantha

FLOWERING CURRANT, *see* Ribes

FORSYTHIA

Capsid Bug, *see* Buddleia

Gall (Cause Unknown)
Abnormal nodular growths develop on the stems.

CONTROL: Cut out affected shoots and spray with a copper fungicide.

ABOVE LEFT: orange-red trumpet flowers of *Campsis grandiflora*
CENTRE LEFT: the Canterbury bell-like flowers of *Cobaea scandens*
LEFT: *Eccremocarpus scaber* has orange-scarlet, tubular flowers
ABOVE: a member of the potato family, *Solanum crispum*

ABOVE LEFT: a self-clinging climber, *Schizophragma hydrangeoides*
ABOVE RIGHT: *Schizophragma integrifolium* has creamy-white bracts
BELOW LEFT: the self-clinging hydrangea, *H. petiolaris*
BELOW RIGHT: *Wisteria sinensis* has pendant trusses of mauve or lilac fragrant flowers

FUCHSIA

Capsids, *see* Buddleia

GARRYA

Weather Damage

Large brown blotches on leaves can be caused by cold winds or frost. Plants lacking in vigour or affected by too dry soil conditions are more susceptible to damage of this type.

HAWTHORN, *see* Crataegus

HEATHER, *see* Erica

HEBE

Leaf Spot, *Septoria exotica* (Fungus)

Numerous small circular spots develop on the leaves. A common disease in S.W. England and the Isles of Scilly.

CONTROL: Pick off affected leaves as soon as first symptoms are seen.

HEDERA

Aphids (Insects)

CONTROL: Spray with malathion whenever observed.

Bryobia Mites, *Bryobia spp.* (Mites)

Very small, blood-red mites causing silvery speckling on green leaves which soon become chlorotic.

CONTROL: Spray with derris whenever seen.

D   49

Leaf Spots (Fungus)

At least four different fungi cause brown blotches on ivy leaves.

CONTROL: Cut off affected leaves and spray with copper fungicide.

Scale insects, *see* Ceanothus

HOLLY, *see* Ilex

HONEYSUCKLE, *see* Lonicera

HORNBEAM, *see* Carpinus

HYDRANGEA

Capsids, *see* Buddleia

Do not use BHC on hydrangea.

Chlorosis (Physiological disorder)

Yellowing of the leaves occurs, starting between the veins and then spreading until the leaves are completely yellow or almost white. The blooms (bracts) are poor in colour. Too alkaline soil conditions are the cause of this trouble.

CONTROL: Dig in acidic materials such as peat. Use a proprietary product containing iron chelates or fritted trace elements.

Powdery Mildew, *Microsphaera polonica* (Fungus)

A white powdery coating develops on brown spots on the leaves.

CONTROL: Spray with dinocap or a sulphur fungicide.

HYPERICUM

Rust, *Melampsora hypericorum* (Fungus)

Small orange pustules develop on the undersurface of the leaves.

CONTROL: Remove badly affected leaves and spray with thiram or zineb.

ILEX

Aphids (Insects)

CONTROL: Spray with malathion as necessary except at flowering time.

Holly Leafminer, *Phytomyza ilicis* (Insect)

Larvae feed in tissues of leaf, causing green and brown blotches and tunnels.

CONTROL: Spray with BHC against egg-laying flies in early May or with BHC or trichlorphon against larvae in the mines.

Tortrix Moth, *Acroclita naevana* (Insect)

Small caterpillars spin the shoots together.

CONTROL: Spray with trichlorphon but not at flowering time.

IVY, *see* Hedera

JUNIPER, *see* Juniperus

JUNIPERUS

Conifer Spinning Mite, *see* Picea

Juniper Scale, *Carulaspis spp.* (Insects)

Small, round whitish scales.

CONTROL: Spray with malathion as necessary.

Juniper Webber, *Dichomeris marginella* (Insect)

Small brown and grey striped caterpillars, spin shoots together to form thickets, causing dead patches.

CONTROL: Spray with trichlorphon when caterpillars are present in midsummer.

Rusts, *Gymnosporangium spp.* (Fungus)

Four different rusts spend part of their life-cycle on juniper (the other stages are on plants belonging to the rose family). Bladder-like or horn-like gelatinous yellowish masses protrude from an affected branch which is swollen at that part.

CONTROL: Cut out and burn affected branches.

LARCH, *see* Larix

LARIX

Adelges, *Adelges abietis* (Insects)

Insects secrete white waxy wool so that the needles appear to be powdered with snow.

CONTROL: Spray with BHC, *see also* Picea.

Canker, *Trichoscyphella willkommii* (Fungus)

The fungus enters through wounds and produces large cankers on branches or main stems. Fruiting bodies of the fungus develop on the cankers and these are small ($\frac{1}{8}$ in. across), yellow or orange, saucer-shaped and borne on short stalks.

CONTROL: Cut out affected branches. Treat wounds with a fungicidal wound paint. Encourage vigour in the tree by good cultivation.

Root Rot, *see* Ligustrum

Rusts, *Melampsora spp.* (Fungus)

Small white, bladder-like pustules full of yellow spores develop on the needles. The fungi concerned do not seriously harm the larches and no control measures are necessary.

LAURUS

Weather Damage

Large brown blotches on leaves can be caused by cold winds or frost. Plants lacking in vigour or affected by too dry soil conditions are more susceptible to damage of this type.

LAVANDULA

Froghoppers, *Philaenus leucophthalmus* (Insect)

The nymphs protect themselves with a frothy secretion or 'cuckoo-spit'.

CONTROL: Spray forcibly with malathion but not when lavender is in flower.

Grey Mould, *Botrytis cinerea* (Fungus)

In wet seasons the flowers are attacked by this fungus which causes them to wilt or turn brown prematurely.

CONTROL: Cut out affected flower stems and spray with captan or thiram.

Leaf Spot, *Septoria lavandulae* (Fungus)

Spotting of the foliage occurs but the disease is rarely serious.

CONTROL: If necessary spray with Bordeaux Mixture.

Shab, *Phoma lavandulae* (Fungus)

Only likely to be troublesome in districts where lavender is grown for commercial purposes. The fungus attacks stems and branches, causing wilting and death of affected plants.

CONTROL: Cut out affected shoots and in bad attacks burn whole plant. Spray with Bordeaux Mixture.

Root Rot, *see* Ligustrum

LAVENDER, *see* Lavandula

LIGUSTRUM

Aphids (Insects)

These sometimes cause malformation of shoots and leaves and much sticky honeydew.

CONTROL: Spray with malathion as necessary, except during flowering period.

Leaf Spot, *Mycosphaerella ligustri* (Fungus)

Discoloured patches with a brown or reddish border develop on the leaves.

CONTROL: Rarely necessary but in severe cases spray with a copper fungicide.

Leafminer, *Caloptilia syringella* (Insect)

Brown blisters on leaves caused by caterpillars feeding in leaf tissue.

CONTROL: Spray with BHC, avoiding flowering period.

Privet Thrips, *Dendrothrips ornatus* (Insect)

Very small, slender insects, the nymphs pale and the adults striped black and silver when wings at rest. Their feeding causes silver blotches on the leaves.

CONTROL: Spray with BHC or dimethoate as necessary, except during the flowering period.

Root Rot, *Armillaria mellea* (Fungus)

Privet hedges are very susceptible to attacks by this root parasite. A plant affected by the fungus dies fairly quickly, and the trouble spreads to adjacent plants so that in a hedge, patches of dead shrubs will be seen with dying ones on either side. When a dead or dying plant is lifted the roots are found to be decayed and beneath the bark of the roots and collar portion of the plant will be seen white, fan-shaped sheets of fungal growth which smell strongly of mushrooms. Long black strands like leather bootlaces are produced by the fungus and these rhizomorphs, as they are called, travel through the soil and spread the trouble. Honey coloured toadstools sometimes develop in autumn at the base of dead tree stumps, which provide ideal conditions for the establishment of this disease.

CONTROL: It is essential to dig up and burn all dead and dying plants, making quite sure that all the roots are also removed. In a hedge, bushes on either side which may look apparently healthy may also be affected, and should also be destroyed. Any rhizomorphs in the soil should be dug out. Once the affected area has been cleared, the soil should be forked over and watered thoroughly with a 2 per cent formalin solution (1 pt. 37–40 per cent commercial formaldehyde to 6 gallons of water). The treated area should be covered with wet sacks for 24 hours, and following removal of these, the soil should be left vacant for up to six weeks.

LILAC, *see* Syringa

LIME, *see* Tilia

LONICERA

Aphids (Insects)

Colonies of aphids may infest the buds, deforming them and preventing flowering.

CONTROL: Spray with malathion when first few insects are seen in developing buds.

Silver leaf, *see* Prunus

MAGNOLIA

Grey Mould, *Botrytis cinerea* (Fungus)

Flower buds are often attacked by this fungus following frost injury. The buds turn brown and become coated with a brownish-grey covering of the fungus which may enter the shoot and cause some dieback.

55

CONTROL: Cut out affected shoots back to clean, living tissues.

MAHONIA

Leaf Spot, *Phyllosticta mahoniae* (Fungus)

Brown spots, in which tiny black dots can be seen, develop on the leaves.

CONTROL: Destroy affected leaves.

Powdery Mildew, *Microsphaera berberidis* (Fungus)

A white powdery covering develops on young leaves and shoots.

CONTROL: Cut out badly affected shoots and spray with dinocap.

Rusts, *Puccinia graminis* and *Cumminsiella mirabilissima* (Fungi)

Small red spots appear on the upper surface of the leaves and on the lower surface brownish, somewhat powdery masses of spores are produced.

CONTROL: Cut out badly affected shoots and spray with thiram.

MAPLE, *see* Acer

METASEQUOIA

Root Rot, *see* Ligustrum

MOUNTAIN ASH, *see* Sorbus

MYRTLE, *see* Myrtus

MYRTUS

Leaf Spot, *Cercospora myrticola* (Fungus)

On the leaves develop spots which are at first small and light yellowish-green but quickly enlarge and become dark reddish-purple in colour surrounded by a light yellow halo.

CONTROL: Burn affected leaves and spray with copper fungicide.

NUT, *see* Corylus

OAK, *see* Quercus

PASSION FLOWER, *see* Passiflora

PASSIFLORA

Mosaic, *Cucumber Mosaic Virus* (Virus)

Leaves become distorted and during the winter months become mottled with yellowish flecks along the lateral veins. Affected plants look very unsightly but the symptoms fade during spring and summer and reappear in the autumn.

CONTROL: Burn affected plants.

PHILADELPHUS

Aphids (Insects)

CONTROL: Spray with malathion except during flowering period.

PHILLYREA

White Fly, *Siphoninus phillyreae* (Insect)

Colonies of flat, oval scales on underside of leaf giving rise to tiny, white-winged moth-like adults.

CONTROL: Spray with malathion when adults are present.

PICEA

Conifer Spinning Mite, *Oligonychus ununguis* (Mite)

Small red mites with black markings cause needles to become mottled and bleached. Eggshells, moultskins and gossamer webbings can be seen with aid of a magnifying glass.

CONTROL: Spray with derris as necessary.

Spruce Aphid, *Elatobium abietinum* (Insect)

Green aphids infest needles which become mottled and may become brown and fall.

CONTROL: Spray with malathion whenever seen.

Spruce Pineapple Gall Adelges, *Adelges abietis* (Insect)

Symptoms of infestation include tufts of white waxy wool secreted by the insects at certain times of the year and pineapple-like galls on shoots in summer. Part of life cycle may be spent on Larix, q.v.

CONTROL: Spray with BHC in April.

PINE, *see* Pinus

PINUS

Pine Shoot Moth, *Rhyacionia buoliana* (Insect)

Caterpillars tunnel in the shoots causing death of the leaders.

CONTROL: Spray with trichlorphon at the beginning of August and again three weeks later.

POPLAR, *see* Populus

POPULUS

Canker, *Aplanobacterium populi* (Bacterial)

Unsightly cankers varying from ¼–6 in. in length develop on the shoots, branches and sometimes on the trunk. Young shoots may die back in early summer.

CONTROL: There is no control for this bacterial disease, but cut out affected shoots. Destroy badly affected plants and replant with a more resistant strain or species.

Leaf Spots, *Marssonina spp.* (Fungus)

Small, irregular, blackish-brown spots develop on the leaves which fall prematurely.

CONTROL: Where possible spray in spring and at least once more in summer with a copper fungicide. Feed larger trees to encourage vigour.

Poplar Beetle, *Melasoma populi* (Insect)

Grubs feed on leaf surface exposing network of veins.

CONTROL: Spray with trichlorphon if feasible.

Poplar Lettuce Aphids, *Pemphigus bursarius* (Insects)

They may form bulbous red pouches on leafstalks. Winged aphids emerge in July to infest roots of lettuce, etc. No control feasible on poplar.

Rusts, *Melampsora spp.* (Fungus)

Yellowish-orange pustules develop on the lower leaf surfaces. Premature defoliation may occur.

CONTROL: Rarely feasible but on small trees, thiram could be tried.

Silver Leaf, *see* Prunus

Yellow Leaf Blister, *Taphrina populina* (Fungus)
Large yellow blisters are produced on the leaves.

CONTROL: Where feasible, spray in dormant period (January or early February) with lime-sulphur or a copper fungicide and repeat a fortnight later.

PORTUGAL LAUREL, *see* Prunus

PRIVET, *see* Ligustrum

PRUNUS (Cherry, Laurel and Plum)

Cherry Black Fly, *Myzus cerasi* (Insect)

Colonies of black aphids cause leaf curl and often death of shoots.

CONTROL: Spray with tar oil winter wash in December against egg stage or with malathion, when first aphids noticed in the growing season but avoiding the flowering period.

Leaf Spot of Cherry Laurel, *Trochila laurocerasi* (Fungus)

Spots at first yellowish, then purplish and finally brown, develop on the leaves. Later, the discoloured spots become separated from the leaf and fall away leaving large holes, either spherical or irregular in outline.

CONTROL: Destroy badly affected leaves. Spray with sulphur during spring and early summer and cut back the bushes only in the autumn.

Powdery Mildew, *Podosphaera oxyacanthae var. tridactyla* (Fungus)

A white powdery coating develops on leaves and shoots of cherry laurel and plum suckers.

CONTROL: Cut out badly affected shoots and spray with dinocap.

Root Rot, *see* Ligustrum

Rusts, *Tranzschelia spp.* (Fungus)

Different species of these rust fungi attack different *Prunus* species. Small brown powdery masses of spores develop on the lower leaf surfaces in late summer and premature defoliation may occur.

CONTROL: If troublesome spray with thiram, but as the disease is only severe on weak trees, see that cultural conditions are suitable, and feed.

Silver Leaf, *Stereum purpureum* (Fungus)

Many types of plants can be affected by this disease but *Prunus* species are very susceptible. Silvering of the foliage sometimes occurs but not always, and this symptom can, in any case, be due to adverse cultural conditions and not disease. True Silver Leaf results in the death of affected branches, and later, flat, purplish fruiting bodies of the fungus appear on dead wood. A purplish-brown stain is produced in the inner tissues of diseased stems, and a cross-section of a branch bearing silvered leaves should be examined for signs of this stain to confirm the presence of the disease.

CONTROL: Cut out affected shoots to a point 4–6 in. behind where the stain ceases to show in the wood. Paint pruning cuts and all wounds with a fungicidal pruning paint.

Winter Moth caterpillars, *see* Carpinus

PYRACANTHA

Aphids (Insects)

CONTROL: Spray with malathion as necessary except during flowering period.

Brown Scale, *see* Ceanothus

Fireblight, *see* Crataegus

Scab, *Fusicladium pyracanthae* (Fungus)

An olive-brown coating covers the berries spoiling their appearance. The leaves can also be attacked and defoliation occurs.

CONTROL: Spray with captan three times in March/April and twice in June.

Woolly Aphid, *see* Cotoneaster

QUERCUS

Cynipid Gall Wasps (Insects)

Small ant-like insects, rarely seen, cause many different galls, e.g. oak apples, marble gall, cherry, pea, artichoke, currant, spangle, silk-button

61

galls and so on. Healthy trees can usually support vast populations of galls and no control measures are needed.

Phylloxera, *Phylloxera quercus* (Insects)

Plump, aphid-like, yellow insects which feed on the underside of leaves causing yellow blotches and later, brown patches on the leaves.

CONTROL: Malathion could be tried if spraying is feasible.

Powdery Mildew, *Microsphaera alphitoides* (Fungus)

A floury-white coating covers the leaves and shoot tips. Young shoots can be severely crippled in growth.

CONTROL: Cut out badly affected shoots and spray with dinocap or a sulphur fungicide.

Tortrix and other caterpillars (Insects)

CONTROL: Trichlorphon controls caterpillars but it is not usually feasible to spray large trees.

QUICKTHORN, *see* Crataegus

RHODODENDRON

Bud Blast, *Pycnostysanus azaleae* (Fungus)

Killed buds turn brown, black or silvery in spring with black, bristle-like spore heads protruding from them.

CONTROL: Pick off and burn affected buds. Control of the Rhododendron Leafhopper checks the spread of this disease.

Chlorosis, *see* Hydrangea

Gall, *Exobasidium vaccinii* (Fungus)

Developing leaves or flower buds swell into small galls which are at first reddish but later turn waxy-white.

CONTROL: Pick off galls. Spray with a copper fungicide such as Bordeaux Mixture.

Lichen, Moss and Algae

Growths such as these can be very unsightly. Unfortunately there is no method of controlling them on evergreen shrubs. Deciduous azaleas can, however, be sprayed in the dormant season with lime sulphur made at a strength of 1 pt. in 2 gal. of water.

Rhododendron Bug, *Stephanitis rhododendri* (Insect)

Colonies of shiny brown bugs cause chocolate staining on underside of leaves and pale speckling on upper surface. The lacy-winged adults lay eggs along the midribs on underside of leaves in late summer.

CONTROL: Spray with malathion in June.

Rhododendron Leafhopper, *Graphocephala coccinea* (Insect)

Young leafhoppers are pale yellow, wedge-shaped; adults have green-and-red-striped wing-cases. Eggs are laid in flower buds in late summer, allowing entry of disease.

CONTROL: Spray with malathion or dimethoate towards the end of July.

Rhododendron Whitefly, *Dialeurodes chittendeni* (Insect)

Clouds of small, moth-like insects with snow-white wings infest shoots in June. Thousands of eggs laid on the young leaves, giving rise to oval, scale-like nymphs.

CONTROL: Spray with malathion when adults are present.

Root Rot, *see* Ligustrum

Silver Leaf, *see* Prunus

RIBES

Aphids (Insects)

CONTROL: Spray with malathion as necessary, except during the flowering period.

63

Brown Scale, *see* Ceanothus

Leaf Spot, *Pseudopeziza ribis* (Fungus)

Small brown spots appear on leaf and coalesce until whole leaf is completely covered. Premature defoliation occurs.

CONTROL: Pick up and burn fallen leaves. Spray with thiram or zineb immediately after flowering and repeat at least twice at fortnightly intervals.

ROSE, *see* Rosa

ROSA

Aphids (Insects)

CONTROL: Spray with malathion as soon as noticed before colonies can build up. Avoid spraying open flowers.

Black Spot, *Diplocarpon rosae* (Fungus)

Circular black spots with fringed edges appear on the leaves and premature defoliation occurs.

CONTROL: Spray with captan or maneb immediately after pruning and repeat regularly throughout the summer. Rake up and burn fallen leaves.

Brown Scale, *see* Ceanothus

Canker and Dieback (Fungus)

Several different fungi can cause cankers in roses but in most cases they first enter through dead wood or wounds such as pruning snags. Once they have entered, however, they cause further dieback of stems.

CONTROL: Cut out all dead wood back to living tissues and paint larger wounds with a fungicidal protective paint. In severe cases, winter spraying of the bushes with a copper fungicide may be worth while.

Capsid Bugs, *Lygocoris pabulinus* (Insect)

64

Glossy, green, long-legged insects which move nimbly and are not often seen on the plants. Their feeding causes tattered leaves and distorted shoots.

CONTROL: Spray with dimethoate, avoiding open blooms, or water roots with formothion.

Caterpillars (Insects)

CONTROL: Spray with trichlorphon as necessary, avoiding open blooms.

Dieback, *see* Rose Canker

Leaf-rolling Rose Sawfly, *Blennocampa pusilla* (Insect)

Small black sawflies lay eggs in the leaf margins and the edges roll so that leaflets form a conical tube. Caterpillar-like green larvae feed inside the folds.

CONTROL: Spray with trichlorphon or BHC several times at 14-day intervals, from the end of April.

Leafhopper, *Typhlocyba rosae* (Insect)

Slender, yellowish, wedge-shaped creatures, the adults being winged; their feeding causes coarse mottling on the upper surface of the leaves and fragile, white moultskins are left on the underside.

CONTROL: Spray with malathion several times at 14-day intervals from the end of April.

Powdery Mildew, *Sphaerotheca pannosa* (Fungus)

A white powdery coating covers the shoots and the young leaves which are crippled. The disease is worse on plants affected by too dry soil conditions.

CONTROL: Spray regularly with dinocap. Mulch plants well and water in dry periods before the soil dries out completely.

Red Spider Mite, *Tetranychus urticae* (Mite)

Very small mites with eggs, empty eggshells and moultskins can be seen on the underside of the leaves with magnifying glass. Cause light freckling on upper surface of foliage, which eventually becomes chlorotic and may shrivel, especially in hot, dry summers.

CONTROL: Spray with derris or malathion as necessary, avoiding open blooms.

Root Rot, *see* Ligustrum

Rust, *Phragmidium spp.* (Fungus)

Orange-coloured pustules develop on the leaves in summer, mostly on the lower surface. In autumn darker brown or black areas develop often on the same spots.

CONTROL: Spray with maneb, thiram or zineb.

Scurfy Scale, *Aulacaspis rosae* (Insect)

Flat, whitish scales give stems a scurfy appearance.

CONTROL: Spray with malathion making two or three applications at 14-day intervals.

Silver Leaf, *see* Prunus

Slugworm, *Endelomyia aethiops* (Insect)

Pale green larvae eat away the leaf surface and the skeletonized areas turn brown and papery.

CONTROL: Spray with malathion or derris whenever larvae are seen, avoiding open blooms.

SALIX

Anthracnose, *Marssonina salicicola* (Fungus)

Small brown spots develop on leaves and small blackish cankers on the shoots. Premature defoliation occurs and also some dieback of shoots.

CONTROL: Rake up and burn fallen leaves. Where possible cut out badly affected shoots and spray with copper fungicide as the leaves unfold and at least once more in the summer. On large trees, control is often not possible, and then feeding to encourage vigour and resistance should be tried.

Aphids (Insects)

CONTROL: Spray with malathion as necessary. This should also control the Large Willow Aphid *Tuberolachnus salignus*, a large brown aphid with iridescent wings which occurs in colonies on the bark. Much honeydew is secreted and sooty moulds may flourish on it, blackening not only the willow leaves but plants growing below. Wasps and flies may also be attracted.

Red Spider Mite, *Schizotetranychus schizopus* (Mites)

Masses of mites on the underside of the leaves cause yellowing and premature defoliation especially in hot, dry summers.

CONTROL: Spray with derris if feasible.

Root Rot, *see* Ligustrum

Sawflies (Insect)

Caterpillar-like larvae, usually green or yellow with black spots, strip the leaves.

CONTROL: Spray with derris or malathion.

Scale (Insects)

Whitish, scurfy scales encrust the stems.

CONTROL: Spray with malathion, making several applications at about 14-day intervals.

Willow Beetles, *Phyllodecta vitellinae* (Insects)

Small metallic beetles and blackish grubs which eat away leaf surface, exposing veins.

CONTROL: Spray with BHC as necessary.
NB. Willow trees should not be sprayed if insecticide is likely to contaminate water containing fish.

SORBUS

Fireblight, *see* Crataegus

Gall-Mite, *Phytoptus piri* (Mite)

Causes yellowish or reddish pustules on leaves of mountain ash.

CONTROL: If feasible, spraying with lime sulphur when leafbuds are just breaking in spring might be tried.

Rust, *Gymnosporangium cornutum* (Fungus)

This is a common disease in certain parts of Scotland particularly where Juniper, the other host for the fungus, grows in close proximity. Orange horn-shaped structures borne in clusters develop on the leaves in late September. In severe cases, every leaf is discoloured, partially rolled up and shrivelled.

CONTROL: Spraying with thiram may give some control. If an affected Juniper is adjacent this should also be treated (*see* Juniperus).

SPINDLEWOOD, *see* Euonymus

SPRUCE, *see* Picea

STRANVAESIA

Fireblight, *see* Crataegus

STRAWBERRY TREE, *see* Arbutus

SWEET BAY, *see* Laurus

SYCAMORE, *see* Acer

SYRINGA

Blight, *Pseudomonas syringae* (Bacterial)

68

Small, angular brown spots develop on the leaves. Young flowers, foliage and shoots blacken and wither away.

CONTROL: Cut out affected shoots back to a healthy bud, and spray with a copper fungicide.

Grey Mould, *Botrytis cinerea* (Fungus)

The flower buds and shoots are often attacked by this fungus following frost injury. The symptoms are very similar to those caused by blight (see above) and the disease can be controlled in the same way.

Lilac Leafminer, *Caloptilia syringella* (Insect)

Large brown blisters contain mining larvae. Later, caterpillars emerge and roll leaves to feed inside folds.

CONTROL: Spray with BHC.

Privet Thrips, *see* Ligustrum

Root Rot, *see* Ligustrum

Scale (Insects)

Whitish, scurfy scales encrust stems.

CONTROL: Spray with malathion as necessary except during flowering periods, making several applications at about 14-day intervals.

TAXUS

Yew Scale, *Parthenolecanium pomeranicum* (Insects)

Dome-shaped brown scales on leaves and shoots often accompanied by sooty moulds growing on deposit of honeydew.

CONTROL: Spray with nicotine and white oil in March or early September, 5 per cent tar oil in winter or malathion in the growing season. Try a small section of the hedge first when using either of the last named, to ensure that the hedge is not sensitive to the chemicals.

Root Rot, *see* Ligustrum

THUJA

Leaf Blight, *Didymascella thujina* (Fungus)

Attacked leaves turn brown and die and very small dark brown spots appear on the upper side. Only serious on young plants.

CONTROL: Spraying with a copper fungicide may give some control.

TILIA

Leaf Spot, *Gloeosporium tiliae* (Fungus)

Brown spots with dark edges develop on the leaves and sometimes on the leafstalks and young shoots. Withering and defoliation may result.

CONTROL: Rarely serious enough to warrant special control measures but all fallen leaves should be raked up and burned.

Nail Galls, *Eriophyes tiliae* (Mite)

Tintack-like crimson or greenish galls on leaves.

CONTROL: If feasible, trees could be sprayed with lime sulphur when the leafbuds are just breaking, but the galls do little harm.

Red Spider Mite, *Tetranychus tiliae* (Mite)

Masses of mites on underside of leaves causing chlorosis and premature defoliation, especially in hot dry seasons. In autumn, the tree trunks may become enmeshed in webbing.

CONTROL: Spray with derris or malathion, if feasible.

TSUGA

Root Rot, *see* Ligustrum

VERONICA, *see* Hebe

VIBURNUM

Aphids (Insects)

Attack shoots early in the season causing malformation.

CONTROL: Spray with malathion as necessary.

Scale, *Aleurotrachelus jelinekii* (Insect)

Flat, oval, black scales with white waxy fringes on underside of leaves of *Viburnum tinus*. Snowy winged, moth-like adults present in early June.

CONTROL: Spray with malathion when adults present.

WILLOW, *see* Salix

WISTERIA

Root Rot, *see* Ligustrum

YEW, *see* Taxus

The Law Relating to Trees, Hedges, Screens and Climbers

by ROBERT S. W. POLLARD, L.A.M.T.P.I.

In the following notes the word 'hedge' will, so far as the context permits, include fences and boundary walls, and the word 'fence' include hedges and walls. The word 'tree' will include 'creepers (bushes and shrubs)', whether or not forming part of a hedge. These notes can only state the law broadly and are intended to be used as a guide to problems which may arise, and a warning of possible risks and dangers. They are not a substitute for legal advice. If they show that there may be a legal problem, a solicitor should be consulted at once.

BOUNDARIES

The boundary is the line which divides two contiguous properties. Where the ownership has not been severed the surface ownership to the boundary carries with it in law the ownership of the air over the land up to the sky and the soil to the centre of the earth. (Acts of Parliament have given aircraft a right of passage and have nationalized certain mineral substances.)

The ownership of the air can be important. For instance, if a projection attached to a neighbour's building projects into the air over one's property this is trespass and is actionable but only on proof of damage.

Fixing of boundaries

Boundaries are generally shown by the deed conveying or transferring a particular property, and it is common to have a plan on the deed. Frequently a 'T' mark inside a boundary line on a plan will indicate that the owner of the land is responsible for some particular fence or hedge, but it is unfortunate that plans too often do not have these marks and are not always, in other respects, entirely accurate. It is often useful in connection with a plan on a deed to use the Ordnance Survey maps. Note that the line of the Ordnance Survey follows the middle of a hedge when this is the boundary. Sometimes a landowner will have a special survey made in order to mark his boundaries and their measurements.

In the case of registered land the Land Registry supply a map upon which the property is marked, but they do not, unless specially requested, show on this plan who are the owners of the several boundary fences or hedges. It may be costly to ask the Land Registry to mark the boundaries exactly, since notice has to be given to all adjoining owners and this may give rise to dispute.

Property owners are advised to see (a) that the plans on their deeds mark their boundaries and the lengths of the several boundary lines as accurately as possible, and (b) that the title deeds, if possible, indicate to whom the several hedges and fences belong. If uncertainty can be avoided there will be fewer disputes. A deed can always be drawn up and signed by one landowner and his neighbour or neighbours declaring the ownership of hedges and fences and the respective liability for repairs.

There are some presumptions of law which may apply where the deeds are not clear. It may be doubted if they are of great value nowadays, but they should be mentioned. The law presumes that when a man makes a ditch he makes it at the very extremity of his own land, forming a bank on his own side with the soil which he takes out of the ditch, and that on the top of the bank a hedge is usually planted. Therefore, when two fields are separated by a hedge or bank and an artificial ditch, the hedge, or bank, and ditch belong to the owner of the field on the other side of the hedge; for this presumption to apply, the ditch must be artificial. Acts of ownership, such as trimming a hedge and clearing a ditch, by an adjoining owner will not negative this presumption. It is sometimes said that there is a rule of law that the owner of a bank or ditch is entitled to 4 ft. of width for the base of the bank and 4 ft. also for the ditch, but this statement is not true. Properties may be divided by two ditches, one on each side of a hedge, or by two hedges, one on each side of a ditch, or by an old hedge without any ditch; in these cases there is no presumption of law and, if the title deeds are not clear, acts of ownership, such as trimming a hedge, may show to whom it belongs. If both owners treat the hedge as theirs, they may be held to own the hedge in

73

common, unless the amount of land which each owner gave to make the hedge is known; in this case the hedge can be notionally divided.

Party hedges

A party hedge or fence is one where there is a notional vertical division but each owner has a right to have it maintained as a dividing hedge and has liability for its maintenance and repair. Legal questions arising out of party hedges, fences or walls tend to be complicated and it is wise to see a solicitor about them.

Duty to fence

There is a general rule of law that owners of adjoining lands are not bound to fence either against or for the benefit of each other, although a man is required to see that his animals do not trespass upon adjoining property and, apart from dogs and cats, is liable for any natural consequence of their trespass. Similarly, there is no general duty to fence against the public. Persons straying from a highway do so as a general rule at their own peril, provided that works on the land are not so near the highway as to be dangerous to its users. Acts of Parliament may modify these rules in the case of certain dangerous works or buildings and obligations to fence are frequently imposed by positive covenants when houses are built.

As between a landlord and a tenant the liability for repair of a fence or hedge should be dealt with by the lease or tenancy agreement. If liability to maintain a hedge is to be cast upon either party, then the agreement must say so expressly.

In the absence of any express provision, there will be no liability on either party in the case of a yearly tenancy or less. But in the case of a lease for more than a year the tenant will be liable to repair fences unless the lease otherwise provides. The Landlord, of course, may be liable to repair fences by virtue of some covenant in his title deeds but this provision is unlikely to benefit a tenant.

Trespassing children

Since there is no general duty to fence, there is no general duty to keep children out of property. Children who get through a defective hedge and trespass normally do so at their own risk and a landowner is under no liability if they suffer damage. However, he should take reasonable care to see that, either by a warning or some other means, he protects against injury any children who are too young to realize the danger of some attractive object or 'allurement' within his knowledge or control, if he knows or ought to know of the possible presence of such children.

A further qualification of the general rule is that a landowner cannot escape liability if, without giving sufficient warning, he suddenly creates a new danger on his land and causes injury to a trespasser who has entered on to the land unaware of the danger. This rule was well illustrated in a case where a woodcutter chased away a crowd of children who were watching him fell a large tree. An hour later the final root was cut and because the woodcutter did not look round and see that his spectators had returned, the child who was hurt by the fall of the tree was able to claim damages.

Animals

If without negligence on the part of its owner a domestic animal enters a garden from a highway, its owner is not responsible for damage caused thereby. The owner of the property is supposed to protect himself by proper fencing. If the trespassing animal is inadvertently injured in the garden no liability will attach to the owner of the garden.

Again, there is no remedy if the cattle have strayed from the highway, unless, of course, there has been negligence on the part of their owner. Straying of animals may cause some danger or may cause some damage to trees and therefore some reference to the Animals Act, 1971, is necessary. This Act conveniently codifies a large part of the law relating to damage by animals. The keeper of any animal belonging to a dangerous species is liable for all damage it may do. The keeper of any other animal is liable for damage caused by it if the damage is of a kind which the animal, unless it was restrained, was likely to cause or which was likely to be severe and the likelihood of this was due to some unusual characteristic in the animal or some characteristic which is only found at a particular time or in particular circumstances and these characteristics were known to the keeper or his servant. When livestock strays on to an adjoining owner's land and damage is done to the land or any property on it the owner of the livestock is liable for the damage. He is also liable for any expenses reasonably incurred in keeping the livestock while it cannot be restored to the person to whom it belongs to while it is detained under the powers given by the Act or in ascertaining to whom it belongs. This liability does not extend to livestock straying on to a highway when it is lawfully there but he may still be liable for negligence. A landowner is not bound to fence against his neighbour's livestock straying and the fact that he did not fence is not to be considered negligence which would debar him from successfully claiming damages. But, if some other person has a duty to fence and livestock escape because of a breach of this other person's duty then the owner of the livestock is not liable. Straying livestock can be detained by the occupier of the land on to which it strays. But, within the following forty-eight hours notice of the detention has to be given to the local police station and to the owner of the livestock if known. Where livestock is detained for more than twenty-one days there may be a right to sell it but these rights need to be exercised strictly in accordance with the Act and anyone proposing to exercise this right of detention would be well advised to get in touch with his solicitor.

TREES AND BOUNDARIES

Obligation to cut hedge

There is no general legal obligation to cut your hedge or to lop or top trees (see paragraphs Right to Light, page 83 and Powers of Public and Local Authorities, page 84). Therefore, a neighbour cannot require a landowner to cut his hedge and, of course, he cannot have an adjoining landowner's hedge trimmed and charge the owner with the cost of doing this work. So far as the law is concerned, it is not difficult to be un-neighbourly and let your property become an eyesore.

Right to use neighbour's fence

There is no legal right to drive nails into a fence or wall belonging to a neighbour or to attach trellis work or a washing line to such a fence. To use a neighbour's property in this way is trespass and the neighbour is entitled to remove the object with which the trespass is committed.

Overhanging branches: the right to lop

Where the branches of a tree belonging to an owner overhang the soil of an adjoining landowner or occupier, the latter may at any time cut off any branch which overhangs his land without notice to the former. But he may not trespass on the adjoining land to do this. On the other hand, the branches which are cut off, and any fruit growing on them, belong

76

to the owner of the tree or hedge, and if they are not returned to him he can sue the neighbour who cut them for the value. Although there is a legal right to cut branches without notice, it would be most discourteous to do this and a neighbour should first be asked to attend to his own trees. An owner is not entitled to lop a neighbouring tree as a precautionary measure before it overgrows his land.

If a man cannot lop his tree without the boughs falling upon his neighbour's land, he is probably permitted to justify the fall of the branches in this way, but he must do the lopping as carefully as possible. Moreover, there is an old authority for saying that if fruit belonging to one landowner falls upon adjoining land the owner of the tree may enter upon the other land to take his fruit, so long as he does not (a) stay on the adjoining land longer than necessary or (b) break his neighbour's hedge. As to trees overhanging highways, see the section on Powers of Public and Local Authorities (page 84).

Entry on neighbour's land to cut hedge

There is no legal right to enter your neighbour's land in order to cut your own hedge.

Roots of trees and hedges

The roots not only of poplar trees but of elm, ash and others spread far and wide. Poplar trees are the worst offenders, but generally speaking it is unwise to plant any forest tree within 20 yd. of any building. The faster a tree grows, the faster its roots grow and in the case of trees such as poplars, the roots spread laterally rather then downwards. If, of course, the surrounding ground is generally wet, roots may not spread so far, but when it is dry, they will spread further. The consumption of water by poplars is prodigious and a dry summer can cause considerable extension and length of root systems. If the ground is covered by paving, then the root system will travel farther to replace the water diverted from it by the paving. Moreover, the root system of a tree may grow farther in one direction, because it is drier, than in another.

Tree roots may cause damage in two ways. They may damage foundations, pipes and the surface by physical pressure. On the other hand, they can also cause subsidence of the soil and undermining of structures by making the soil contract because it is deprived of its water. Buildings on a clay soil are particularly vulnerable to these dangers.

A difficult question arises when roots in neighbouring land do not

77

spread into an owner's land but, by being near the boundary, they deprive it of water and so cause injury. It was held in the nineteenth century that a man was free to drain water off from his own land, although in doing so he deprived his neighbour of the support which the water in his soil gave to his neighbour's land and his neighbour's land therefore subsided. This principle suggests that no action will lie for damage caused by roots which do not cross the boundary.

A person has the same right to cut the roots of any tree or hedge which encroaches on his land as he has to cut overhanging boughs.

Roots and branches of creepers

The same principles apply to branches, tendrils and roots of creepers on walls as apply to branches and roots of trees and shrubs and any which extend on to a neighbour's property may be cut off.

Compensation

If the encroaching roots or branches cause injury to a person's property, an action can be brought for the damage actually caused. This action is for nuisance and there must be proof of actual damage. An owner of land had some oak and elm trees which had been growing near the boundary for 20 years. Their branches overhung the adjoining land and damaged the neighbour's orchard by depriving the orchard trees of sun and moisture. The neighbour succeeded in an action for damages and also obtained an injunction forbidding the continuance of this nuisance. If a creeper grows on to an adjoining house and obstructs a gutter, an action for damages can be brought. It is now clear that there is no distinction between damage caused by trees which have been deliberately planted and trees which are self-sown and, if a tree is cut down and suckers spring from the decapitated roots, the owner of the original tree is liable for any damage caused by the suckers. A complaint under this heading can only be made about a tree which belongs to the owner of adjoining land. It appears that a tree which was planted in one person's land and has grown partly on to the land of his neighbour belongs to the owner of the land where it was first sown or planted or from which it grew. The position where a tree is planted directly on a boundary line is not clear.

Liability

Frequently the owner and occupier of land will be the same, but when different persons own and occupy land the occupier in many cases is the person primarily liable for damage done by trees and in practice, of course, he is often the only person who can manage them. A landowner has, however, been held liable for damage caused by roots, although he has never been in actual occupation of a property because it is subject to a lease. It was said in this particular case that he had retained control of the premises although they were let, and he was accordingly liable. He may be considered to retain some control where the lease gives him a right to enter and inspect and do repairs. This clause appears in most leases and is never intended to apply to trees. Moreover, if a landlord lets land with trees on it growing in such a way that they are likely to cause damage to adjoining property, he remains liable, particularly if the letting is for a short tenancy, such as a monthly tenancy, unless he removes the tree or branch which may cause damage.

The landlord will also be liable either directly or as third party under a notice served by the tenant occupier if he has reserved the timber when letting the land. The lease may go further than reserving the timber (oak, ash and elm generally, and other trees in certain areas, e.g. beech in Buckinghamshire and chestnut in Kent), or by implication—e.g. ornamental trees and shrubs in a lease of a dwelling house, or orchard trees. The doctrine of waste has to be considered in this context. In practice a tenant who fells any substantial tree of any kind which might be described as ornamental or useful for shelter or shade or who grubs up hedgerows without prior consent of the landlord will be taking a risk; the more so with productive trees such as apples, hazelnuts and holly, even though the lease is silent.

A landlord may incur some liability to third parties when he has some control over felling.

It is very desirable for all tenancy agreements and leases to define specifically the liability for trees and the responsibility for their care and maintenance as between landlord and tenant.

Insurance

The danger of planting the wrong trees cannot be too strongly emphasized. The present writer knows of a case where a newly-married woman planted a little poplar tree at the bottom of her garden. Thirty years later her husband had to pay £1,000 damages for the cracks caused in the adjoining building by injury to its foundations by the poplar roots.

Some comprehensive insurance policies of buildings or contents will

THE LAW RELATING TO TREES, HEDGES, SCREENS AND CLIMBERS

provide insurance against liability for damage caused by tree roots or branches, but property owners would do well to look at their policies and make sure that they are covered for this liability. An insurance company might properly require the report of a tree expert to be obtained before covering this liability.

Right to grow trees in neighbouring properties

No right can be obtained to have tree roots or branches growing in or over someone else's land. The fact that roots or branches have been growing in this way for many years does not and cannot establish such a right because, since trees make continued growth during every year, the right claimed could never be the same in any one year.

DAMAGE AND NUISANCE

Poisonous trees

The law does not consider that a man ought to have any responsibility for trimming or lopping his neighbour's trees and the owner of trees must take full responsibility for them. If a person plants poisonous trees, such as yews, near a boundary and permits the branches to grow over his neighbour's land, he will be liable if his neighbour's cattle eat them and die.

If, however, the cattle of an adjoining owner put their heads over a hedge and eat poisonous foliage of trees on the other side, the owner of the poisonous trees is under no liability. His trees are wholly within his land and he has done nothing wrong. A landlord who lets part of his land and leaves a poisonous tree growing on the part he retains which overhangs the part let is under no liability, since the tenant has notice of the state of the land at the time of the letting and takes it in that state. The position is not clear as to the liability of an owner of a poisonous tree when its leaves blow on to adjoining land. The law books have in the past drawn a distinction between trees naturally grown and trees artificially planted and said there was no liability for damage caused by drifting poisonous leaves which come from trees grown naturally, whereas the owner of poisonous trees artifically planted could be liable for damage caused by drifting leaves. A recent authority, however, suggests that there may be no difference in law between the ways in which trees are planted, and a landowner of a poisonous tree may be liable in either event.

The same principles appear to apply to children who are lawfully using adjoining property and eat poisonous leaves or berries. If the children are trespassers, an occupier of land is generally under no liability to them but, if he expressly or tacitly allows children to come on to his land, he must take reasonable precautions to protect them from being injured by dangerous objects on the land, which may allure them and which a child is not likely to know about. A landowner should, therefore, not grant permission to children who are unaccompanied by a responsible person to play near poisonous berries and, if they enter his land without his permission to play near such berries, he should take steps to stop them.

The moral is, of course, do not plant any tree or shrub with poisonous leaves or berries anywhere where either cattle or children can easily get at it.

Dangerous hedges and trees

A person who has a hedge or tree in such a state as to constitute danger to occupiers of adjoining land or persons lawfully using a highway—(see page 84) is liable for any damage which may result to such persons. But mere apprehension of injury from barbed wire does not give a right to damages.

Barbed wire

Under Section 143 of the Highways Act, 1959, a local authority may by notice require the removal of any barbed wire which constitutes a nuisance to a highway. If the land is occupied by the local authority any ratepayer can take proceedings to require the removal of the wire. If the wire is not removed within six months from the date of the notice, the authority or ratepayer can apply to a magistrates' court and if an order by them is not obeyed the authority or ratepayer can remove the wire and charge the occupier of the land with the cost of doing this.

Nuisance caused by use of land

A person must use his land in such a way as not to injure people on the highway. In a recent case a man lit a large bonfire of hedge clippings near a highway and the dense smoke blowing across the road caused two cars to collide because the vision of the drivers was obscured. The owner of the bonfire was held liable to the owners of the cars.

F   81

Generally speaking, however, the mere fact that an owner uses his land in a way which inconveniences a neighbour does not give the neighbour any right of action. To be actionable the conduct must be such as to constitute what the law terms a private nuisance, and this is judged by what the courts consider would be the reasonable standards of a reasonable man. Smoke from an occasional bonfire, is therefore, something quite different from a factory chimney belching smoke, and normally no action can be brought about a bonfire.

The question has been raised whether the Clean Air Act, 1956, applies to bonfires. Section 11 of the Act dealing with Smoke Control Areas, refers specifically to smoke which is emitted 'from a chimney of any building within a Smoke Control Area'. The smoke from a bonfire is not emitted from a chimney, and therefore, there is no control over it in a Smoke Control Area.

It would be possible, although in practice it is doubted if the provision will be used for this purpose, for smoke from bonfires to be dealt with under Section 16 of the Act. This relates to smoke other than that emitted from the chimney of a private dwelling, or other than dark smoke emitted from industrial chimneys. Unlike the preceding parts of the Act this section relates to 'smoke nuisances', and it is necessary for the emission to be proved to be a nuisance to the inhabitants of the neighbourhood.

Trees adjoining roads

An owner or occupier may be liable for damage caused by falling trees adjoining a highway although he does not know of the fact that the tree is dangerous, but negligence must be proved against him. If a tree overhangs a highway, the owner of the tree is liable for any damage caused by its roots or branches as a nuisance in the same way as he is liable when branches of his tree overhang his neighbour's property.

He is under a duty to manage his property in accordance with the principles of good estate management so that it is not in a condition likely to cause damage to persons lawfully using highways in the immediate vicinity. Good estate management may mean the inspection and trimming of trees from time to time. This principle does not mean that the owner of a tree is liable for damage, for instance, caused by a tree falling owing to rot in its roots where inspection would not have revealed this rot. He will be liable if he ought to have appreciated a danger which he would have been warned of if he had made proper inspections. It is a wise precaution, however, say, every four years to have any trees of a type which may become dangerous (e.g. elms) in-spected by a properly qualified and experienced tree expert. A land-owner is wise if he also inspects his trees himself every year when they are in leaf.

A tree may be dangerous not only because of decay or disease but because its top is too large or because it is growing on the side of a bank with few roots on one side.

Spraying

Spraying of plants, crops, hedgerows and trees with various poisons has become common and is too frequently undertaken thoughtlessly and with a reckless disregard of the effect of the sprays on the balance of nature and the property of neighbours. Spray, whether in the form of liquid or dust, drifts very easily, and, if a neighbour's crop or land is injured in any way by sprayed material from adjoining land, he can sue for damages without proof of any negligence on the part of the man using the spray; but he must, of course, prove that his property has been damaged by the spray. If the spraying were repeated continuously he could also apply for an injunction to stop the spraying. It is a pity that the law is not invoked more often against the selfish people who spray in disregard of the interests of others. A judge stated the law in 1704 thus: 'He whose filth it is must keep it in.'

Right to light

It is well known that there is no general right to the free passage of light to a house or building, and a right to the free passage of air to land or buildings can only be acquired in unusual circumstances—e.g. any right to the flow of air can subsist as an easement if it is claimed in respect of some definite channel, such as a ventilator in the flank wall of a build-ing. But a right to light can be acquired by grant from an adjoining owner or, what is more important, by actual enjoyment of such light for a period of at least twenty years without interruption. When a right to light has been acquired it is a breach of that right to erect a building on adjoining land which causes a substantial privation of light sufficient to render the occupation of the house with the right to light uncomfortable according to the ordinary notions of mankind or, in the case of business premises, which prevents the owner enjoying the light from carrying on his business as profitably as before.*

* Owners of property should note the provisions of the Right of Light Act, 1959, providing for a registration of a light obstruction notice, instead of a screen, to

Trees often obstruct light, but they differ from buildings, which are quickly erected, by growing comparatively slowly so that light is only gradually taken away over a period of years. Nevertheless it must often happen that the owner of a building has cause to complain of the reduction of his light which is caused by neighbouring trees. What is his position? Where the tree encroaches on to his land by root or by branch, there is an encroachment and, as we have said, an action for nuisance will lie whether the damage caused by the encroachment is to light, crops or buildings, provided there is damage. Where the tree grows in a boundary hedge there will in practice almost always be an encroachment.

The position, however, where trees are obstructing light without encroaching on neighbouring land at all, is much more difficult and, extraordinary as it may seem, no case has been found dealing with this point. Whether this is due to the reasonableness of landowners and the fact that they always have their trees or hedges pruned upon complaint, is not known. It may, of course, be due to their unwillingness to pay costs in making new law. Until English law is codified, too many areas of it will remain uncertain and will be resolved only at the expense of private litigants. Eminent counsel have considered this problem and one took the view that, in an acute case, the interference of light by trees where there was no encroachment would be actionable. But most counsel disagree. It would seem obvious that owners of trees and hedges should be required to behave in a neighbourly way, but the common law of England has in the past made little provision for enforcing habits of good conduct upon neighbours. The issue remains to be decided by some landowner who will be glad to see his name in the Law Reports.

POWERS OF PUBLIC AND LOCAL AUTHORITIES

Trees or hedges obstructing highways

By Section 65 of the Highways Act, 1959, a highway authority may,

---

prevent a right of light being acquired. Under this Act, an owner who is threatened by the acquisition of a right of light by a neighbour can apply to the Lands Tribunal for a certificate that notice of application for registration of a certificate has been given to all persons who may be affected. When the certificate is issued the notice accompanied with a plan and £10 must be registered with the local authority and has the same effect as if an actual screen had been erected to prevent a right of light coming into existence. It is no longer necessary to erect an unsightly screen for this purpose. There is no hearing of a case before the Lands Tribunal. If there is a dispute about the right of the applicant to register a notice, legal proceedings must be stated.

84

in relation to a highway which consists of or comprises a made-up carriageway, plant and remove trees, shrubs, grass and other vegetation, either for ornament or in the interests of safety, on any works which separate parts of the carriageway or on works at cross roads or other junctions, for regulating the movement of traffic.

By Section 82 a highway authority may, in a highway maintainable at the public expense by them, plant, alter and remove trees and shrubs and lay out grass verges, and may erect and maintain guards or fences and otherwise do anything expedient for the maintenance or protection of trees, shrubs and grass verges planted or laid out by them.

These powers may also be used in respect of land acquired for the construction of a highway.

A parish council or a local authority which is not the highway authority may, with the consent of the highway authority, also exercise these powers.

No tree, shrub, grass verge, guard or fence may be planted, laid out or erected or allowed to remain, in such a situation as to hinder the reasonable use of the highway or so as to be a nuisance or injurious to the owner or occupier of premises adjacent to the highway. If damage is caused to the property of any person by anything done in exercise of the powers conferred by this section, he is, unless his negligence caused the damage, entitled to recover compensation therefore from the authority or council by whom the powers were exercised, but if by his negligence he contributed to the damage the compensation is to be reduced accordingly.

Subject to these provisions, Section 123 provides that no tree or shrub shall be planted in a made-up carriageway, or within 15 ft. from the centre of a made-up carriageway. If this law is broken the highway authority may, by notice to the owner or to the occupier of the land in which the tree or shrub is planted, require him to remove it within 21 days.

A person who fails to comply with this notice is liable to a fine not exceeding 50p, and if the offence continues after conviction to a fine not exceeding 50p, for each day on which the offence is continued.

Although public and local authorities have these special powers to plant trees in streets, they owe the same duty of care to users of the highway as private owners of land adjoining the highway. If, however, a tree causes injury to a user of the highway, and the tree was not planted by the authority, it is likely but by no means certain that the authority is not liable under the present law.

It is also a nuisance at common law to allow trees to hang over a highway so as to obstruct its passage and any person may lop them so far as is necessary to remove the obstruction. Notwithstanding this law, however, it is clearly not advisable to take the law into one's own hands. In a case decided in 1888 H cut off the high blossoms, valued at 10d., from a chestnut tree growing on B's land and overhanging part of the highway to within a few feet of H's premises, and claimed a right to do the act complained of, as he had no other remedy to abate a nuisance caused by the branches of the tree interfering with the light and air to his dwelling, and by boys throwing stones at the blossoms and breaking his glass. It was contended for H that the cutting of the blossoms was a trifling trespass which did not come within the Malicious Damage Act. The High Court held that H was properly convicted for wilfully damaging the tree. A local authority should be asked in the case of obstruction to use its powers under the Highways Act hereafter set out.

Section 81 of the 1959 Act contains provisions to prevent danger of obstruction to the view of the users of a highway on or near any corner or bend or junction. A notice with a plan showing the land referred to may be served on the owner or occupier of the land and may direct the alteration of the height or character of any hedge, tree, shrub or vegetation, whether part of a hedge or not, and may forbid any fence, hedge, tree, etc., to be erected or planted on the land. This notice can be by the Department of the Environment or other highway authority. Any dispute about the reasonableness of the notice is decided by a court. The cost of doing the work can be recovered from the highway authority and, if the authority does the work, it cannot recover the cost from the owner. It is also a criminal offence, punishable by a fine of not more than £5, to fail to comply with the notice, and there is a further penalty of up to £2, for each day on which the offence continues. Compensation is payable for any loss or when property is injuriously affected by restrictions about planting imposed by such a notice.

Section 134 deals with a hedge, tree, shrub or vegetation which overhangs a highway or any other road or footpath to which the public has access so as to endanger or obstruct the passage of vehicles or pedestrians, or to obstruct or interfere with the view of drivers of vehicles or the light from a public lamp. In such a case the Department of the Environment or appropriate local authority may, by notice either to the owner of the hedge, or to the occupier of the land on which it is growing, require him, within 14 days, so to lop or cut it as to remove the cause of the danger, obstruction or interference. A person aggrieved by such notice may, within 21 days, appeal to a magistrates' court.

If a person fails to comply with a notice within the time limited the authority may carry out the work themselves and recover the expenses from the person in default. This section does not apply to trees adjoining the highway which are dangerous because of their position or diseased state. In London similar powers are given by Section 39 of the London County Council (General Powers) Act, 1928.

A final provision, which should be mentioned, although it is of less importance than it was because (a) of the powers given by Section 134, and (b) highways are not nowadays generally constructed so as to be liable to damage by sun or wind, is contained in Section 120. If a highway which comprises a carriageway is being damaged in consequence of the exclusion from it of the sun and wind by a hedge or tree (other than a tree planted for ornament, or for shelter to a building, courtyard or hop ground), a magistrates' court may, on a complaint made by the highway authority by order require the owner or occupier of the land so to cut, prune or plash the hedge or prune or lop the tree as to remove the cause of damage. Any person against whom an order is made who fails to comply with it within ten days from a specified date is liable to a fine not exceeding £2, and the highway authority may carry out the work required by the order and recover the expenses thereof from the person in default.

No person may be required by an order nor may any person be permitted by the authority to cut or prune a hedge at any time except between the last day of September and the first day of April. This useful restriction might well be borne in mind by authorities exercising their powers of lopping, etc., under other sections.

Planting of trees in roads

The Highways Act 1971 (Section 43) gives a new power to plant trees in highways. The highway authority may by a licence permit the occupier or the owner of any premises adjoining the highway to plant and maintain, or to retain and maintain, trees, shrubs, plants or grass in a specified part of the highway.

A licence may be granted to the occupier of premises and transfer of the licence may be prohibited. A licence may also be granted to the owner of premises and his successors in title but it is a condition of every such licence that within one month after any change in the ownership of the premises the licensee shall inform the highway authority of it.

A highway authority may by notice served on the licensee withdraw a licence granted by them:

(a) on the expiration of such period as may be specified in the notice, being a period of not less than seven days, if any condition of the licence is contravened by the licensee;

(b) on the expiration of such period as may be so specified, being a period of not less than three months, if the authority consider the withdrawal of the licence is necessary for the purpose of the exercise of their functions.

Where a licence expires or is withdrawn or surrendered, the highway authority:

(a) may remove all or any of the trees, shrubs, plants or grass to which the licence relates and reinstate the highway and recover the expenses reasonably incurred by them in so doing from the licensee; or

(b) if satisfied that the licensee can, within such reasonable time as they may specify, remove such trees, shrubs, plants or grass and reinstate the highway, may authorize him to do so at his own expense.

The licensee must indemnify the highway authority against any claim in respect of injury or loss arising out of the planting or presence of the trees or shrubs or works in connection therewith. If any person plants a tree or shrub in a highway without a licence he can be prosecuted under section 123 (which restricts the planting of trees or shrubs in or near a made-up carriageway) referred to above.

A highway authority retains its rights to authorize any person to plant anything in land it owns.

Electricity and telegraph lines

Under the Electricity (Supply) Act, 1926 (Sec. 34), statutory electricity authorities may lop hedges and lop or fell trees which obstruct or interfere with electric lines. They must, of course, give due notice, and an order of the Department of Trade and Industry can be required if the application is opposed. Any such lopping or cutting of trees and hedges must be done in a woodmanlike manner.

The Post Office has similar powers (under Section 5 of the Telegraph (Construction) Act, 1908) to require a tree to be lopped which obstructs or interferes with telegraph or telephone lines on a street or road. Disputes about any lopping required are decided by the county court. Compensation may be payable if the Post Office itself arranges for the work to be done and, if it does, it must be done in a husbandlike manner so as to avoid injury to the growth of the trees. It is encouraging to find an Act of Parliament recognizing the importance of not mutilating trees.

The British Railways Board, under an Act of 1868, has power

to get an order from magistrates for the removal of a tree which is in danger of falling on a railway line.

Improvement of amenities of open land

Section 65 of the Town and Country Planning Act, 1971, seems to give all the powers which are necessary for requiring the proper maintenance of gardens and open land. It appears to apply when the local planning authority considers that the amenity of any part of the authority's area, or of any adjoining area, is seriously injured by the condition of any garden, vacant site or other open land. In such a case, and subject to any directions given by the Department of the Environment, the authority may serve on the owner or occupier of the land a notice requiring him to take such steps for abating the injury to the neighbourhood as may be specified in the notice and the period within which these steps are to be taken may also be specified. The powers conferred by this section were reduced in value by a decision of the High Court in 1960 when it decided that the section does not apply where the garden or land is attached to a building.

Weeds

It is of some interest under this heading to note the provision of the Weeds Act, 1959, which gives the Ministry of Agriculture power to require an occupier of land to prevent the spreading of injurious weeds. The Ministry, if they consider that there are such weeds on a piece of land, may serve the occupier with a notice requiring him, within the time specified, to take such action as may be necessary to prevent the weeds from spreading. The Act applies to the following weeds:

Spear thistle (*Circium vulgare* (Savi) Ten)
Creeping or Field Thistle (*Circium arvense* (L.) Scop.)
Curled Dock (*Rumex crispus* L.)
Broad-leaved Dock (*Rumex obtusifolius* L.)

and to such additional weeds as may be prescribed.

When a person unreasonably fails to comply with a notice he is liable to a fine not exceeding £75 or, in the case of a second or subsequent offence, to a fine not exceeding £150.

Any person authorized by the Minister may, after notice, enter on and inspect any land and, if any person prevents or obstructs this entry, he is liable to a fine not exceeding £50.

The Minister may authorize the council of any county or borough to exercise on his behalf any of these powers. Complaints about these weeds should, therefore, first be made to the appropriate council.

Ownership of trees in highways

There is a presumption of law that the owner of land adjoining a highway owns the soil of one half the highway, i.e. up to its centre and trees in his half of a highway would, therefore, belong to him. The legal term 'highway' include footpaths and bridleways and this ownership may, therefore, well be of importance. Most highways which are roads or streets are, however, now vested in the Minister of Transport or in some local authority and in the case of these roads the property in the surface of the road and so much of the soil underneath as may be required for the proper use of the road is vested in the Minister or local authority. Trees in streets which are vested in a public authority belong to the authority. It is immaterial when the trees were planted.

Tree preservation orders

The Town and Country Planning Act empowers local planning authorities to make preservation orders for the protection of trees 'in the interests of amenity'.

This Act gives local planning authorities the power to make orders for the protection of specified single trees and groups of trees or woodlands, and specifies the provisions which an order may include. These may include the necessity of obtaining the consent (with or without conditions) of the local planning authority for the lopping, topping or felling of trees, the replanting of trees felled in accordance with the order and the payment of compensation.

When making a tree preservation order the local planning authority must serve notice on the owners and occupiers of the land, and where known, on other persons entitled to fell trees on the site, and the Minister is required to consider any objections or representations made by them. If necessary he holds a public inquiry. Any person who objects to the decision of a local planning authority to withhold consent to fell or the imposition of conditions governing consent or conditions requiring replanting may appeal to the Minister within 28 days or such longer period as the Department of the Environment may allow.

Preservation and planting of trees

The local planning authority must ensure whenever it is appropriate, that in granting planning permission adequate provision is made for the

90

preservation or planting of trees, and it must make such tree preservation orders as appear to be necessary in connection with the grant of such permission.

The policy now is to promote a planting policy for trees and to authorize an order for a tree not yet planted to operate as from the time the tree is planted.

The law is changed to ensure replacement of trees covered by an order. If any tree for which an order is in force (except a tree to which the order applies as part of a woodland) is removed or destroyed in breach of the order, or is removed, or destroyed, or dies when cutting down is authorized, the owner of the land must plant another tree of an appropriate size and species at the same place as soon as he reasonably can, unless the local planning authority dispense with this requirement.

The relevant order continues to apply as it applied to the original tree.

The duty applies even if the owner is not at fault, e.g., if a tree is destroyed by vandals. Statutory undertakers and government departments, such as the electricity boards and the Post Office, are exempt from these requirements, though it is said that appropriate discussions and concessions will take place.

Default in replanting

In the event of alleged default to replant, the local planning authority may serve an enforcement notice on the owner of the land, requiring him within a specified period to plant a tree or trees of such size as may be specified.

An appeal lies to the Department of the Environment on the grounds that: (a) the replanting does not apply (e.g., woodland) or has been complied with; (b) the requirements of the notice are unreasonable in respect of the period or the size or species of trees specified; (c) the planting of a tree or trees in accordance with the notice is not required in the interests of amenity or would be contrary to the practice of good forestry; (d) the place on which the tree is, or trees are, required to be planted is unsuitable for that purpose.

Penalties

The penalties for contravention of an order by cutting down or wilfully destroying a tree, or of topping or lopping a tree in such manner as to be likely to destroy it, are a fine of up to £250, or twice the sum which appears to the court to be the value of the tree, whichever is the greater. Alec Samuels comments in the Solicitors Journal, 8th September 1967 on these provisions as follows:

'Hitherto the small maximum fine has often been taken by the developer as part of the cost of development, and he has profited financially from deliberate defiance and flouting of the law. It is odd how often the bulldozer accidentally bumped into a tree, or the foreman of the site forgot to tell the bulldozer driver, or the driver misunderstood his instructions, or the tree unexpectedly died because somebody removed the bark in a fork, drilled a hole, filled it with salt, and replaced the bark. There is no statutory provision, largely because of drafting and enforcement difficulties, regarding the problem of mutilation not causing death, variously described as insensitive pollarding, unskilful surgery, and tree brutality.'

The problem essentially is one of educating owners to employ properly qualified persons to carry out pollarding, i.e. members of the Association of British Tree Surgeons and Arborists. The Department of the Environment has dealt with the problem in its publication *Trees in Town and City*, 1966.

The Forestry Commission advises the Ministry. The British Standards Institution has issued British Standard No. 3998 of 1966 on proper techniques for pollarding.

In anticipation of confirmation of an order, the owner or developer used often quickly to cut the tree down. Now a provisional order takes effect immediately, without waiting for a ministerial confirmation, and runs for six months pending such confirmation.

Powers of the Forestry Commission

The Forestry Act, 1967,* prohibits (except under licence) the felling of all growing trees other than those specifically exempt. The Act does not apply to trees in London.

An owner may without licence fell trees containing not more than 825 cu. ft. in any one quarter of a year, or sell trees containing not more than 150 cu. ft. in any one quarter. Other exemptions include the felling of small trees of a diameter not exceeding 3 in. or, in the case of coppice or underwood, not exceeding 6 in.; felling of fruit trees or any trees in an orchard, garden, churchyard or public open space; felling of trees for prevention of danger, and felling of trees of a diameter not exceeding 4 in. to improve the growth of other trees and the lopping or topping of trees or the trimming or laying of hedges.

* See also the Trees Act, 1970.

The Forestry Commission may direct an owner to fell trees when, in their opinion, it is expedient to do so in the interests of good forestry, or for the promotion of the establishment and maintenance of adequate reserves of growing trees, but they must have regard to the interests of agriculture and certain local amenities of the district. The Commission may also make the issue of a felling licence conditional on the restocking or stocking with trees of the land on which the felling takes place, and the maintenance of the trees for a period not exceeding ten years in accordance with the rules and practice of good forestry.

In cases where it appears to the Commissioners to be expedient in the interests of good forestry or agriculture, or of the amenities of the district or for promoting the establishment and maintenance of adequate reserves of growing trees, the Commission may: (a) refuse to grant a licence; or (b) grant a licence subject to conditions as above. In all other cases licences are granted unconditionally.

The countryside

The Countryside Act, 1968, has as its main purpose to provide for the improvement of facilities for the enjoyment of the countryside by the public. The Countryside Commission replaces the National Parks Commission and the re-constituted commission is given new powers which range from keeping under review matters relating to natural beauty, amenity, recreation and access to the countryside, to carrying out research and engaging in publicity about the countryside.

For what it is worth the Act provides in Section 11 that in the exercise of their functions relating to land under any Act of Parliament, every Minister and government department and public body shall have regard to the desirability of conserving the natural beauty and amenity of the countryside.

Section 15 amends the law relating to areas of specific scientific interest, i.e., those which are of interest because of their flora, fauna or geological or physiographical features, and the Natural Environment Research Council may enter into agreements with land owners and occupiers about such A.S.S.I.

Sections 23 and 24 empower the Forestry Commission to provide recreational and other facilities on land acquired for forestry and to acquire and plant land for amenity purposes. Section 25 provides for compensation of owners denied a forestry planting grant on replanting required under the terms of a replanting direction given by a local planning authority under a tree preservation order.

THE CRIMINAL LAW AND TREES

Theft

The law about the theft of trees and shrubs is contained in the Theft Act, 1968. Under this Act it is a criminal offence to steal a tree or plant or shrub in whole or part. It is also an offence to pick flowers, fruit, fungi or foliage from a plant growing wild for the purposes of sale, reward or other commercial purposes. It is therefore punishable to up-root and take away trees or cut off branches and remove them and it is also an offence to pick holly or primroses for sale.

The penalty for these offences is a fine of up to £100 or six months imprisonment on conviction before magistrates or up to ten years imprisonment on conviction before a higher court.

The 1966 report of the Criminal Law Revision Committee on which this Act is based proposed that any picking of flowers, fruit or foliage should be punishable if it injured the growth of the tree or shrub. Parliament unfortunately did not enact this provision. Therefore too much picking of plants continues.

Malicious damage

The whole of the law relating to damage to trees and shrubs is now covered by a comprehensive statute—the Criminal Damage Act, 1971 which deals with any damage to property. It creates several offences but that which is of most interest to readers is that contained in the first section which makes it a criminal offence without lawful excuse to damage or destroy another's property. This covers the destruction or damage to any type of property by any means. There must be an intention to destroy or damage or recklessness in relation to the destruction or damage of property; for instance to throw a stone at a motor-car which misses and breaks a shop window could lead to a criminal charge for damaging the shop window because the thrower of the stone was reckless.

There is also the more serious offence of destroying or damaging property if life might be endangered and if destruction or damage to property includes damage by fire this offence is arson. There are other offences created by the Act, such as threatening to destroy or damage property and having in one's custody or under one's control anything

94

for the purpose of using it or letting someone else use it to destroy or damage someone else's property. If a person damaging property raises the defence of lawful excuse the law becomes more complicated and it would be advisable to consult a solicitor. The penalty for this offence is on conviction before magistrates imprisonment of up to six months or a fine up to £400 or both. If the offence is regarded as more serious and sent to a Crown Court then the offender can be sent to prison for up to ten years.

Under the Act it is an offence to destroy or damage any wild creatures which have been tamed or which are ordinarily kept in captivity. It is not an offence to destroy or damage mushrooms growing wild or the fruit, flowers or foliage of a plant growing wild on any land. 'Mushroom' is defined to include any fungus and 'plant' includes any shrub or tree. Therefore, the wild fruits or flowers or leaves of a tree can be picked but it could be a criminal offence to break off a whole branch. It is a question of degree as to when a person taking, e.g., foliage, in fact does more than remove the foliage and removes a branch of a tree.

None of the penalties mentioned in this chapter is changed by the Criminal Justice Act of 1967 which increased many maximum fines to adjust them to the falling value of money.

6

Selective Lists
of Climbing and Twining Plants
and Plants for Hedges and Screens

When one is planting a climbing or twining plant or a hedge or screen, choice must often be governed by the nature of the soil. The purpose for which the climbing or twining plant or hedge or screen is required must be considered, its situation—whether it is in town or country or by the sea, and so on—and the extent to which it is to serve as a screen or windbreak. I have, therefore, set out in alphabetical sequence a selection of climbing and twining plants, also hedge and screen plants for various soils and situations. Full descriptions of those recommended are given in Chapter 7.

Deciduous = d. Evergreen = e. Semi-evergreen = s-e.

SOILS

Chalk soils

CLIMBING AND TWINING PLANTS

d.   Actinidia in variety
d.   Ampelopsis
d.   Celastrus species
d. e. Clematis in variety
d.   *Clianthus puniceus* (Lobster-claw)
e.   *Ercilla volubilis*
e.   *Euonymus fortunei* and its varieties

ABOVE LEFT: the fragrant flowers of *Chimonanthus praecox*
ABOVE RIGHT: *Jasminum nudiflorum*, the winter jasmine, has bright yellow flowers
BELOW LEFT: the Japanese Quince, *Chaenomeles speciosa*, in fruit
BELOW RIGHT: *Chaenomeles speciosa* 'Cardinalis' bears crimson-scarlet flowers

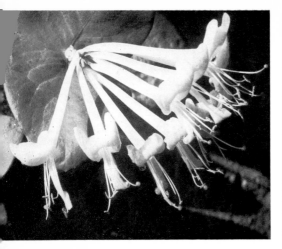

ABOVE LEFT: a striking honeysuckle, *Lonicera tragophylla*, with large, bright yellow, scentless flowers

ABOVE RIGHT: our common honeysuckle, *Lonicera periclymenum*

BELOW LEFT: the free flowering, evergreen *Lonicera japonica halliana* has sweetly scented, white flowers

BELOW RIGHT: golden-yellow variegated netted, evergreen foliage of *Lonicera japonica* 'Aureoreticulata'

e.   Hedera (Ivy) in variety
d.   *Hydrangea anomala*
d.   *H. petiolaris*
d. e. Jasminum (Jasmine), in variety
d. e. Lonicera (Honeysuckle) in variety
d.   *Lycium chinense* (Chinese Box-thorn)
d.   *Muehlenbeckia complexa*
d.   Parthenocissus (Virginia Creeper) species and varieties
d.   *Periploca graeca* (Silk Vine)
d.   *Polygonum baldschuanicum* (Russian Vine)
d.   Rosa species and varieties
d.   Rubus species (Bramble)
d.   *Schizophragma hydrangioides*
d.   *S. integrifolium*
d.   *Senecio scandens*
d.   Vitis (vine) species
d.   Wisteria in variety

WALL AND FENCE PLANTS

d.   *Abeliophyllum distichum*
d.   *Abutilon megapotamicum*
d.   *A. vitifolium*
d.   Actinidia species
d.   Ampelopsis
e.   *Azara dentata*
e.   *Carpenteria californica*
d. e. Ceanothus species and varieties
d.   *Celastrus orbiculatus*
d.   Chaenomeles in variety (syn. Cydonia) (Japanese Quince, Japonica)
d.   *Chimonanthus praecox* (Winter Sweet)
e.   *Choisya ternata* (Mexican Orange-blossom)
d. e. Clematis species and varieties
d.   *Clianthus puniceus* (Lobster-claw)
d. e. *Coronilla glauca*
d. e. Cotoneaster species and varieties
e.   *Ercilla volubilis*
e.   Escallonia in variety
e.   *Euonymus fortunei*
d.   Forsythia species and varieties
d.   *Fremontodendron californicum*
e.   *Garrya elliptica*

G   97

e.   Hedera (Ivy) species and varieties
d.   *Hydrangea petiolaris*
d. e. Jasminum (Jasmine) in variety
d.   *Kerria japonica* 'Pleniflora' (Jew's Mallow)
d.   *Lippia citriodora* (Lemon-scented Verbena)
d. e. Lonicera (Honeysuckle) species and varieties
e.   *Magnolia grandiflora*
e.   *Osmanthus delavayi*
d.   Parthenocissus (Virginia Creeper) species and varieties
d.   *Polygonum baldschuanicum* (Russian Vine)
d.   *Punica granatum* (Pomegranate)
d.   Pyracantha (Firethorn) species and varieties
d.   *Ribes laurifolium*
d.   *R. speciosum*
d.   *Schizophragma hydrangioides*
d.   *S. integrifolium*
d.   *Senecio scandens*
e.   *Sophora tetraptera* (Kowhai)
e.   *Teucrium fruticans* (Shrubby Germander)
e.   *Viburnum × burkwoodii*
d.   *V. macrocephalum*
d.   Vitis (Vine) species
d.   Wisteria species and varieties

HEDGES

d.   *Acer campestre* (Common Maple)
e.   *Atriplex halimus* (Tree Purslane)
e.   *Aucuba japonica*
e.   Bamboo
d. e. Berberis (Barberry) species and varieties
d.   *Buddleia davidii* in variety
e.   *Bupleurum fruticosum*
e.   Buxus (Box)
e.   *Cassinia fulvida* (syn. *Diplopappus chrysophyllus*)
d.   *Ceratostigma willmottianum*
d.   Chaenomeles in variety (syn. Cydonia) (Japanese Quince, Japonica)
e.   *Chamaecyparis lawsoniana* and its varieties
e.   *Choisya ternata* (Mexican Orange-blossom)
e.   Cistus (Rock Rose)
d.   *Cornus mas* (Cornelian Cherry)
d.   *Corylus avellana* (Hazel)

d. e. Cotoneaster species and varieties
d.   *Crataegus* (Hawthorn, Quickthorn)
e.   *Cryptomeria japonica* 'Elegans'
e.   *Cupressocyparis leylandii* (Leyland Cypress)
e.   *Cupressus macrocarpa* (Monterey Cypress)
d.   Deutzia in variety
d.   Diervilla, *see* Weigela
e.   *Erica carnea* (Heather) and varieties
e.   *E. mediterranea*
e.   *E. terminalis*
e.   Escallonia in variety
d.   *Euonymus europaeus* (Spindle Tree)
e.   *E. fortunei*
e.   *E. japonicus*
d.   *Fagus sylvatica* (Beech)
d.   *Forsythia intermedia* 'Spectabilis'
d.   Fuchsia in variety
e.   *Griselinia littoralis*
e.   Hebe (syn. Veronica)
e.   Hedera (Ivy) (for a fedge, *see* page 190)
d.   *Hibiscus syriacus* varieties
d.   *Hippophae rhamnoides* (Sea Buckthorn)
e.   *Hypericum calycinum* (Rose of Sharon)
e.   *H. patulum*
d.   *Hyssopus officinalis*
e.   *Ilex aquifolium* (Holly) in variety
e.   Juniperus species and varieties
d.   *Kerria japonica*
d.   *K. j.* 'Pleniflora' (Jew's Mallow)
e.   *Laurus nobilis* (Sweet Bay)
e.   Lavandula (Lavender)
d.   *Leycesteria formosa* (Himalayan Honeysuckle)
e.   Ligustrum (Privet)
e.   *Lonicera nitida* (Chinese Honeysuckle)
d.   *Lycium chinense* (Chinese Box-thorn)
e.   *Mahonia aquifolium* (Oregon Grape)
e.   *Myrtus communis* (Myrtle)
d.   Nothofagus
e.   Olearia, particularly *O. haastii* and *O. macrodonta*
e.   Osmanthus
e.   *Osmarea burkwoodii*

d. *Perovskia atriplicifolia*
d. Philadelphus (Mock Orange, Syringa, in variety)
e. Phillyrea
e. Pittosporum
e. *Podocarpus andinus* (syn. *Prumnopitys elegans*)
d. *Potentilla fruticosa*
d. *Prunus cerasifera* (Myrobalan Plum) and varieties
e. *P. laurocerasus* (Common or Cherry Laurel)
e. *P. lusitanica* (Portugal Laurel)
e. Pyracantha (Firethorn) species and varieties
e. *Quercus ilex* (Evergreen or Holm Oak)
d. *Ribes sanguineum* (Flowering Currant)
d. Rosa (Rose) species
e. Rosmarinus (Rosemary)
e. *Ruscus aculeatus* (Butcher's Broom)
e. Ruta (Rue)
d. Sambucus (Elder)
e. *Santolina chamaecyparissus* (Lavender Cotton)
e. Sarcococca
e. *Senecio greyi*
d. *Sorbus intermedia*
d. *Spartium junceum* (Spanish Broom)
d. Spiraea species and varieties
e. Stranvaesia
d. Symphoricarpos (Snowberry)
d. Syringa (Lilac)
d. Tamarix (Tamarisk)
e. *Taxus baccata* (Yew)
e. *Teucrium fruticans*
e. Thuja
e. Tsuga
e. *Ulex europaeus* (Gorse)
d. Ulmus (Elm)
e. Veronica, *see* Hebe
d. *Viburnum opulus* (Guelder Rose)
e. *V. tinus* (Laurustinus)
d. Weigela (syn. Diervilla)

Damp and clay soils

CLIMBING AND TWINING PLANTS

d. Actinidia species
d. Ampelopsis
e. *Asteranthera ovata*
d. Campsis species (Trumpet Vine)
d. Celastrus species
d. e. Clematis species and varieties
d. *Decumaria barbara*
d. *Eccremocarpus scaber*
e. *Ercilla volubilis*
e. *Euonymus fortunei*
e. Hedera (Ivy) species and varieties
d. Humulus (Hop) species
d. *Hydrangea anomala*
d. *H. petiolaris*
d. Jasminum (Jasmine) species
d. e. Lonicera (Honeysuckle) species and varieties
d. *Lycium chinense* (Chinese Box-thorn)
d. *Menispermum canadense* (Moonseed)
d. *Muehlenbeckia complexa*
e. Mutisia species
d. Parthenocissus (Virginia Creeper) species and varieties
d. *Passiflora caerulea* (Passion-flower)
d. *Periploca graeca* (Silk Vine)
e. *Pileostegia viburnoides*
d. *Polygonum baldschuanicum* (Russian Vine)
d. Rubus species (Bramble)
d. Schizophragma species
d. *Senecio scandens*
d. *Smilax rotundifolia*
d. Solanum species and varieties
e. *Trachelospermum jasminoides*
d. *Tropaeolum speciosum* (Scotch Creeper)
d. Vitis (Vine) species
d. Wisteria species and varieties

WALL AND FENCE PLANTS

d. *Abeliophyllum distichum*
d. *Abutilon vitifolium*

d. e. Ceanothus species and varieties
d. Chaenomeles (syn. Cydonia) (Japanese Quince, Japonica)
d. *Chimonanthus praecox* (Winter Sweet)
d. *Choisya ternata* (Mexican Orange-blossom)
d. e. Cotoneaster species and varieties
e. *Eriobotrya japonica* (Loquat)
e. Escallonia species and varieties
e. *Feijoa sellowiana*
d. Forsythia species and varieties
e. *Garrya elliptica*
d. *Kerria japonica* 'Pleniflora' (Jew's Mallow)
e. *Magnolia grandiflora*
d. *M. soulangiana*
e. *Osmanthus delavayi*
e. Pyracantha (Firethorn) species and varieties
d. *Ribes laurifolium* (Flowering Currant)
e. *Sophora tetraptera*
e. *Viburnum × burkwoodii*
d. *V. macrocephalum*

HEDGES

d. *Acer campestre* (Common Maple)
d. *Alnus glutinosa* (Alder)
e. Arundinaria, *see* Bamboo
e. Aucuba
e. Bamboo
d. e. Berberis (Barberry) species and varieties
d. Betula (Silver Birch)
d. *Buddleia davidii* varieties
e. *Bupleurum fruticosum*
d. *Carpinus betulus* (Hornbeam)
e. *Cassinia fulvida*
d. Chaenomeles (syn. Cydonia) (Japanese Quince, Japonica)
d. *Cornus alba* (Dogwood) and varieties
d. *Corylus avellana* (Hazel)
d. Crataegus (Hawthorn, Quickthorn)
d. *Kerria japonica*
d. *K. j.* 'Pleniflora' (Jew's Mallow)
d. *Leycesteria formosa* (Himalayan Honeysuckle)
d. Lycium
e. *Mahonia aquifolium* (Oregon Grape)

102

e. Phyllostachys, *see* Bamboo
e. *Prunus laurocerasus* (Common or Cherry Laurel)
e. *Rhododendron ponticum* (Common Rhododendron)
d. *Ribes sanguineum* (Flowering Currant)
d. *Salix alba* (Willow)
d. *S. a.* 'Chermesina'
d. *S. viminalis* (Common Osier)
d. *Sambucus nigra* (Elder)
e. *Skimmia japonica*
d. Spiraea species and varieties
e. Stranvaesia
d. Ulmus (Elm)
d. *Viburnum lantana* (Wayfaring Tree)
d. *V. opulus* (Guelder Rose)

Dry and sandy soils

CLIMBING AND TWINING PLANTS

d. Actinidia
d. Ampelopsis
d. Campsis species (Trumpet Creeper)
d. Celastrus species
d. *Cobaea scandens*
d. Cucurbita
d. *Decumaria barbara*
e. *D. sinensis*
e. *Eccremocarpus scaber*
e. *Ercilla volubilis*
e. *Euonymus fortunei* and its varieties
e. *Hedera helix* (Ivy) in variety
e. *Holboellia coriacea*
d. *Jasminum officinale*
e. *Kadsura japonica*
e. *Lapageria rosea*
d. *Muehlenbeckia complexa*
e. Mutisia species
d. Parthenocissus (Virginia Creeper) species and varieties
e. *Passiflora caerulea* (Passion Flower)
d. *Periploca graeca* (Silk Vine)
d. Pharbitis
e. *Pileostegia viburnoides*

d.   *Polygonum baldschuanicum* (Russian Vine)

d. e. s-e. Rubus species (Bramble)

d. e. Schisandra species

d.   *Schizophragma hydrangoides*

d. e. Smilax

e.   *Stauntonia hexaphylla*

e.   *Trachelospermum jasminoides*

d.   Tropaeolum

d.   Vitis (Vine) species

d.   Wisteria species and varieties

WALL AND FENCE PLANTS

s-c. Abelia species

d.   *Abeliophyllum distichum*

d.   Abutilon species and varieties

e.   *Azara dentata*

e.   *Berberidopsis corallina* (Coral Plant)

d.   Campsis species (Trumpet Creeper)

e.   *Carpentaria californica*

e.   Ceanothus

d.   Chaenomeles (syn. Cydonia) (Japanese Quince, Japonica) species and varieties

d.   *Chimonanthus praecox* (Winter Sweet)

e.   *Choisya ternata* (Mexican Orange-blossom)

e.   *Coronilla glauca*

e.   Cotoneaster species and varieties

d.   *Dendromecon rigida*

e.   *Eccremocarpus scaber*

e.   *Eriobotrya japonica*

e.   Escallonia in variety

e.   *Euonymus fortunei* and its varieties

e.   *Feijoa sellowiana*

s-e. *Fremontiodendron californicum*

e.   *Garrya elliptica*

e.   Hedera (Ivy) species and varieties

e.   *Holboellia coriacea*

d.   *Hydrangea anomala*

d.   *H. petiolaris*

e.   *Itea ilicifolia*

d.   *Jasminum nudiflorum* (Winter Jasmine)

d.   *Kerria japonica* 'Pleniflora' (Jew's Mallow)

d.   *Lippia citriodora* (Lemon-scented Verbena)
e.   *Magnolia grandiflora*
d.   *M. soulangiana*
e.   *Osmanthus delavayi*
d.   Parthenocissus (Virginia Creeper) species and varieties
e.   *Piptanthus laburnifolius*
d.   *Prunus triloba*
d.   *Punica granatum* (Pomegranate)
e.   Pyracantha (Firethorn) species and varieties
e.   *Ribes laurifolium*
d.   *R. speciosum*
d.   Schisandra
d.   *Schizophragma hydrangioides*
d.   *S. integrifolia*
d.   *Senecio scandens*
d.   *Sophora tetraptera* (Kowhai)
e.   *Teucrium fruticans* (Shrubby Germander)
s-e. *Viburnum* x *burkwoodii*
d.   *V. macrocephalum*
d.   *Watakaka sinensis*
d.   Wisteria species and varieties

HEDGES

d.   *Acer campestre* (Common Maple)
e.   *Atriplex halimus* (Tree Purslane)
d. e. Berberis (Barberry) species and varieties
d.   *Betula pendula* (Silver Birch)
d.   *Buddleia davidii* in variety
e.   *Bupleurum fruticosum*
e.   Buxus (Box)
d.   *Carpinus betulus* (Hornbeam)
e.   *Cassinia fulvida* (syn. *Diplopappus chrysophyllus*)
d.   Chaenomeles (syn. Cydonia) (Japanese Quince, Japonica)
e.   *Choisya ternata* (Mexican Orange-blossom)
e.   Cistus (Rock Rose) species and varieties
e.   *Corokia cotoneaster*
d.   Crataegus (Hawthorn, Quickthorn)
d.   Cytisus (Broom)
e.   Escallonia in variety
d.   *Fagus sylvatica* (Beech)
d.   Fuchsia in variety

105

e. *Griselinia littoralis*
e. Hebe (syn. Veronica) species and varieties
e. *Hedera helix* (Ivy)
d. *Hibiscus syriacus*
d. *Hippophae rhamnoides* (Sea Buckthorn)
d. Hypericum in variety
e. *Ilex aquifolium* (Holly)
d. *Kerria japonica*
d. *K. j.* 'Pleniflora' (Jew's Mallow)
e. *Laurus nobilis* (Sweet Bay)
e. Lavandula (Lavender)
d. *Leycesteria formosa* (Himalayan Honeysuckle)
e. Ligustrum (Privet)
e. *Lonicera nitida* (Chinese Honeysuckle)
e. *L. yunnanensis*
d. *Lycium chinense* (Chinese Box-thorn)
e. *Mahonia aquifolium* (Oregon Grape)
e. *Myrtus communis* (Myrtle)
e. *Olearia haastii*
e. *O. macrodonta*
e. *Osmarea burkwoodii*
e. Phillyrea
e. Pittosporum
d. *Potentilla fruticosa*
e. *Prunus laurocerasus* (Common or Cherry Laurel)
e. *P. l. schipkaensis*
e. *P. lusitanica* (Portugal Laurel)
d. *P. spinosa* (Blackthorn, Sloe)
e. Pyracantha (Firethorn) species and varieties
e. *Rosmarinus officinalis* (Rosemary)
e. *Ruscus aculeatus* (Butcher's Broom)
d. *Sambucus nigra* (Elder)
e. *Santolina chamaecyparissus* (Lavender Cotton)
e. *Senecio greyi*
d. *Spartium junceum* (Spanish Broom)
d. Spiraea species and varieties
d. Symphoricarpos (Snowberry)
d. Tamarix (Tamarisk)
e. Ulex (Gorse)
e. Veronica, *see* Hebe
d. *Viburnum lantana* (Wayfaring Tree)

106

d.   *V. opulus* (Guelder Rose)
e.   *V. rhytidophyllum*
e.   *V. tinus* (Laurustinus)

HEDGES FOR VARIOUS PURPOSES

CONIFER HEDGES

e.   *Chamaecyparis lawsoniana* (Lawson Cypress)
e.   Cryptomeria
e.   *Cupressocyparis leylandii* (Leyland Cypress)
e.   *Cupressus macrocarpa* (Monterey Cypress)
e.   *C. m.* 'Lutea'
d.   *Metasequoia glyptostroboides* (Dawn Redwood)
e.   Picea (Spruce) in variety
d.   *Podocarpus andinus* (syn. *Prumnopitys elegans*)
e.   *Taxus baccata* (Yew) and varieties
e.   Thuja (Arbor Vitae) in variety
e.   Tsuga (Hemlock Spruce) in variety

FARM HEDGES

d.   *Acer campestre* (Common Maple)
d.   *Carpinus betulus* (Hornbeam)
d.   *Crataegus oxyacantha* (Hawthorn, Quickthorn)
d.   *Corylus avellana* (Hazel)
d.   *Fagus sylvatica* (Beech)
e.   *Ilex aquifolium* (Holly)
d.   *Prunus cerasifera* (Myrobalan Plum)
d.   *P. spinosa* (Blackthorn, Sloe)
e.   *Ulex europaeus* (Gorse)
d.   *Ulmus procera* (English Elm)

FLOWERING HEDGES

d.   Azalea, *see* Rhododendron
e.   *Berberis candidula*
e.   *B. darwinii*
e.   *B. gagnepainii*
e.   *B. stenophylla*
e.   *B. thunbergii*
e.   *B. verruculosa*
d.   *Buddleia davidii* in variety

107

e. Calluna (Ling)
e. *Cassinia fulvida*
d. Ceanothus
d. *Ceratostigma willmottianum*
d. Chaenomeles (syn. Cydonia) (Japanese Quince, Japonica)
e. *Choisya ternata* (Mexican Orange-blossom)
e. Cistus (Rock Rose)
d. e. Cotoneaster species and varieties
d. *Cytisus scoparius* (syn. *Sarothamnus scoparius*) and its varieties.
d. Deutzia species and varieties
d. Diervilla, *see* Weigela
d. Erica (Heather)
e. Escallonia in variety
d. Forsythia in variety
d. Fuchsia in variety
e. Hebe (syn. Veronica)
d. *Hibiscus syriacus*
d. *Hydrangea macrophylla* (syn. *H. hortensis*)
d. e. Hypericum (St. John's Wort)
d. *Kerria japonica*
d. *K. j.* 'Pleniflora' (Jew's Mallow)
e. Lavandula (Lavender)
d. *Leyesteria formosa* (Himalayan Honeysuckle)
d. *Lycium chinense* (Chinese Box-thorn)
e. *Mchonia aquifolium* (Oregon Grape)
e. *Mayrtus communis* (Myrtle)
d. Nuttallia, *see* Osmoronia
e. *Osmanthus delavayi*
e. *Osmarea burkwoodii*
d. Osmoronia (syn. Nuttallia) (Oso Berry)
d. *Perovskia atriplicifolia*
d. Philadelphus (Mock Orange, Syringa)
d. *Potentilla fruticosa*
e. Pyracantha species and varieties
e. *Rhododendron ponticum* (Common Rhododendron) when allowed
    to grow informally
d. Ribes (Flowering Currant)
d. Rosa (Rose) species and varieties
e. Rosmarinus (Rosemary)
e. *Santolina chamaecyparissus* (Lavender Cotton)
d. Sarothamnus, *see* Cytisus

108

e. *Senecio greyi*
e. Skimmia
d. Spiraea species and varieties
d. Syringa (Lilac) species and varieties
d. Tamarix (Tamarisk)
e. Ulex (Gorse)
e. Veronica, *see* Hebe
d. *Viburnum opulus* 'Sterile' (Snowball Tree)
e. *V. tinus* (Laurustinus)
d. Weigela (syn. Diervilla)

FRAGRANT HEDGES
(All have fragrant flowers: ff. = also fragrant foliage)

e. ff. Artemisia
d. Azalea, *see Rhododendron luteum*
e. *Berberis stenophylla* (Barberry)
d. *Buddleia davidii* varieties
e. Buxus (Box)
d. Cytisus (Broom)
e. *Erica arborea alpina* (Tree Heath)
e. ff. Lavandula (Lavender)
e. *Mahonia aquifolium* (Oregon Grape)
d. Nuttallia, *see* Osmaronia
d. *Osmanthus delavayi*
d. *Osmarea burkwoodii*
d. *Osmaronia cerasiformis* (Oso Berry)
d. Philadelphus (Mock Orange, Syringa)
e. *Rhododendron luteum* (Yellow Azalea)
e. ff. Rosmarinus (Rosemary)
e. ff. Rosa species and varieties
e. ff. Santolina (Lavender Cotton)
e. *Skimmia japonica*
d. Syringa (Lilac) species and varieties

INDUSTRIAL AND TOWN HEDGES

e. *Aucuba japonica* and varieties
e. *Berberis darwinii*
e. *Berberis stenophylla*
e. Buxus (Box)
s-e. *Cotoneaster simonsii*
e. *Euonymus japonica*

d.   *Fagus sylvatica* (Beech)
d.   Forsythia
e.   *Griselinia littoralis*
e.   *Hebe brachysiphon* (syn. *Veronica traversii*)
d.   *Hibiscus syriacus* in variety
e.   Ilex (Holly)
e.   Ligustrum (Privet)
e.   *Lonicera nitida* (Chinese Honeysuckle)
e.   *Mahonia aquifolium* (Oregon Grape)
e.   *Olearia haastii*
e.   *Osmarea burkwoodii*
d.   *Prunus cerasifera* (Myrobalan)
e.   *P. laurocerasus* (Common or Cherry Laurel)
e.   *P. lusitanica* (Portugal Laurel)
e.   Pyracantha (Firethorn)
e.   *Rhododendron ponticum* (Common Rhododendron)
e.   *Quercus ilex* (Evergreen or Holm Oak)
d.   *Ribes sanguineum* (Flowering Currant)
e.   *Veronica traversii, see* Hebe
e.   *Viburnum tinus* (Laurustinus)

INTERIOR HEDGES

d.   Azalea, *see* Rhododendron
e.   *Berberis darwinii*
e.   *B. gagnepainii*
e.   *B. stenophylla*
e.   *B. verruculosa*
e.   *Buxus sempervirens* (Box)
e.   *B. suffruticosa* (Box used for edging)
d. e. Ceanothus
d.   Chaenomeles (syn. Cydonia) (Japanese Quince, Japonica)
e.   Cistus (Broom)
d.   *Corylus avellana* (Hazel) and varieties
d. e. Cotoneaster species and varieties
d.   Cytisus (Broom)
e.   Erica (Heather)
e.   Escallonia in variety
d.   Forsythia
d.   Fuchsia in variety
e.   *Hebe* (syn. Veronica) *speciosa*
d.   *Hibiscus syriacus*

110

d.   *Hydrangea macrophylla* (syn. *H. hortensis*)
d.   Hypericum (St. John's Wort)
e.   Lavandula (Lavender)
d.   *Leycesteria formosa* (Himalayan Honeysuckle)
e.   *Mahonia aquifolium* (Oregon Grape)
e.   *Myrtus communis* (Myrtle)
e.   *Osmanthus delavayi*
e.   *Osmarea burkwoodii*
e.   *Pernettya mucronata* varieties
d.   Philadelphus (Mock Orange, Syringa)
d.   *Potentilla fruticosa* varieties
e.   Pyracantha (Firethorn)
e.   *Rhododendron luteum* (Yellow Azalea)
d.   Ribes (Flowering Currant)
d. e. Rosa (Rose) species and varieties
e.   Rosmarinus (Rosemary)
e.   Ruta (Rue)
e.   Santolina (Lavender Cotton)
e.   *Senecio greyi*
d.   Spiraea species and varieties
e.   Veronica, *see* Hebe
e.   *Viburnum tinus* (Laurustinus)

ROSE HEDGES

Agnes
Alba maxima
Belle de Crecy
Blanc Double de Coubert
Bloomfield Abundance
Bonn
Buff Beauty
Capitaine John Ingram
Cecile Brunner
Celestial
Charles de Mills
Chinatown
Commandant Beaurepaire
Cornelia
Dorothy Wheatcroft
Eglantine—see *Rosa rubiginosa*
Elmshorn

111

Felicia
Fellemberg
Frau Dagmar Hastrup
Frensham
Heidelberg
Hermosa
Iceberg
Kassel
Kathleen Ferrier
Kathleen Harrop
Korona
Lavender Lassie
Lilli Marlene
Louisie Odier
Lubeck
Madame Isaac Pereire
Maidens Blush, Great
Masquerade
Nypel's Perfection
Old Blush
Penelope
Prosperity
Queen Elizabeth
Rosa Mundi
Rosemary Rose
Roseraie de L'Hay
rubiginosa
rugosa
Saarbrucken
Sarah Van Fleet
scabrosa
Schneezwerg
Stanwell Perpetual
Tuscany Superb
Wilhelm
Will Scarlet
Zéphirine Drouhin

SEASIDE HEDGES

d. e. *Atriplex halimus* (Tree Purslane)
d. e. Berberis (Barberry)

ABOVE LEFT: the fruits of *Celastrus orbiculatus* are scarlet and orange-yellow
ABOVE RIGHT: the leaves of *Hedera canariensis* 'Variegata' are green, silvery-grey and white
BELOW LEFT: *Abeliophyllum distichum* has white, forsythia-like blossoms
BELOW RIGHT: a variegated Persian ivy, *Hedera colchica* 'Dentata Variegata'

ABOVE LEFT: *Garrya elliptica*, an evergreen, is aptly named the Tassel Bush—its greyish-green male catkins are often 6–10 in. long

ABOVE RIGHT: the deep blue flowered *Ceanothus impressus*

BELOW LEFT: camellias make a useful evergreen covering for a trellis

BELOW RIGHT: the Jew's mallow, *Kerria japonica* 'Pleniflora' and *Cotoneaster horizontalis* (far left)

d. *Buddleia davidii* for an informal hedge
e. *Buxus sempervirens* (Box) if given partial shelter
e. Calluna (Ling)
e. *Cassinia fulvida* (syn. *Diplopappus chrysophyllus*)
e. *Corokia virgata*
e. Cotoneaster species and varieties
d. Crataegus (Hawthorn, Quickthorn)
e. Erica (Heather)
e. *Escallonia macrantha*
e. *Euonymus japonica*
e. *Griselinia littoralis*
e. *Hebe brachysiphon* (syn. *Veronica traversii*)
e. *H. speciosa*
d. *Hippophae rhamnoides* (Sea Buckthorn)
d. *Hydrangea macrophylla* (syn. *H. hortensis*)
e. Lavandula (Lavender)
e. *Lonicera nitida* (Chinese honeysuckle)
e. Ligustrum (privet)
d. *Lycium chinense* (Chinese Box-thorn)
e. *Olearia haastii*
e. *O. macrodonta*
e. Osmanthus
e. *Osmarea burkwoodii*
e. *Pernettya mucronata* and varieties
e. Pittosporum
d. *Potentilla fruticosa*
d. *Prunus cerasifera* (Myrobalan Plum)
d. *P. spinosa* (Blackthorn or Sloe)
e. Pyracantha (Firethorn) species and varieties
e. *Quercus ilex* (Evergreen or Holm Oak)
e. Rosmarinus (Rosemary)
d. *Sambucus nigra* (Elder)
e. *Santolina chamaecyparissus* (Lavender Cotton)
e. *Senecio greyi*
e. *S. rotundifolius*
e. *Skimmia japonica*
d. *Spartium junceum* (Spanish Broom)
d. Tamarix (Tamarisk)
e. *Ulex europaeus* (Gorse)
e. Veronica, *see* Hebe
e. *Viburnum tinus* (Laurustinus)

d.   Weigela (syn. Diervilla) in variety

SCREENS AND WINDBREAKS FOR VARIOUS PURPOSES

CONIFER SCREENS AND WINDBREAKS

e.   *Chamaecyparis lawsoniana* (Lawson Cypress) and its many varieties
e.   *Cupressocyparis leylandii* (Leyland Cypress)
e.   *Cupressus macrocarpa* (Monterey Cypress)
e.   *C. m.* 'Lutea'
d.   Larix (Larch)
e.   Picea (Spruce)
e.   Pinus (Pine)
e.   Pseudotsuga (Douglas Fir)
e.   *Thuja occidentalis* (Arbor-Vitae)
e.   *T. plicata*
e.   Tsuga (Hemlock Spruce)

SEASIDE CONIFEROUS SCREEN TREES

e.   *Cupressocyparis leylandii* (Leyland Cypress)
e.   *Cupressus macrocarpa* (Monterey Cypress)
e.   *C. m.* 'Lutea'
e.   *Pinus mugo* (Mountain Pine)
e.   *P. nigra* (Austrian Pine)
e.   *P. n. maritima* (Corsican Pine)
e.   *P. muricata* (Bishop Pine)
e.   *P. pinaster* (Cluster or Maritime Pine)
e.   *P. radiata* (Monterey Pine)
e.   *P. sylvestris* (Scots Pine)
e.   *Taxus baccata* (Yew)

SEASIDE SCREEN TREES

d.   *Acer platanoides* (Norway Maple)
d.   *A. pseudoplatanus* (Sycamore)
d.   Betula (Birch)
d.   *Carpinus betulus* (Hornbeam)
d.   Crataegus (Hawthorn or Quickthorn)
d.   Fagus (Beech)
d.   *Fraxinus excelsior* (Common Ash)
d.   Laburnum
d.   *Populus alba* (Abele or White Poplar)

d.   *P. nigra* (Black Poplar)
d.   *P. n.* 'Italica' (Lombardy Poplar)
d.   *Prunus avium* (Wild Cherry or Gean)
d.   *P. cerasifera* (Myrobalan Plum) and varieties
d.   *P. padus* (Bird Cherry)
d.   *Quercus cerris* (Turkey Oak)
e.   *Q. ilex* (Evergreen or Holm Oak)
d.   *Q. robur* (syn. *Q. pendunculata*) (Common English Oak)
d.   *Salix alba* (White Willow)
d.   *S. caprea* (Goat Willow)
d.   *Sorbus aria* (Whitebeam)
d.   *S. aucuparia* (Mountain Ash)
d.   *S. intermedia* (Swedish Whitebeam)
d.   *Ulmus sarniensis* (Guernsey or Jersey Elm)

SCREEN TREES AND WINDBREAKS

d.   *Acer campestre* (Common Maple)
d.   *A. platanoides* (Norway Maple)
d.   *A. pseudoplatanus* (Sycamore)
d.   *Alnus glutinosa* (Alder)
e.   Arundinaria (*see* Bamboo)
e.   Bamboo
d.   *Betula alba* (Birch)
d.   *Carpinus betulus* (Hornbeam)
d.   *Castanea sativa* (Sweet Chestnut)
d.   *Cotoneaster frigidus*
d.   *Crataegus monogyna* (Hawthorn or Quickthorn)
d.   *C. prunifolia*
e.   *Eucalyptus gunnii*
d.   *Fagus sylvatica* (Beech)
e.   *Ilex aquifolium* (Holly) and other species and varieties
e.   *Olearia macrodonta*
e.   Phyllostachys (*see* Bamboo)
e.   *Pittosporum tenuifolium*
d.   Populus (Poplar) in variety
d.   *Prunus cerasifera* (Myrobalan Plum) and varieties
e.   *P. laurocerasus* (Common or Cherry Laurel)
e.   *P. lusitanica* (Portugal Laurel)
d.   *Quercus cerris* (Turkey Oak)
d.   *Q. ilex* (Evergreen or Holm Oak)
d.   *Q. robur* (syn. *Q. pendunculata*) (Common English Oak)

e.   *Rhododendron ponticum* (Common Rhododendron)
d.   Salix (Willow)
d.   Syringa (Lilac)
d.   Tilia (Lime)
d.   Ulmus (Elm)
e.   *Viburnum rhytidophyllum*

CLIMBING PLANTS FOR VARIOUS PURPOSES

CLIMBING AND TWINING PLANTS—For North and East Aspects

e.   *Berberidopsis corallina*
e.   *Decumaria sinensis*
e.   *Hedera helix* (Ivy) species and varieties
d.   *Hydrangea petiolaris*
d.   *Jasminum nudiflorum* (Winter Jasmine)
d.   *Parthenocissus henryana*
e.   *Pileostegia viburnoides*
d.   *Schisandra species*

CLIMBING PLANTS FOR TUBS AND POTS

d. e. Clematis in variety
d.   *Eccremocarpus scaber*
e.   *Hedera helix* (Ivy) species and variety
d.   *Hydrangea petiolaris*
d.   Jasminum (Jasmine) species
d.   *Lathyrus latifolius*
d. e. Lonicera in variety
d.   *Passiflora caerulea* (Passion Flower)
d.   *Solanum jasminoides*
d.   *Vitis coignetiae*
d.   Wisteria species and varieties

CLIMBING AND TWINING PLANTS FOR LARGE TREES

d.   *Actinidia arguta*
d.   *Aristolochia macrophylla* (Dutchman's Pipe)
d.   *Campsis grandiflora* (Trumpet Creeper)
d.   *C. radicans*
d.   *Celastrus orbiculatus*
d.   *Clematis montana*

116

e. *Holboellia coriacea*
e. *H. latifolia*
d. *Hydrangea anomala*
d. *H. petiolaris*
d. *Polygonum baldschuanicum* (Russian Vine)
d. *Rosa filipes* 'Kiftsgate'
d. *R.* 'Wedding Day'
d. *Schizophragma hydrangeoides*
d. *S. integrifolia*
e. *Stauntonia hexaphylla*
d. *Vitis coignetiae*
d. *V. quinquefolia*
d. Wisteria

CLIMBING AND TWINING PLANTS FOR TREES OF MEDIUM SIZE

d. Akebia species
d. Clematis, large flowered hybrids
d. *C. macropetala*
d. *C. m.* 'Markhams Pink'
d. *C. montana rubens*
d. *C. orientalis*
d. *C. tangutica*
d. *Jasminum officinale* (Summer Jasmine)
d. e. Lonicera species and varieties
e. *Mutisia ilicifolia*
d. *Rosa* 'Alberic Barbier'
d. *R.* 'François Juranville'
d. *R. helenae*
s-e. *R. longicuspis*
d. *R.* 'New Dawn'
d. *R.* 'Wedding Day'

VARIOUS TYPES OF CLIMBING PLANTS

ANNUALS

Cobaea scandens (Cup and Saucer Plant)
Convolvulus, *see* Pharbitis
Cucurbita species and varieties
Humulus (Hop) species and varieties
Ipomoea, *see* Pharbitis

117

Lathyrus odoratus (Sweet Pea)
Pharbitis purpurea
Tropaeoleum majus (Nasturtium)

PERENNIALS OF A HERBACEOUS NATURE

Aristolochia macrophylla (Dutchman's Pipe)
Humulus (Hop) species and varieties
Lathyrus species and varieties
Tropaeolum speciosum (Scotch Flame Flower)

CLIMBING ROSES

Bourbon
  Zéphirine Drouhin
Bracteata
  Mermaid
Climbers
  Allen Chandler
  Aloha
  Casino
  Chaplin's Pink Climber
  Clair Matin
  Copenhagen
  Coral Dawn
  Danse du Feu
  Dortmund
  Elegance
  Golden Showers
  Goldilocks, Climbing
  Guinée
  Handel
  Hamburger Phoenix
  Leverkusen
  Maigold
  Mme Gregoire Staechelin
  Meg
  Parade
  Parkdirektor Riggers
  Paul's Lemon Pillar
  Pink Perpetué
  Ritter von Barmstede
  Royal Gold

Soldier Boy
Climbing Hybrid Teas
  Crimson Conquest
  Ena Harkness
  Golden Dawn
  Lady Sylvia
  Mme Caroline Testout
  Mme Edouard Herriot
  Mrs. Sam McGredy
  Shot Silk
Noisettiana Climber
  Mme Alfred Carrière
Ramblers
  Albéric Barbier
  Albertine
  American Pillar
  Crimson Shower
  Dorothy Perkins
  Dr. W. van Fleet
  Emily Gray
  Excelsa
  François Juranville
  Helenae
  Minnehaha
  New Dawn
  Paul's Scarlet Climber
  Purity
  Sanders' White
  Veilchenblau
  Violette

SELF-CLINGING CLIMBING PLANTS

e.   *Asteranthera ovata*
d.   Campsis species (Trumpet Creeper)
d.   *Decumaria barbara*
e.   *Ercilla volubilis*
e.   *Euonymus fortunei*
e.   Hedera (Ivy) species and varieties
d.   *Hydrangea anomala*
d.   *H. integerrima*
d.   *H. petiolaris*

119

d.   Parthenocissus (Virginia Creeper) species and varieties
e.   *Pileostegia viburnoides*
d.   Schizophragma
d.   Vitis in variety

7

Alphabetical List
of Climbing and Screening Plants

ABELIA

These attractive shrubs are not strictly climbers but wall shrubs as they enjoy the warmth and protection which a south or west wall can give. Abelias grow satisfactorily on chalk soils. All need to be tied to wires or trellis.

A. floribunda

Semi-evergreen shrub, with rosy-red tubular flowers which are freely borne. Height not more than 5 ft. and as much or a little wider. Flowering July to September.

A. × grandiflora

Semi-evergreen, with dark, glossy green foliage and bearing white, tinged-pink flowers abundantly. It is the hardiest of the abelias. Height 5 ft. Flowering July to September.

A. schumannii

A deciduous shrub, having an almost continuous display of soft rose-lilac tubular flowers from June to October. Height 5 ft. and as wide or more.

Planting is best done in early autumn or spring. Very little pruning is needed, apart from tidying up in the spring.

Propagation is by cuttings of half-ripened shoots in June-July, 2–3 in.

long, preferably taken with a heel of older wood, and inserted in a propagating frame.

ABELIOPHYLLUM

A. distichum

This is a much branched deciduous shrub, related to forsythia, and is one of the wall shrubs which gives us blooms in February. Its fragrant, white, tinged pink, 4-petal flowers are borne on naked wood. It is very hardy, and not fussy over soil. It will need tying to wires or trellis against a wall or fence. Plant it in autumn. Prune after flowering by pinching tips out of young shoots when they have made some 4-5 in. of growth. Propagate by cuttings of half-ripened wood in June-July, placed in a propagating frame or under mist. Height 4–6 ft.

ABUTILON

A. megapotamicum (syn. *A. vexillarium*)

A deciduous shrub of unusual beauty. Its quaint, chinese-lantern-like flowers, which consist of a red calyx and yellow petals from which protrude brown anthers, are freely borne on wiry shoots. A warm south or west wall suits it best, and if trained out on wires or trellis will make a spectacular show. It flowers from April onwards. Plant in spring from pots. It thrives on most soils, but avoid damp or heavy soils. Prune in spring by removing all parts damaged by frost, also cutting out any unwanted older growth and any weak shoots. Propagation is by cuttings of half-ripened shoots in July, inserted in sandy soil in a propagating frame, preferably with a little bottom heat under mist. It grows to a height of 6–7 ft. and as wide.

A.m. 'Variegatum' has similar flowers, but with golden variegated foliage. In other respects, see *A. megapotamicum*.

A. vitifolium

A deciduous, soft-wooded shrub which, being slightly tender, enjoys the protection and warmth of a south or west wall. The single hollyhock-like, pale to deep mauve flowers are borne in clusters, often of four, in the axils of the grey-vine-shaped leaves, first appearing in May. It is a tall, handsome shrub. To prevent bud-drop see that it has ample moisture before the flowers begin to open. It requires to be securely tied to supporting wires or trellis. Plant in spring from pots. Prune in spring by removing all parts damaged by frost, also cutting out any unwanted older growth and any weak stems to make room for new shoots. Propagate from seed sown in January under glass in warmth. Cuttings of soft-wood can also be taken in May or July in a propagating frame, under mist, where there is some warmth. Height 15–20 ft.

ACER (Maple)

A. campestre (Common or Field Maple)

A hardy, deciduous tree, which makes a strong hedge either on its own or when mixed with other subjects. Has a rough, curiously cork-like bark, with 5-lobed leaves which turn yellow in autumn. When unclipped the 'keys' (fruits) are decorative. Plant 1 ft. apart, October to March, in sun or shade. Good on clay soils or chalk. Trim in late summer or winter. Propagate by seed sown in beds out of doors, as soon as ripe; remove wings from seeds. Height 6–20 ft.

A. platanoides (Norway Maple)

A hardy, deciduous tree, too strong-growing for a formal hedge, but excellent as a screen or windbreak in blustery positions. It will grow by the sea. Its large, 5-lobed heart-shaped leaves are bright green above and below, lovely and fresh in the summer and handsomely coloured in autumn in varying shades of red, brown and buttery-yellow. In April the Norway maple produces greenish-yellow flowers which are followed by attractive keys in autumn. Plant young trees 9 ft. apart, October to March. Propagate by seed as for *A. campestre*. Height up to 60 ft.
A.p. 'Reitenbachii'. Its green leaves change to rich red in autumn. It grows to a height of up to 60 ft.
A.p. 'Schwedleri'. The leaves are bright red when young, changing to green in the summer. Cultivation for these varieties is as for Norway maple, except that propagation is by budding in June, on to stocks of *A. platanoides*. Its height is up to 60 ft.

123

A. pseudoplatanus (Sycamore)

Hardy deciduous tree, too strong-growing for a formal hedge, but excellent as a screen or windbreak in a blustery position, and stands up to salt-laden winds by the coast. Large 5-lobed leaves, changing colour in autumn. Yellow flowers followed by attractive keys when not pruned. Plant screen trees 6–8 ft. apart, October to March. It thrives on any soil. Propagate by seed as for *A. campestre*. Height up to 70 ft.

A. p. purpureum. This makes a handsome tree to plant in a belt of mixed trees. The dark green leaves being rich purple beneath show to considerable advantage when blown by the wind. Its height is 60–70 ft.

A. platanoides and *A. pseudoplatanus* and their respective varieties can be pruned during October to March.

ACTINIDIA

This is a hardy, deciduous twining shrub of vigorous habit and is not fussy over soil. It will thrive in full sun or some shade. Plant in spring. No pruning is needed. Propagation is by seeds sown in April or cuttings of well-ripened wood, taken in late autumn, inserted in a sheltered bed out of doors.

A. arguta

This has large, shining green foliage, with white, slightly fragrant flowers, enriched by purple anthers, followed by greenish-yellow, 1-in. long berries. It is very vigorous and is, therefore, excellent for climbing up tall trees. Its height is indeterminate.

A. chinensis (Chinese Gooseberry)

Not so vigorous as *A. arguta*, but it has even larger leaves, being 6–9 in. wide. The fragrant, creamy-white flowers, $1\frac{1}{2}$ in. across, which are produced in summer, later change to buff-yellow, and are followed by edible egg-shaped fruits, covered with brownish hairs. As male and female flowers are usually on separate plants, both must be grown if fruit is expected. Height up to 30 ft.

124

A. kolomikta

This scores over the other two species because of its tri-coloured variegated leaves, which in spring are a striking metallic green, but are even more striking during the summer when they become suffused with pink and white. To obtain good variegated foliage, plant against a south or west wall and in full sun. Height up to 20 ft.

AEGLE, *see* PONCIRUS

AKEBIA

This genus has two vigorous, semi-evergreen, twining shrubs which are worth growing, bearing attractive foliage and flowers, followed by purplish sausage-like fruits—some 4 in. long. They like an acid soil.

A. lobata, *see A. trifoliata*

A. quinata

A semi-evergreen twiner, with usually 5 leaflets to one stalk, its fragrant chocolate-purple female flowers are borne during April. It is a useful plant for a wall, trellis or pergola, and does best on an acid or loamy soil. Height up to 30–40 ft.

A. trifoliata (syn. *A. lobata*)

Almost evergreen—an elegant climber with 3 leaflets to a stalk. It has deep purple female flowers in April. Plant in spring; no pruning needed. Propagate by cuttings of half-ripened wood in spring, or layering out of doors in spring. Height up to 30 ft.

ALDER, *see* ALNUS

ALNUS (Alder)

A. glutinosa (Common Alder)

This is a hardy, deciduous tree. It can be used as a hedge, though it is more often seen as a screen tree. It is also used for holding together banks of rivers and streams. It has male catkins which persist from autumn until spring, when the cone-like female catkins appear. Place plants 1½ ft. apart for a hedge, and for screen trees 6 ft. apart, October to March. It grows best in a rich soil; dislikes acid peat soils. Trim in late summer. Propagate by seed gathered in the autumn and sown in spring. Height up to 50 ft.

ALOYSIA, *see* LIPPIA

ALTHAEA, *see* HIBISCUS

AMPELOPSIS

A. brevipedunculata (syn. *A. heterophylla, Vitis brevipedunculata*)

This attractive vine has interesting 3-lobed leaves resembling those of the hop. It is a vigorous climber which has the added attraction of porcelain blue grapes, which are freely produced after a hot dry summer. Ideal for a pergola. Plant in autumn or spring. Propagate by soft-wood cuttings in July, inserted singly in small pots in a propagating frame or under mist. It is not fussy over soil. Its height is indeterminate.

ARBOR-VITAE, *see* THUJA

ARBUTUS

A. unedo (Strawberry Tree)

This is an attractive evergreen shrub, bearing white and pink pitcher-shaped blossoms and round strawberry-like fruits at the same time, from October to December. Makes an informal hedge, screen or wind-break, especially in warmer coastal districts. Plant 3–4 ft. apart in September or April, but farther apart where more shapely bushes are needed. As they transplant rather badly, they are best planted out of pots. The strawberry tree will grow in lime soils, though it succeeds best

126

in peaty or loamy soils. Trim lightly when required in April. Propagated by seed sown as soon as ripe. Separate seed from pulp and mix with sand before sowing. It grows to a height of 15–25 ft.

ARISTOLOCHIA

A. macrophylla (Dutchman's Pipe) (syn. *A. sipho, A. durior*)

This is a deciduous, hardy perennial, climbing or twining plant, having heart-shaped leaves. Its siphon-shaped flowers are yellowish-green without, brownish-purple within, and appear from May to July. It is ideal for growing up an old tree, on a pillar, over an archway, or wire netting or trellis. A loamy, peaty soil suits it best. Plant it in April. Propagate by layers, or half-ripe cuttings taken with a heel inserted in slight heat during the summer, or division of the roots in April. Sometimes a little thinning may be required as pruning; this is best done in March. Its height is 15–30 ft.

ARTEMISIA

A. abrotanum (Southernwood, Lad's Love, Old Man)

This is a popular deciduous semi-shrubby plant, for a low hedge. The dull green foliage is at first covered with grey down. It is fragrant and much used in herb gardens. Plant 1 ft. apart, October to March. Thrives in any soil and likes a well-drained sunny spot. Trim in early spring before growth starts, and cut out old wood when necessary. Propagate by taking heel cuttings in July and August. Height $2\frac{1}{2}$–3 ft.

ARUNDINARIA, *see* BAMBOO

ASH, COMMON, *see* FRAXINUS

ASH, MOUNTAIN, *see* SORBUS

ASTERANTHERA

A. ovata

This is an evergreen, self-supporting creeper, introduced in 1926 having aerial roots; hardy only in mild localities. It is most successful when grown on a shaded wall where it has moist, leafy soil. In southern England it can be grown successfully on a north wall. The red tubular flowers, mostly in pairs, are borne in June. Plant it in spring. Propagate by seeds or half-ripened cuttings taken in the summer and inserted in a sand and peat mixture in a shady frame. Height 10–15 ft.

ATRIPLEX

A. halimus (Tree Purslane)

This is a semi-evergreen shrub, silvery-grey foliage, hardy on southern and western coasts. A first-class seaside, wind-hardy hedge; inland it tends to be damaged by frosts in severe winters, though it soon recovers in spring. Plant 18–21 in. apart, October to April. It does best in a well-drained and manured soil, whether limy or otherwise, and likes full sun. Trim in early spring. Propagate by half-ripened cuttings in July or hard-wood cuttings in October or November. Height 4–6 ft.

AUCUBA

A. japonica

This is a hardy, evergreen shrub, with leathery, glossy, laurel-like leaves; the female bushes bear scarlet berries. It makes a good hedge or windbreak and is an ideal seaside or town shrub. As it is dioecious, a male plant must be present in order for bushes to bear berries. There are green and variegated forms, and also a white-fruited variety.
A.j. 'Variegata' is golden spotted and *A.j.* 'Fructu-albo' is the white-berried form. Plant 2–3 ft. apart. It thrives in any open soil, whether lime or otherwise, in sun or shade. Trim it in April; those who have the patience should use secateurs. Propagate by hard-wood cuttings, 6–9 in. long, inserted in October to November, in a sheltered bed out of doors. Height 6–9 ft.

128

ABOVE LEFT: the orange peel clematis, *Clematis orientalis*
ABOVE RIGHT: feathery seed heads of *Clematis tangutica*
BELOW LEFT: *Clematis montana* 'Elizabeth' produces masses of sweetly scented flowers
BELOW RIGHT: the pale yellow, cowslip scented flowers of *Clematis rehderiana*

ABOVE LEFT: the coral pink shaded climbing rose 'Mme Grégoire Staechelin' in the author's garden. Its orange-yellow hips in autumn and winter are equally striking

LEFT: *Rosa filipes* 'Kiftsgate' has large clusters of creamy-white flowers

BELOW LEFT: a lovely repeat flowering, climbing rose, 'Pink Perpetué'. Its pink blooms have a carmine-pink reverse

ABOVE: the rambling rose 'New Dawn' produces clusters of fragrant, silvery-pink flowers; here it is seen growing beside the Palm House Pond, at the Royal Botanic Gardens, Kew

AZALEA, *see* RHODODENDRON

AZARA

A. serrata

This evergreen, though not a true climber, is worth inclusion as it needs the protection of a south or west wall or fence. It has shining green oval leaves and fragrant yellow flowers in July. Plant in spring. No regular pruning is needed, extra long shoots can be cut back at the end of April. Best in chalk or sandy soil. Propagate by cuttings of ripened wood, in August, inserted in a propagating frame. Height 8–12 ft.

BAMBOO

The bamboos are perhaps one of the most beautiful and graceful evergreens we grow in our gardens. They are hardy, and particularly suitable and adaptable as screens and less formal hedges and windbreaks, though they resent the cutting blasts of cold north and east winds and, where exposed to these, will require some kind of shelter themselves. In cold districts during hard winters many will lose much or all their foliage, but given adequate protection, such disfigurement will largely be avoided. As a rule bamboos grow for many years without producing any flowers, however, when they do flower the plants usually die afterwards. Soil should be loamy, neither too light nor too heavy, and not liable to become waterlogged. Bamboos are greedy feeders and benefit from an annual mulch of leafmould or rotted manure, with an application of sulphate of ammonia at the rate of 1 oz. per sq. yd. Although bamboos will tolerate full sun, they prefer a little shade during the hottest part of the day.

The ground should be well dug before planting, this being done in the autumn, when well-rotted manure should be worked in. Never plant from late autumn to early spring, but either in early autumn or in late spring; May is the ideal month. The best planting size is 3–5 ft. and the plants should be spaced 3–4 ft. apart. It will take a clump of bamboo at least two years to become established. Little or no pruning is necessary. When it is, do the work from mid-April to mid-May. The canes can be used in the garden for staking plants. Tie them in bundles and stand

I   129

them on end in an open, airy shed or underneath a hedge to dry and mature for three to four months. Propagation is by division in May. Height 10–25 ft.

Nomenclature of bamboos has for many years been very confused, so for ease of reference both present names and their synonyms are given.

Arundinaria anceps

Stems are erect, purplish at first, changing to brownish-green, and its branches are purple and slender. The leaves are brilliant green, glaucous beneath. Height 10–15 ft.

A. fastuosa (syn. *Semiarundinaria fastuosa*)

The stems are erect, hollow, dark green; branches are short and very leafy. The leaves are dark lustrous green above, glaucous beneath. Height 20–25 ft.

A. japonica (syn. *Bambusa metake, Pseudosasa japonica*)

This bamboo, often known as *Bambusa metake*, is the common bamboo. Stems erect, round and hollow. The leaves are 7–12 in. long, glossy, dark green above, glaucous beneath. Height 10–12 ft.

A. murieliae (syn. *Sinoarundinaria murieliae*)

An elegant bamboo with plumes of soft green foliage, it has arching, slender canes. Height 8–12 ft.

A. nitida (syn. *Sinoarundinaria nitida*)

The stems are erect, round and hollow, very dark purple. The leaves are $2\frac{1}{2}$–$3\frac{1}{2}$ in. long, vivid green above, somewhat glaucous beneath. It is very hardy and vigorous in growth. It needs a semi-shaded spot, does not like full sun and requires plenty of moisture. Height up to 10 ft.

Phyllostachys bambusoides

The stems are hollow, bright yellow, alternately jointed and dark green on the flattened side. The leaves are 2–5 in. long and uniformly striped with creamy yellow lines, above, glaucous beneath. Height 8–10 ft.

P. flexuosa

The stems are bright green at first, darkening with age, and sometimes almost to black. Leaves 2–4 in. long, dark green above, glaucous beneath. An elegant bamboo. Height 12–14 ft.

P. nigra

The stems are hollow, at first green, later quite black. The leaves grow in plume-like masses, dark green above, glaucous beneath. Height 10–20 ft.
P.n. 'Henonis'. This tall, handsome bamboo has graceful canes and dark green shining foliage which is never scorched or damaged by the sharpest frost in winter. Height 10–14 ft.

P. viridi-glaucescens

The stems are hollow, yellowish-green and purplish at the joints. The leaves are bright green above, glaucous beneath. Height 14–18 ft.

BAMBUSA, *see* BAMBOO

BARBERRY, *see* BERBERIS

BAY LAUREL, *see* LAURUS

BAY, SWEET, *see* LAURUS

BEECH, *see* FAGUS

BEECH, ROBLE, *see* NOTHOFAGUS

BELLFLOWER, CHILEAN, *see* LAPAGERIA

131

BERBERIDOPSIS

B. corallina (Coral Plant)

An unusual and beautiful evergreen from Chile, introduced over 100 years ago (1862) and still not sufficiently well known. I first remember seeing this shrub in flower at Kew in July 1935, with its crimson-red globose flowers, hanging among dark green, leathery leaves, which are glaucous beneath. It is semi-twining but must have wall support and protection from north and east winds. Choose a south or west wall, where there is shade from nearby trees or shrubs. It dislikes lime or hungry soils. Plant in spring, adding peat or leafmould to the soil. No regular pruning is required but when it is, prune in April, or in September or October. Propagate either by layers or half-ripened cuttings in early July, inserted in a sandy-peaty soil under a large glass jar or under mist—a little bottom heat is helpful. Height 6–10 ft.

BERBERIS (Barberry)

Hardy, deciduous and evergreen flowering shrubs armed with few or many thorns. In autumn and winter many barberries produce colourful fruits and brilliant foliage, which varies in size and shape. They make good hedges either by the sea or inland. They will thrive in all soils. The most popular for this purpose are *Berberis stenophylla* and *B. darwinii*, both evergreen, and the decidous *B. thunbergii*. Plant 9–24 in. apart according to the species, from October to April, the deciduous kinds being planted when the foliage is off. Trim deciduous kinds in February, and evergreens in April, or those such as *B. stenophylla* directly after flowering. Height varies from 2–12 ft.

B. aquifolium, *see Mahonia aquifolium*

B. buxifolia 'Nana'

This is a tufted, unarmed evergreen, perfect for a dwarf hedge. Plant it 9 in. apart, October to March. Trim in early spring when necessary. Propagate by division in spring. Height up to 1½ ft.

B. candidula

Compact evergreen, dark green shining leaves, blue-white beneath, flowers bright yellow. Makes a good dwarf hedge if planted 1 ft. apart, October to March. Trim in early spring when necessary. Propagate by hard-wood cuttings October to November. Height 2–2½ ft.

B. darwinii (Darwin's Barberry)

This has evergreen, dark glossy green, stalkless, shield-shaped leaves. The deep golden or orange-yellow flowers, tinged with red, are produced in April and May and are followed by plum coloured berries in autumn. It does best on loamy soils. Plant 1½–2 ft. apart October to March. Trim after flowers fade for informal hedges, otherwise in late summer. Propagate by seed, which should be collected as soon as ripe and stratified, and sown in pots or boxes in a cold frame the following February; or by half-ripened wood cuttings August or September. Height 6–8 ft.

B. gagnepainii

This is an evergreen of dense, erect habit with dark dull green foliage, bright yellow flowers in May, followed by jet-black berries. It has formidable spines. Plant 15–18 in. apart October to March. Good on chalk. Trim after flowering or in late summer. Propagate by seed or hard-wood cuttings, October to November. Height 4 ft.
B.g. 'Fernspray'. As *B. gagnepainii* in treatment, but foliage is a fresh green with narrow crinkled leaves which gave a fern-like effect. Height 5–7 ft.

B. hookeri

Evergreen, dense thicket of erect stems, leathery dark green leaves, glaucous-white beneath. Three-forked spines ½–1 in. long; solitary pale-yellow flowers tinged red followed by black-purple tapering berries. It makes a useful impenetrable hedge. Plant 1½ ft. apart October to March. Trim in April, after flowering or in late summer. Propagate by hard-wood cuttings October to November. Height 4–5 ft.

B. × stenophylla

Evergreen, small narrow leaves, deep green above, glaucous beneath,

133

and spine-tipped. In April and May the long slender branches are wreathed to their ends in golden-yellow flowers. Hedges left untrimmed produce globose berries covered with a blue-white bloom. Plant 1½–2 ft. apart October to March, trim as flowers fade, and when necessary cut hard back in April. Propagate by hard-wood cuttings October to November. Height 8–10 ft.

B.s. 'Irwinii'. Evergreen, similar to *B. stenophylla* in many respects but of denser and dwarfer habit. Ideal for a low hedge. Orange-yellow flowers in April and May. Plant 15 in. apart October to March. Trim after flowers fade. Propagate as for *B. stenophylla*. Height 2 ft.

B. thunbergii (Thunberg's Barberry)

Hardy, deciduous shrub, reddish-brown bark, red-and-yellow flowers, followed by bright red berries and brilliant autumn foliage. Makes a very good hedge. Plant 15–18 in. apart October to March. Trim in February. Propagate by seed or hard-wood cuttings in October or November. Height 4–6 ft.

B.t. atropurpurea. Similar to above, but with purple foliage, which is more brilliant and finally scarlet in autumn. Other remarks as for *B. thunbergii*. Height 3–4 ft.

B.t. 'Erecta'. Hardy deciduous erect-growing shrub, which colours brilliantly in autumn. Good for a short and narrow hedge. Plant 12–15 in. apart, October to March. No trimming needed. Height 2½–3 ft.

B. verruculosa

Hardy evergreen shrub, dark lustrous green leaves above, glaucous beneath. Three-parted spines. Golden-yellow flowers followed by black berries covered with a blue bloom. Makes a close low hedge. Plant 15–18 in. apart, October to March. It will thrive in sun or partial shade. Trim very lightly after flowering. Propagate by hard-wood cuttings in October or November. Height 3–4 ft.

B. wilsoniae (Mrs. Wilson's Barberry)

A hardy deciduous shrub which makes an attractive low hedge and is also a good bank coverer. Pale yellow flowers in July, followed by coral or salmon-red berries freely produced, and vivid red autumn foliage. On light, sandy and chalk soils its colour is particularly brilliant. Plant 1–1½ ft. apart. Trim lightly in late summer. Propagate by seed or by hard-wood cuttings in October or November (especially where a good form is available). Height 2½–3 ft.

BERCHEMIA

B. racemosa

This is a deciduous scandent climber, with bright green, heart-shaped leaves, turning yellow in autumn. In late summer it bears panicles of greenish-white flowers followed by red berries, which later turn to black. It needs a south wall or fence. It is best in acid or loamy soils. Plant in October or March. Propagate by cuttings of ripened wood in October, inserting them in a sheltered bed out of doors. Height 10–15 ft.

BETULA

B. pendula (Common Birch)

Hardy deciduous tree, mostly used as a screen or shelter tree, but makes a useful hedge. Trees grown as screens and allowed to develop catkins are most decorative, and the white trunks of birches are equally beautiful. It makes a quick growing hedge. Plant 1½–2 ft. apart as a hedge, or as a screen or shelter tree 8–10 ft. apart. Thrives on any soil, but light sandy soils suit it best. Trim hedges and screen trees November to March. Propagate by seed, sowing it as soon as gathered. Height as a hedge 8–10 ft., as a screen 40–50 ft.

BIGNONIA

B. capreolata (Cross Vine)

A very beautiful evergreen or semi-evergreen though unfortunately not fully hardy and, therefore, needs the protection of a warm south or west wall or fence, except in more favoured parts of the country, such as Cornwall or Devonshire. Its lanceolate, evergreen or semi-evergreen leaves attach themselves to walls, by branched tendrils. During June and July clusters of funnel-shaped flowers are produced, varying from yellowish-red to orange-red. Plant in spring, in well drained and well

135

cultivated loamy soil. No regular pruning necessary. Propagate by layers or by cuttings of well-ripened shoots taken in winter and inserted in a propagating frame with bottom heat or under mist. Height when grown up a tree will reach as much as 40 ft.

BIRCH, *see* BETULA

BLACKTHORN, *see Prunus spinosa*

BOX, *see* BUXUS

BOX-THORN, CHINESE, *see* LYCIUM

BRAMBLE, *see* RUBUS

BRIDGESIA, *see* ERCILLA

BROOM, *see* CYTISUS

BROOM, BUTCHER'S, *see* RUSCUS

BROOM, SPANISH, *see* SPARTIUM

BUCKTHORN, SEA, *see* HIPPOPHAE

BUDDLEIA

B. davidii

Hardy, deciduous shrub for an informal screen. There are many

136

varieties which produce panicles of mauve, purple and white flowers at the ends of their branches. My favourite variety is Ile de France. Ideal for town or country and flourishes near the sea. Plant 3–4 ft. apart October to March. Thrives on any soil, including chalk soils. Trim each year in February or March by cutting the bushes hard back to within a few buds of the old wood. Propagate by hard-wood cuttings in October or November. Height 8–10 ft.

B. d. nanhoensis. Hardy, deciduous shrub, smaller than *B. davidii*, making close screen or informal hedge. Suitable for coastal areas. Panicles of mauve flowers in July and August. Plant 3 ft. apart, October to March. Trim and propagate as for *B. davidii.* Height 4–6 ft.

BULL BAY, *see Magnolia grandiflora*

BUPLEURUM

B. fruticosum

This is an evergreen or semi-evergreen shrub, with blue-green narrow leaves, and purplish young shoots bearing umbels of yellow flowers in July. Useful as a dwarf windbreak near the sea. I saw a fine hedge of *B. fruticosum* at Slapton Sands, S. Devon in August 1967. It is, however, quite hardy in Sussex. Plant 15 in. apart in September to October or March to April. It does not seem fussy as to soil, whether chalk, clay or sand. Trim in February or March. Propagate by cuttings, using firm side shoots inserted in cold frame in August. Height 4–6 ft.

BUTCHER'S BROOM, *see* RUSCUS

BUXUS (Box)

B. sempervirens (Common Box)

A hardy evergreen and, still in my estimation, ranks as one of the best dozen evergreen hedge shrubs. No one who has visited Box Hill in Surrey when box bushes are in flower could fail to remember their musky fragrance. The flowers are pale yellowish-green. For many years box has been used for topiary as well as hedges. The leaves are dark green and leathery. It does best on any light, well-drained soil, likes chalk and succeeds well by the sea. To keep a hedge in good condition an occasional mulch of manure is beneficial and the ground should be well enriched before planting a hedge. Plant 1½–2 ft. apart, March to April or September to October.

Box is excellent for planting beneath the shade of trees and does not object to sites facing north. Trim formal hedges and topiary in summer, but when dealing with overgrown hedges or bushes cut hard back in April. Propagate by cuttings, choosing mature side shoots 3–4 in. long in August or September. There are also silver and gold variegated forms: *B.s.* 'Elegantissima', silver, and *B.s.* 'Aureo variegata', golden. The height of hedges is up to 10 ft., a screen 15–18 ft.

B.s. 'Handsworthensis' (Handsworth Box). More vigorous than the species and more upright in habit with larger leaves. Cultivation as for common box.

B.s. 'Suffruticosa' (Edging Box). Hardy, evergreen dwarf shrub. Used extensively two centuries ago to form parterres, knot gardens and many other elaborate designs. Also used as an edging in the kitchen garden, but it is a great refuge for snails. It has the attractive musky fragrance of the common box. It is sold by the yard, and one nursery yard—i.e., a number of rooted pieces close together occupying a yard in the nursery, should be enough to produce 2–3 yd. of box edging when planted out. Plant March to April or September to October. Trim two or three times during the summer. Propagate by division in spring. Do any hard pruning in April. Height as a rule not more than 3 ft. and frequently much lower.

CALLUNA

C. vulgaris (Heather or Ling)

Hardy, evergreen shrub which, with its many varieties, can be used to form low divisional informal hedges. I shall not list the many varieties, but these can be obtained from any good grower of heathers. Suitable for coastal areas and is best on acid or loamy soils. Plant 1–1½ ft. apart. April and May are the best planting months, but if this is not possible then plant in September or October. Trim by removing old flower heads from the bushes in early spring before new growth commences. Shears or secateurs can be used. Propagate by cuttings in July or August, or by layering at almost any time of the year, except during very bad or frosty weather. Height 1½–2 ft.

CAMELLIA

C. japonica

At one time this most handsome of evergreen shrubs was mothered and cosseted in the conservatory or greenhouse but, fortunately, today it is grown freely out of doors. Nevertheless there are certain reservations that must not be overlooked. The most important is that camellias will not succeed in chalk soils; also they do not appreciate too hot or dry a position in the garden, certainly not at their roots. What they do enjoy is what one might term a full bodied soil, containing plenty of leaf-mould or peat (well moistened), in fact a good acid soil, such as suits azaleas and rhododendrons.

Camellias can be planted against a wall, provided their roots are going to be sufficiently moist, especially during the summer or in dry seasons. They like some shade—and such conditions suit them well. They can be grown successfully in tubs, which are ideal where the natural soil is at all chalky. When grown by a wall they can be allowed to grow more or less naturally or tied in formally. I have known them planted as a hedge, and they are excellent to form a screen, particularly under semi-shady conditions.

In America today a popular way of growing camellias is as espaliers, although I have neither seen nor tried this method. It cannot be very different from the way *C. sasanqua* is trained on the outer wall of the Duke's Garden at the Royal Botanic Gardens, Kew. However, all one has to do is to first fit wires or trellis to a wall or fence, and then tie in the main stem or stems and all laterals (side shoots) in a way similar to that in which espalier fruit trees are trained. With thickish shoots care must be taken not to fracture the stem when bending it, indeed it is often necessary to bend and tie it by degrees. Use fairly strong string, such as 4-ply fillis. The final result of the espalier-trained camellia should be almost flat against the wall. Plant from November to March, though in extremely cold districts never plant before March. Prune right at the end of the flowering season, when necessary, in order to keep them well shaped and flat against the wall, to two or three buds. Propagate by seeds, grafting or cuttings; the last named is probably the easiest for the amateur, of half-ripened wood in July and August or hard-wood from November to February, placed in either case in a propagating frame. Height 5–10 ft. and as wide.

Some attractive species and varieties are:

C. japonica, deep scarlet, single; *C.j.* 'Magnoliiflora', flesh-pink, semi-double; *C.j.* 'Nobilissima', white, double; *C. sasanqua*, white or flesh-pink, single or semi-double; *C.* 'Donation', soft pink, semi-double; *C.* 'Francis Hanger', white, single; *C.* 'Inspiration', a clear pink, rather similar to 'Donation' but a slightly paler shade, and *C.* 'Salutation', silvery-pink, semi-double.

CAMPSIS

These are probably the most spectacular creepers we have for a south or west wall. Their rich scarlet, trumpet-shaped blooms which grace our walls in July and August or until frost comes, give any garden an exotic splendour. They are deciduous woody climbers, doing best in a good loam.

C. grandiflora (syn. *C. chinensis*)

A native of China, and is a twiner or scandent climber. Among the long leaves, made up of seven to nine leaflets, are borne panicles of six to nine large, orange-scarlet trumpets, being 3 in. wide at the mouth. This climber can be pruned like a vine, by having its young shoots pruned back to the old wood. Hardy, though not as hardy as *C. radicans*. Height up to 20 ft.

C. radicans (Trumpet Vine)

This American species is much more rampant, and supports itself by aerial roots, and will climb up a tree as freely as *Hydrangea petiolaris*. What a wonderful spectacle the two could be together, though I have never seen it done. It is very hardy. There are nine to eleven leaflets to a leaf and its trumpet-shaped, orange-coloured flowers are borne in terminal clusters of four to twelve, but only 1½ in. wide at the mouth. Prune as for *C. grandiflora*. Height 30–40 ft.

C. × tagliabuana 'Madame Galen'

This is a hybrid between *C. grandiflora* and *C. radicans*. It has vivid

140

salmon-red trumpets borne in shorter crowded panicles. It is as hardy as *C. radicans*. Plant in spring. Prune by cutting out old worn out or unwanted wood. Where plants must be kept in check, spur back all side shoots to the old wood as with a vine. Propagate by layering root cuttings or ripened wood cuttings taken in July or August. Its height is 30 ft. or more.

CARAGANA

C. arborescens (Pea Tree)

Hardy, deciduous flowering shrub, rather upright in habit with a stiff, grey look. The leaves are pinnate and the main stalk of each leaflet ends in a spine. This gives the shrub additional effectiveness as a barrier or hedge plant. Yellow, pea-shaped flowers produced singly in May. As in the case with many of the pea family, caragana thrives best in poor, stony ground. Best planting 1–1½ ft. spaced at 15–18 in. apart. Plant in March or April, or in early autumn. Trim after flowering. Propagate by seed. Its height is up to 10 ft., though as an isolated shrub it will reach 15–20 ft.

CARPENTERIA

C. californica

This evergreen from California, though rather tender, is worth a place at the foot of a south or west wall, where the soil is well drained. It thrives in a lime, acid or peaty soil. In late June and July it bears fragrant white flowers 3 in. wide. It is not a long lived plant, but worth growing. Plant in April. No pruning needed. Propagate by seed, layers or cuttings. Height 6–9 ft.

CARPINUS (Hornbeam)

C. betulus (Hornbeam)

Hardy, deciduous shrub or tree; a first-rate hedge plant. Has leaves similar to those of beech, but rough textured on either side of the leaf;

141

it is also more prominently veined. Another difference is that hornbeam has a serrated leaf edge, whereas beech is smooth. Good for planting in exposed positions. Mixes well with quickthorn or hawthorn, for which purpose it should be planted at the rate of one hornbeam to six quickthorn. Plant double rows, 15 in. between the rows. In single rows the plants should be 1 ft. apart. Do not prune during the first two years after planting. Trim young hedges in July, established ones in late summer. Thrives on rich deep soil, clay or chalk, and does not mind shade. Propagate by seed. Height 10–20 ft.

CASSINIA

C. fulvida (syn. *Diplopappus chrysophyllus*)

Evergreen of erect habit, branches closely packed, small leaves dark green above and yellowish and downy beneath. Makes a low hedge, especially useful by the sea, growing in sun or shade as it is wind hardy. Plant 1 ft. apart, October to April. Trim in summer. Propagate by cuttings, using mature shoots 4–6 in. long, August to September. Height 3–4 ft.

CASTANEA (Chestnut)

C. sativa (Sweet or Spanish Chestnut)

Deciduous tree, not a hedge plant but a useful shelter-belt tree inland and when sheltered from the sea. Plant young trees 4–5 ft. high, 3–6 ft. apart, October to March. Trim in winter. Thrives best on a good deep sandy loam. Not so good on heavy wet clay soils. Height up to 60 ft.

CEANOTHUS

Evergreen and deciduous shrubs best suited, when used as a hedge or shelter, for the warmer parts of the country and near the sea. Several species and varieties are suitable when trained on wires or trellis or walls or fences. It is the evergreen kinds which are chiefly used for such purposes. The flowers of most varieties are in shades of blue, though there are pink forms. They bloom from May to October. They do not make dense formal hedges and are more suitable for informal hedges. The delinianus group to which 'Gloire de Versailles' belongs, is tidier and bushier in habit than the evergreen kinds, and *C.* × *delinianus* and its forms are suitable for informal hedges. Plant young pot-grown plants 1½–2 ft. apart, March to April. They thrive in most soils, including chalk. All like good drainage and prefer poor soil to rich. Prune spring flowering evergreen kinds immediately after flowering, by shortening their longest shoots, and by generally tidying up the bush; deciduous kinds, such as 'Gloire de Versailles' prune back drastically each February or March. With wall or fence grown plants prune back all side shoots to within 1–2 in. of the main stems after flowering. Propagate by taking cuttings of half-ripened wood in July or August; with the spring flowering kinds take cuttings with a heel.

C. 'Burkwoodii'

Evergreen and an ideal wall shrub where space is limited, its rich blue flowers are freely borne throughout summer and autumn. Height 6–8 ft.

C. × delinianus

A deciduous shrub. The variety 'Gloire de Versailles' has deep powder-blue flowers. Other forms of *C.* × *delinianus* are 'Indigo' (deep blue), 'Henri Desfosse' (bright blue), 'Ceres' and 'Marie Simon' (both pink). All flower June to October. Height 4–6 ft.

C. dentatus

Evergreen, grey-blue flowers in May and June. This also makes an excellent wall shrub. Height 6 ft.

C. impressus

An evergreen and a well-named plant. I cannot think of a more impressive sight than a plant I saw at Coles, Col. Nicholson's garden at Privet, Hants., growing on a south-facing wall. It was a sheet of small bright blue flowers covering its closely trained stems and small rugose dark green leaves. Even its tight, unopened dark red flower buds are attractive, flowering in May. Height 15 ft.

143

C. rigidus

Evergreen, making a fairly compact plant, and is usually considered not fully hardy, but given the protection of a south or west wall it will bear a mass of purplish-blue flowers, which are borne in tightly packed clusters from May to June. Height 8–10 ft.

C. thyrsiflorus

Evergreen, pale blue flowers in May and June. Height 12–15 ft.
C.t. 'Cascade'. Evergreen, vigorous and very hardy, bearing bright, sea-blue flowers on long stems in clusters during May. Height up to 20 ft.

C. × veitchianus

Evergreen, powder-blue flowers in May and June. As this is particularly hardy it makes an ideal wall shrub in less favoured localities. Height 10–12 ft.

CELASTRUS

C. orbiculatus (syn. *C. articulatus*)

Hardy deciduous, vigorous twining climber best suited to growing on trees or over large shrubs, or against a wall or fence, where its spectacular fruits will be shown to advantage. In autumn the orange-yellow fruit capsules when fully ripe split open into three and display the bright scarlet seed-coat, during November, December and January. For full measure the leaves turn a clear yellow. It is not fussy about soils. Plant October to March. Prune, when grown where it is necessary to restrict growth, by cutting away any weak shoots and tips of the main shoots in February. Propagate by layering in August, root cuttings in December or by seeds which are best overwintered in dry sand and sown in February. Height 30–40 ft.

C. scandens

Hardy, deciduous twining climber, its small yellowish flowers are borne on panicles 2–4 in. long and are unisexual or bisexual. The yellow cap-

144

LEFT: the thick, creamy-white petals of *Magnolia grandiflora* are richly fragrant
BELOW: a fine mature specimen of the evergreen *M. grandiflora* 'Lanceolata'

ABOVE LEFT: *Parthenocissus henryana* foliage is veined with white and pinkish-purple
ABOVE RIGHT: in autumn the leaves of *Parthenocissus tricuspidata* 'Veitchii' are red and crimson
LEFT: *Vitis coignetiae* turns rich crimson in autumn
BELOW: the author's birthplace at Lingfield, Surrey, covered with Virginia creeper (*Parthenocissus quinquefolia*)

sules, when fully ripe, split open into three and display their bright red seed-coats. Other remarks as for *C. orbiculatus* except that this species is not quite so vigorous, so can be trained on a wall or trellis. Height up to 20 ft.

CERATOSTIGMA

C. willmottianum

Hardy, dwarf deciduous shrub. It is sometimes severely hit by frost, and even cut back to ground level, but it recovers in the spring. The wiry reddish-brown stems bear rich blue flowers from July to October. Makes an attractive low semi-formal hedge up to 3 ft. high. Plant from pots 15 in. apart in May. Thrives in almost any soil, but prefers hot dry soil and a sunny position. Suitable for coastal areas. Prune in April by cutting back all frosted growth until live wood is reached. Propagate by taking soft-wood cuttings rooted under glass in March, or half-ripe cuttings in June–July under glass. Height 2–3 ft.

CHAENOMELES (Japanese Quince)

C. japonica

The genus has had so much change in its nomenclature that it is difficult to know which is the correct name for this or that species. However, most nurserymen of repute will by now know what one requires when a chaenomeles or Japanese Quince, is asked for. It is a hardy, deciduous shrub, thorn-bearing, with scarlet, red, pink or white flowers in March to April, followed in autumn by greenish-yellow fruits which make excellent jelly. Although the Japanese quince is not commonly seen as a hedge, it makes a formidable informal one, being attractive both in spring and autumn. The Japanese quince is without doubt one of our brightest spring flowering wall shrubs, and being a shrub it does need some kind of support to which it can be tied. It is one of our toughest shrubs, thriving on any wall or fence at any point of the compass. Wall-grown plants should be pruned at the end of April or early May, by cutting back secondary shoots after flowering. There are several varieties. Plant from pots (as open ground plants transplant badly) 1–1½ ft. apart, for hedges October to March. Trim at the end of April or early in

K
145

May after flowering, shortening back young wood to two buds. The Japanese quinces thrive in any well-drained loamy soil, whether alkaline or acid. Propagation by seeds sown in April, heel or nodal cuttings of half-ripened wood in June or July, or hard-wood cuttings in January. Height 2–10 ft.

C. j. alpina (syns. *C. sargentii, C. maulei*)
Bright-red flowers, March to May. Height 2–2½ ft.

C. speciosa (syns. *C. lagenaria, Cydonia japonica, Pyrus japonica*)
Bright red flowers, yellow fruits. Height 6 ft.
    Cultivars of the species are as follows:
C.s. 'Cardinalis'. Bright cardinal-red flowers in March and April. Height 8 ft.
C.s. 'Falconet Charlet' (syn. *C. rosea flore pleno*). Double salmon-pink flowers in March and April. Height 8 ft.
C.s. 'Moerloosii'. Apple-blossom pink flowers, white within, in March and April. Height 6–8 ft.
C.s. 'Nivalis'. Pure white flowers, March and April. Height 6–8 ft.
C.s. 'Simonii'. Crimson flowers, March to May. Height 2–2½ ft.
    All the preceding chaenomeles should be treated and planted as for *C. japonica*.
    Cultivars obtained from a cross between *C. speciosa* and *C. japonica* are as follows:
C.j. 'Boule de Feu'. Vermilion flowers, yellow fragrant fruits. Height 8 ft.
C. 'Crimson and Gold'. A most handsome variety, rich crimson flowers with a host of golden stamens. Height 6–10 ft.
C. 'Firedance'. A beautiful red. Height 3–6 ft.
C. 'Knap Hill Scarlet'. Mandarin-red flowers in March and April. Height 5 ft.
C. 'Pink Lady'. An outstanding, clear rose-pink, its flowers are closely set and freely borne, on a sheltered wall in February, otherwise March to April. Height 3–6 ft.
C. 'Rowallane'. Deep red flowers, March and April. Height 3–4 ft.

CHAMAECYPARIS

C. lawsoniana (syn. *Cupressus lawsoniana*) (Lawson's Cypress)

Some nurserymen still call this plant by its older name, *Cupressus lawsoniana*. Lawson's cypress was introduced as long ago as 1854 from

146

Oregon and California. As W. J. Bean says in *Trees and Shrubs Hardy in the British Isles*: 'No conifer has produced so much variety in foliage and habit under cultivation.' *C. lawsoniana* has foliage that ranges from deep green to a glaucous green, gold, yellow and silver; the bark is reddish-brown; the flowers are crimson-red; the cones are glaucous, finally brown. The cones are mostly found only on screens or hedges that have not been clipped or trees that have been allowed to grow naturally.

The Lawson cypress is a first-class hedge plant. It is also equally suitable as a wind screen. W. Arnold-Forster, in *Shrubs for the Milder Counties*, says: '*C. lawsoniana* stands wind fairly well: the grey and gold-leaved forms, such as the blue-green *C.l.* 'Allumii' resist wind and spray better than the green ones. Thujas, on the contrary, are useless in sea wind.' The Lawson cypress and its varieties thrive on most soils apart from very dry sandy or gravel soils.

Preparation, as for all hedge and screen planting, must be thorough, and it is even more important with an evergreen than a deciduous plant, because an evergreen has to support foliage all the time it is making new roots, whereas a deciduous tree is, each year, producing a mulch of fallen leaves. Fortunately, the Lawson cypress and its varieties are equally happy in clay, chalk or sandy soils. It does, however, like an open position, and resents drip from other trees and root interference from them. It tolerates annual clipping—in fact, it is all the better for it. For the gardener who has the time and energy, secateurs are best, but shears may be used, or any of the mechanical hedge trimmers.

Dig the ground two spits deep and incorporate well-rotted manure or good garden compost at the time of digging. Best planting size is 1½–2 ft. high, spaced at 1½–2 ft. apart. For screens plant at 5 ft. apart, and as soon as the trees start to touch one another remove every other tree. Plant in late September to October, or March to April. Propagate by seed sown in March or cuttings taken from July to September. Height 10–15 ft. for hedges, 40–50 ft. for screens.

C.l. 'Allumii'. Glaucous blue foliage and pyramidal in habit. For a hedge space the plants 1½–2 ft. apart, but for a screen 5–10 ft. apart. Height for hedges 10–12 ft., for screens 25–30 ft.

C.l. 'Erecta' (syn. 'Erecta Viridis'). Bright green erect and monumental in habit; transplants well. In 1939 I planted a quantity many of which were of poor quality and had not been recently transplanted. All grew and today they form a useful hedge. Height 20–40 ft.

C.l. 'Green Pillar' (syn. *C.l.e.* 'Jackman's Variety'). Rich green foliage, good conical habit. Space them 2–2½ ft. apart. Height 20–25 ft., width 5–8 ft.

C.l. 'Fletcheri'. Attractive bluish-grey feathery foliage. Space 5 ft. apart for a screen and 12–18 in. apart for a hedge. Height for screens 8–12 ft., for hedges 4–6 ft.

C.l. 'Fraseri'. Grey to grey-green foliage; spire-shaped or columnar in habit; most useful as a screen. Space 5–8 ft. apart. Height 35–40 ft., width 12–15 ft.

C.l. 'Green Hedger'. This cultivar, as its name implies, is green in colour, and a very rich green. Green Hedger originated in George Jackman and Son's nursery at Woking during the 1920's, when it was picked out of a batch of Lawson seedlings by Mr. G. Rowland Jackman. The first hedge of 'Green Hedger' was planted just before the Second World War (1939 –45) to screen an old barn at Mayford in Surrey. But by 1958 this hedge was 15 ft. high, and thick right down to the ground. To ensure that the stock is kept true to form it is propagated vegetatively. This increases the price a little, but the tree's habit is so good that it is worth the extra cost. Space the plants 1½–2 ft. apart. Other remarks as for *C. lawsoniana*.

C.l. 'Lutea'. A beautiful golden cultivar ideal for screening and equally suitable as a hedge plant. For a screen space at 5–10 ft. apart, and for a hedge 18–21 in. apart. Height for screens 30–50 ft., width 9–12 ft.; height for hedges 5–8 ft.

C.l. 'Stewartii'. Another handsome cultivar rich gold in colour. The original tree was still alive when I saw it at D. Stewart and Son's nursery at Ferndown, Dorset in 1951. It looked remarkably healthy, though it was 60 years old. The first sport was found in Stewarts' nursery around 1890. Space trees for a screen 8–10 ft. apart and for hedges 18–21 in. apart. Height as a specimen or screen 30–35 ft., with a width of 12–15 ft.

C.l. 'Triomf van Boskoop' (syn. 'Triomphe de Boskoop'). Named after the famous nursery centre of Boskoop in Holland, where every square inch of soil is cultivated as nursery land. This cultivar has beautiful glaucous blue foliage. It is pyramidal in habit and makes a useful screen tree and an attractive hedge. For a screen space 8–10 ft. apart, and for a hedge 1½–2 ft. apart. Height as a screen 45–55 ft., width 12–15 ft. Height as a hedge 6–9 ft.

C.l. 'Winston Churchill'. This handsome conifer was raised by the late Mr. J. Hogger of Felbridge, Surrey, in 1938. I well remember him telling me what a winner it would be. In 1945 he named it after W.S.C. It has a dense habit and is broadly columnar having rich golden yellow foliage throughout the year. Ideal where a few stately conifers are wanted as a screen. Space them 5–8 ft. apart for a screen and 2–2½ ft. apart for a hedge. Height 25–30 ft.

148

C. pisifera 'Plumosa Aurea' (syn. *Retinospora pisifera* 'Plumosa aurea')

This conifer was for many years known under the generic name of *Retinospora*. In habit it is closely branched and rather squat, but it makes a good screen or hedge plant. It has soft, golden feathery foliage. For a screen space 8–9 ft. apart, and for hedges 1½–1¾ ft. apart. Height as a screen 10–30 ft., width 10–15 ft. For hedges, height 5–8 ft.

CHERRY LAUREL, *see Prunus laurocerasus*

CHERRY PLUM, *see Prunus cerasifera*

CHERRY, WILD, *see Prunus avium*

CHESTNUT, SWEET, *see* CASTANEA

CHILEAN BELLFLOWER, *see* LAPAGERIA

CHILEAN GUAVA, *see Myrtus ugni*

CHILEAN JASMINE *see* MANDEVILLA

CHIMONANTHUS

C. praecox (syn. *C. fragrans*) (Winter Sweet)

This attractive deciduous, sweetly scented shrub, is best planted beside a wall or fence. Its 1 in. wide flowers of yellow petals, tinged green with purple inner petals, appear on the bare branches during the winter. Once the flowers are over the shrub is of little interest; this can however, be remedied by planting a clematis such as *C. alpina* to climb over the bush. It thrives in most soils other than acid.

There are two cultivars: *C.p.* 'Grandiflorus' with slightly larger

149

flowers of yellow and deeper purple inner petals; and *C.p.* 'Luteus', yellow. This rough leaved shrub can be disappointing by not flowering but correct pruning will ensure plenty of blossom. Prune as soon as flowers fade by spurring back all secondary shoots to within an eye or two of the base. Plant from October to March. Propagation is by cuttings of the current year's half-ripened wood inserted in sandy soil in July in a warm frame or under mist; by seeds sown as soon as ripe, or by layering in spring. Height 8–10 ft.

CHINESE GOOSEBERRY, *see Actinidia chinensis*

CHOISYA

C. ternata (Mexican Orange-blossom)

Evergreen, hardy in all but the very coldest districts, its rich dark, glossy leaves are each made up of three leaflets. It has white flowers with a sweet hawthorn-like fragrance April to May, and again in late summer and sometimes in autumn. The leaves when crushed have a pungent smell. This makes a fine hedge by the sea and is also a good town hedge. It also makes a very useful and attractive wall, fence or trellis plant, in fact, at one house I lived in, I always tied the plant to a fence where it flourished. Plant from pots 2–3 ft. apart, for a hedge, September or April. Thrives in sun or shade but needs shelter from cold winds. In late winter and in the first months of the year foliage will sometimes suffer from frost and wind damage, causing the tips of the leaves to look like pieces of parchment, but as the year advances these will gradually disappear by eventually dropping off. It does well in clay, and also on lighter soils and on chalk. Trim at the end of May after flowering. It does not resent hard pruning. Propagate by half-ripened wood cuttings in July or mature ones in September. Height 6–10 ft.

CINQUEFOIL, SHRUBBY, *see* POTENTILLA

CISSUS

C. striata (syn. *Ampelopsis sempervirens*)

This is the only evergreen vine. It is self-creeping and has foliage similar to the small-leaved Virginia creeper. It is a quick and vigorous climber. Not being fully hardy it is more suitable for southern and western districts of the British Isles. Plant in March or April. Propagate by soft-wood cuttings in July and treat as for *Ampelopsis brevipedunculata*. Its height is indeterminate.

CISTUS (Rock Rose)

Evergreen, free-flowering dwarf shrub, the rock roses are hardy in the milder climates, though plants survive elsewhere in most winters except in the coldest districts. They are especially useful for seaside planting, and grow best on light, well-drained soils, including lime soils, and above all in full sun, but with shelter from cold winds. Their foliage is usually rough and dark green, sometimes glutinous; they flower in June and July. Best used as informal hedges. Plant $1\frac{1}{2}$–2 ft. apart, late March to April, and always use pot-grown plants. Trim in early spring, but never cut back into old wood. With young plants pinch out tips of shoots to induce bushiness. Propagate by seeds sown in spring or by half-ripened wood cuttings in July and August. Height varies from 2–8 ft.

C. × corbariensis

Fresh green leaves, crimson tinted buds followed by white flowers, yellow at the base. One of the hardiest of the species. Height $2\frac{1}{2}$–3 ft.

C. × cyprius

Olive-green foliage changing to pewter in winter. Large white flowers with crimson blotches at the base of each petal. Height 3–5 ft.

C. ladanifer (Gum Cistus)

Aromatic foliage, large solitary flowers, 3–4 in. wide, white with blood-red blotch at the base of each petal. Height 3–5 ft.

C. laurifolius

Hardiest of the rock roses. Dark green aromatic sticky foliage, white flowers, 2½–3 in. wide. Height 6–8 ft.

C. × pulverulentus (syn. 'Sunset')

A compact bush, with purplish-pink flowers, 1½ in. wide, fairly hardy. Height 2 ft.

C. × purpureus (syn. 'Betty Taudevin')

For sheltered positions. Rosy-crimson flowers with a chocolate blotch on base of each petal. Height 3–4 ft.

CLEMATIS

The Virgin's Bower, as clematis is sometimes known, was first introduced to England in 1569 in the reign of Elizabeth I. And today no other climber is more popular, not even the rose. The main reason for the popularity of the clematis is its ease of growth and great adaptability to grow in almost any soil and in any position. All climbing species and hybrid varieties need some form of support, and this can be a wall, fence, trellis, tree or large shrub, which can be evergreen or deciduous.

Clematis can also be grown in tubs, in large earthenware jars, where they can be trained either on a frame or allowed to climb over their container if it is placed in a suitable position. Tubs or pots must have adequate drainage. Fill them with good compost such as John Innes, some well-rotted manure and a good handful of bonemeal. To shield the roots from the sun place pebbles or broken pieces of paving stones on top of the soil.

It is often thought, and frequently recommended, that the clematis must have lime in the soil; this is not, however, the case. I have grown excellent plants in a soil with a reading of pH 6·5, which is acid—in fact it is an ideal soil in which to grow most plants. It is also generally considered that the clematis must have sun; again, this is not absolutely necessary, and I have seen many a fine plant flourishing and flowering freely on a north wall. Two examples that I always think of are 'Nelly Moser' and 'Henryi'. Clematis can be grown north, south, east or west.

What they do not like is sun at their roots. The ideal is roots in the shade and shoots and flowers in the sun. Therefore, when planting them beside a sunny wall whether south or west, shade the roots with a large slab of stone, or some small shrub such as rosemary, lavender, *Senecio greyi*, *Mahonia aquifolium*, *Cotoneaster horizontalis* or similar shrubs.

Planting

Now, when planting a clematis, do not be mean over the preparation of the planting site. Dig the ground two spits deep, incorporate well-rotted farmyard manure, if you can get it, or well-rotted garden compost, or leafmould or peat. Of the last do see that it is properly moist before use. To any of these organic substances add bonemeal at the rate of 4–6 oz. per sq. yd.

As clematis are pot grown, they can be planted at almost any time, though I favour from November to March or early April. At one time most clematis were grafted on to stocks of Old Man's Beard, *C. vitalba*, but today many of the leading clematis growers are propagating them from cuttings. It is to be hoped that this method of cultivation may help to prevent clematis wilt (see page 44). This plant pays for patience— on one occasion in May I planted on the south-west corner of our house a plant of *C. jackmanii* 'Gipsy Queen', grown from a cutting, to clamber through one of my favourite climbing roses—'Albertine'. The clematis had its top removed, leaving it 1 ft. above ground-level. It died back, but by the following March three young healthy shoots appeared. Similarly, I planted an 'Etoile Violette' beside the climbing rose 'Zéphirine Drouhin'; this, too, did little at first, but again by the following March it was flourishing.

Training

When dealing with young plants it is as well to tie in the young shoots in the early stages of growth, but once they are established they will more or less look after themselves, apart from an occasional tie here and there.

Pruning

This is a vexed question. So often books and catalogues say something slightly different, yet basically much of what is written says the same thing. However, the following basic rules will cover the pruning needs of most clematis species and varieties.

METHOD A. *Clematis alpina* and varieties which flower April–May, *C. armandii* and cultivars 'Apple Blossom' and 'Snowdrift' flowering from the end of March to mid-April, *C. calycina* flowering in January–February, *C. macropetala* and cultivars flowering in May. *C. montana* and cultivars flowering during April–May, and *C. m. wilsonii* flowering in June–July, are all pruned after flowering—when trained to a wall, fence or trellis—by cutting all side branches hard back, almost to their base and above a node, i.e. leaf joint. By this method plenty of flower buds will be formed for the next year's blooms.

METHOD B. *Clematis florida* and *patens* cultivars which mostly flower May–June, some June–July, and 'The President' which flowers in June, July and October, require the minimum of pruning, by training out the main branches to prevent them becoming entwined. As soon as they have finished flowering cut all old flowers off above a pair of strong buds.

METHOD C. *Clematis lanuginosa* and its many varieties which flower from May to August should be pruned as for group (B) or more severely as in group (D) like *C. jackmanii* and *C. viticella*, in February or March. Alternatively prune by using both methods and so ensure a longer season of flowering, though the flowers from the later pruning will not be as large as those on the shoots pruned immediately after flowering.

METHOD D. *Clematis jackmanii* and *C. viticella* and its varieties, which for the most part flower from July to October, need to be cut back each year, close to the base of the previous year's growth and immediately above a leaf joint, doing this in February or early March. I prefer to get my plants pruned in February before too much new growth appears, though enough to see what I am doing. From time to time it may be necessary to cut some old stems hard back to within a foot or more of the ground level.

METHOD E. *Clematis flammula*, *C. tangutica*, *C. taxensis* and other miscellaneous species can be hard pruned in February; though frequently such species are allowed to ramble through shrubs or over old apple trees and then little pruning need be done.

As regards newly planted clematis, all plants should be cut back during late February or early March to within 6–12 in. of ground level.

Feeding

The clematis appreciates good living, just as I do—though not bone-meal and dried blood such as the clematis enjoys. An annual application of 50 per cent each of bonemeal and dried blood at 2 oz. per sq. yd. should be given in early March. Also, an annual manuring of well-rotted farmyard manure or well-rotted compost will make all the difference to the plant's well-being. The manure and fertilizer can be lightly forked in, or a few holes can be made around the plant and the bonemeal and dried blood trickled in.

Moisture

Although *Clematis vitalba* (Old Man's Beard) is often seen flourishing in the hedgerow and in a chalk soil, in a sunny and possibly dry position, it would be found that the roots are in the shade and probably growing where they can obtain sufficient moisture for their needs. So do see that the plants in the garden, particularly when growing against a house wall, have a liberal supply of water during the summer, especially in their growing season, May and June.

Pests and Diseases

Earwigs can quickly disfigure flowers and foliage by eating them away. However, a spraying with trichlorphon on stems and leaves should deal with these unpleasant pests.

Mildew is more unsightly than serious, as the foliage and flowers become covered with a white powdery deposit. Attacks are worst when the weather is cold and showery, and in such seasons it is wise to take precautions by spraying with dinocap.

Slugs are extremely fond of young clematis shoots and attack them as they emerge through the ground. Damage can be averted by little mounds of coal or coke ashes placed around the young succulent stems, preferably before the stems appear. Also apply a slug-killer which can now be obtained in liquid or pellet form.

Wilt can be a very alarming occurrence for an amateur who has no knowledge of clematis wilt. I well remember coming home from the office one evening and seeing—what was, when I left in the morning, a flourishing specimen of 'William Kennet'—a limp, browned-off plant. It was cut back until healthy growth was reached. It flowered again, but

155

the same thing happened a second time, so it was cut down to ground level and again new shoots were produced.

Apart from cutting back, also spray the plant with clean water morning and evening; and see that there is an ample supply of moisture at the roots. Cheshunt Compound also helps to ward off the fungus, but at present there is no known cure (see also page 44).

I give now, an alphabetical list of clematis species and varieties, which I am setting out in their respective groups according to the times and methods of pruning (see methods of pruning, page 154).

Pruning method (A)
Alpina, armandii, calycina, chrysocoma, macropetala, montana and *vedrariensis*

C. alpina 'Columbine'

Soft lavender-blue, bell-shaped flowers, long-pointed sepals, flowering April to May.
C.a. 'Pamela Jackman'. Oxford-blue flowers, with four sepals, flowering April to May.
C. a. sibirica. Pure white, small flowers in May.
C.a.s. 'Ruby'. Rosy-red nodding flowers in April to May.
C.a.s. 'White Moth'. Double, white, nodding flowers, pointed sepals, flowering in May.

C. armandii

This species and its cultivars need a warm and sheltered wall. *C. armandii* has deep green, leathery trifoliate leaves, creamy-white flowers, 2 in. across. In severe winters frost can cause injury. Flowers in April.
C.a. 'Apple Blossom'. White sepals shaded pink, flowering in April.
C.a. 'Snowdrift'. The largest of this species, bearing huge clusters of white flowers at the end of March to April.

C. calycina

Nodding creamy-white flowers which are freckled inside, evergreen foliage, flowering in January to February.

156

C. chrysocoma

The shapely flowers are a soft pinkish-mauve and borne on long stalks.
Free flowering June to October.
C.c. sericea
Large, pure white, four-sepaled flowers, with yellow centres in June.

C. macropetala 'Lagoon'

Deep lavender, semi-double, nodding flowers, pointed sepals. Flowering
in May.
C.m. 'Maidwell Hall'. Oxford and Cambridge blue, semi-double, nodding flowers in May.
C.m. 'Markham's Pink'. Soft pink flowers in May.

C. montana (The Mountain Clematis)

An abundance of starry, white flowers in May to June.
C.m. 'Elizabeth'. A beautiful pink montana with large long-stemmed
flowers which are richly fragrant. The foliage is also most attractive.
The flowers are in May.
C.m. grandiflora. A vigorous, large flowered form of *C. montana*, white
flowers in April to May.
C.m. 'Pink Perfection'. Deep pink flowers in May.
C.m. wilsonii. Attractively twisted white sepals, very free-flowering in
June to July.

C. × vedrariensis 'Highdown Variety' (syn. *C. spooneri rosea*)

Pink flowers with deeper reverse in May.

Pruning Method (B)
Florida and *patens*

C. florida 'Belle of Woking'

Double pale mauve, rosette-shaped flowers in May to June.
C.f. 'Sieboldii' (syn. *C. f. bicolor*). Cream sepals changing to white, with
deep purple petal-like stamens, rosette shaped. Flowers in June to
August.

C.f. 'Duchess of Edinburgh'. Pure white, rosette-shaped flowers in May to June.

C. patens 'Barbara Dibley'

Rich violet, with purple bars in the centre of each sepal, free-flowering May to June.

C.p. 'Barbara Jackman'. Soft petunia, with plum-coloured bar, in centre of each sepal, cream stamens. Its colour is most intense on a north or north-west aspect. Flowers in May to June.

C.p. 'Daniel Deronda'. Semi-double, violet-blue flowers—the edges of its pointed sepals are shaded a deeper blue—are produced on last year's shoots in late May. These are followed by single flowers with yellow stamens. Flowers from May to July.

C.p. 'Elsa Spath'. Bright blue flowers, very free-flowering and vigorous. Flowers in May to June.

C.p. 'Lasurstern'. Deep purplish-blue flowers, with yellow stamens, very large—it occasionally blooms on the young wood in May, but usually flowers June to September.

C.p. 'Miriam Markham'. Large rich lavender flowers, double and single blooms appear on the young and old wood respectively. Flowers from May to July.

C.p. 'Miss Bateman'. Large pure white flowers, with attractive purple stamens, vigorous and free-flowering, May to June.

C.p. 'Mrs. George Jackman'. Satiny white flowers, with brown stamens from May to June.

C.p. 'Mrs. P. B. Truax'. Periwinkle blue, with a yellow centre, large and free-flowering in June.

C.p. 'Nelly Moser'. Next to *jackmanii*, this must be the best known and best loved clematis; pale mauve-pink flowers with deep carmine bar. Free-flowering May to June and again in September.

C.p. 'Sealand Gem'. Mauve with a petunia-coloured bar down the centre of the sepals, which have waved edges. Flowers from June to July.

C.p. 'The President'. Deep violet, with paler bar down the centre of each sepal, dark anthers. It produces flowers on young and old wood. Blooms do not fade. Flowers June to July and again in October.

Pruning method (C)
Lanuginosa, alternatively method (D) can be used

C. lanuginosa 'Beauty of Richmond'

Soft, clear mauve with slightly darker bars, a very beautiful clematis. Flowers in June to July.

C.l. 'Beauty of Worcester'. Deep violet-blue, producing double and single blooms on old and young wood respectively, flowering from May to July.

C.l. 'Belle Nantaise'. The long-pointed sepals are a delicate, translucent lavender, making it a real aristocrat. Flowers in June to July.

C.l. 'Lady Northcliffe'. The deep lavender flowers are tinted bright blue, with a centre of white stamens. Flowers from June to October.

C.l. 'Lawsoniana'. Large lavender flowers, the sepals being very long, with a centre of brown stamens, appearing in June to August.

C.l. 'Lord Neville'. Rich plum coloured, shapely flowers with wavy edged sepals. Flowers in June to August.

C.l. 'Marie Boisselot' (syn. 'Mme le Coultre'). Pure white, with yellow stamens, the flowers are full and the sepals are rounded. Flowers from June to August.

C.l. 'Mrs. Cholmondeley'. The long, narrow-reflexed sepals are wisteria blue. It blooms freely and continuously from May to June and later.

C.l. 'Prins Hendrik'. Large flowers, sky blue having pointed sepals. Flowers from July to August.

C.l. 'Proteus'. Pink, suffused soft plum purple; double and single blooms are produced on old and young wood respectively. Flowers from May to July.

C.l. 'W. E. Gladstone'. Extra large lavender flowers, the centre of each rippled sepal being a lighter shade. Blooms freely and is a vigorous grower. Flowers July to August.

C.l. 'William Kennet'. Large, lavender-mauve flowers, with crimped edges to the sepals, each being ribbed down the centre. Brown stamens. This is a magnificent flower, appearing June to July.

Pruning method (D)
Jackmanii, viticella large flowered (l.f.)
and small flowered (s.f.)

C. jackmanii, the most famous of all clematis

159

Known and loved by all. Violet-blue flowers which are freely borne, appearing July to August.

C.j. 'Comtesse de Bouchard'

Charming saucer-shaped flowers of a soft pink with a tint of mauve. Free-flowering, June to October.

C.j. 'Gipsy Queen'. Large flowers of a rich dark purple, having a velvety sheen. Flowers July to August.

C.j. 'Hagley Hybrid'. Deep shell-pink blooms with pointed sepals, and brown anthers. Free-flowering and a vigorous grower. Flowers June to September.

C.j. 'Madame Edouard André'. Beautiful medium-sized flowers, deep red with yellow stamens and pointed sepals, appearing from July to August.

C.j. 'Perle d'Azur'. Light blue, very early and free-flowering, striking blooms. Also flowers on old wood. Blooms mid-July to mid-August.

C.j. 'Star of India'. Similar to *jackmanii*, having medium-sized flowers, its violet sepals have a red bar down the centre of each. Flowers July to August.

C.j. 'Superba'. Dark violet-purple, broader sepals than *C. jackmanii*. Flowers July to August.

C.j. 'Victoria'. Its almost transparent flowers are a soft heliotrope, a fine variety. Flowers July to August.

C. viticella (l.f.) 'Ascotiensis'

Bright blue, having pointed sepals, very free-flowering. Flowers August to September.

C.v. (l.f.) 'Ernest Markham'. A beautiful clematis, its glowing petunia-red flowers have a velvety sheen. Free- flowering, but sometimes requires a little patience to do so. Flowers July to September.

C.v. 'Etoile Violette'. Deep violet, medium-sized flowers with yellow stamens. A most attractive variety and lavish with its blooms, at the end of June to August.

C.v. (l.f.) 'Huldine'. The pearly-white, translucent flowers have a distinct mauve-pink bar on the reverse side of each sepal. To see the blooms at their best advantage they need to be grown over a pergola where the sun can be seen shining through their masses of flowers, which appear July to September.

C.v. (l.f.) 'Lady Betty Balfour'. Rich violet-blue, with yellow stamens. A strong grower and free-flowering, from September to October.

C.v. (l.f.) 'Venosa Violacea'. The rich violet flowers are distinctly and

ABOVE LEFT: *Actinidia kolomikta* has green, pink and white foliage
ABOVE RIGHT: the Passion Flower, *Passiflora caerulea*, is both interesting and beautiful
BELOW LEFT: an old favourite among clematis is the variety 'Nelly Moser', its pale mauve-pink sepals are marked with a deep carmine bar
BELOW RIGHT: *Clematis flammula* covered with a mass of sweetly scented, white star-like flowers

ABOVE LEFT: white, hawthorn-like blossom on Firethorn, or pyracantha
ABOVE RIGHT: *Pyracantha rogersiana* 'Flava' bears bright yellow berries very freely
in autumn
BELOW LEFT: *Skimmia japonica* covered with sealing wax red berries
BELOW RIGHT: the white flowers of *Skimmia japonica* are richly scented

prettily pencilled through to the base of each sepal. Their dark anthers are topped by white filaments—making the blooms particularly attractive. Flowers from July to September.

C.v. (l.f.) 'Ville de Lyon'. The bright, carmine-red flowers have deeper colouring around the edges of the sepals. It occasionally flowers on the old wood. Blooms July to September.

C. viticella (s.f.)

The purple-blue nodding, saucer-shaped blooms, are very free-flowering. George Jackman & Son have an exceptionally good form of this species.

C.v. (s.f.) 'Abundance'. The soft purple flowers are distinctly veined, and freely produced in each leaf axil. Flowers from July to September.

C.v. (s.f.) 'Kermesina'. Bright red flowers, freely produced. A very hardy variety. Flowers from July to September.

C.v. (s.f.) 'Little Nell'. Slaty-mauve flowers which are especially dainty and very freely produced, from August to September.

C.v. (s.f.) 'Minuet'. A most striking small-flowered variety, its delicately shaped cream-centred flowers are ringed with a broad band of purple covering the ends of each sepal. Free-flowering August to September.

C.v. (s.f.) 'Royal Velours'. The velvet-like flowers are a deep purple. Free-flowering, July to September.

Pruning method (E)
includes m.s. = miscellaneous species

C. × durandii (m.s.)

A hybrid between a large-flowered clematis and the herbaceous species *C. integrifolia*. The gentian-blue funnel-shaped, 3 in. wide flowers are carried on 5 ft. growths, which need tying to some form of support as their leaves do not cling. Flowers from July to August.

C. fargesii (m.s.)

The six-sepalled, 1 in. wide, white flowers are freely produced, in large clusters from June to September.

C. flammula (m.s.) (The fragrant Virgin's Bower)

Masses of sweetly-scented small, white star-like flowers. Flowers from August to September.

C.f. 'Rubro marginata' (m.s.). This attractive hybrid has a rosy-purple margin to each sepal, with green stamens in the centre—also sweetly scented. Flowers August to September.

C. jouiniana (m.s.)

The clusters of small dainty lavender flowers are produced in August to October. Especially good for a north wall, or for growing over trees. It needs tying to its supports.

C. orientalis (m.s.) (syn. *C. graveolens*) (The Orange-peel Clematis)

The reason for its common name is that this species has four thick orange-yellow sepals, which hang down like little divided fairy caps. The flowers are followed by feathery seed heads. Little pruning needed. Free-flowering, August to October.

C. rehderana (syn. *C. nutans*) (Nodding Virgin's Bower)

A vigorous species, ideal for growing in and over trees. Its rather in-different straw-coloured bell-shaped flowers are fully compensated by its delicious cowslip-like fragrance. August–October.

C. tangutica 'Gravetye' (m.s.)

Bright yellow chinese lantern-like flowers, followed by large, yellow, feathery seed heads. Flowers August to October.

C. texensis 'Countess of Onslow' (m.s.)

There is a deep pink bar down the centre of each sepal, while the edges are a soft pink. Flowers July to September.
C.t. 'Gravetye Beauty' (m.s.). This, not much more than 6 ft. high, has rich deep red flowers, of an open habit. Flowers July to September.

C. vitalba (m.s.) (Traveller's Joy or Old Man's Beard)

This is one of our most lovely hedgerow sights during July when its masses of white flowers smother hedges and tree tops, followed by clouds of white, frothy seed heads in September that hang on throughout the autumn and early winter. Flowers from July to September.

CLIANTHUS

C. puniceus (Lobster Claw or Parrot's Bill)

This member of the pea family with pinnate, semi-evergreen foliage, is one of our brightest New Zealand, slightly tender, scandent shrubs. Those who can grow it well are the envy of those who cannot. It needs the protection of a south or west wall or fence and prefers a warm locality and a well-drained soil. Then its brilliant red parrot-shaped flowers will reward its owner during June and July. In districts where its winter hardiness is at all doubtful some protection should be given by covering the plant with sacking, polythene, bracken and so on. Planting is best done in spring. As for pruning, little is needed except an occasional trim to keep it tidy. Propagation is by seed, sown in a warm greenhouse or frame in the spring, or by half-ripened cuttings rooted in sandy soil with heat during July. Height 6–8 ft.

COBAEA

C. scandens (Cups and Saucers)

This is so called because of its Canterbury-bell-like flowers set in a saucer-like frill. The flowers are at first green, later changing to violet, before finally falling, when they are followed by large acorn-shaped fruits. This perennial climber is not hardy out of doors all the year round, but is one that should be grown annually. It is a real Jack-in-the-Beanstalk plant. Frequently I have had plants reach the gutter by midsummer. In fact my boys called it the drainpipe flower, because one year it completely covered a pipe. Plant it in early June. As for pruning the frost will do it for you. Propagate by seed sown in February or March in gentle heat. Height up to 25 ft.
C. s. flore albo. The white form is not so common, and I had several plants in a batch of seedlings, for the first time, in 1965. It is not as vigorous as *C. scandens.*

CONVOLVULUS, *see* PHARBITIS

CORAL PLANT, *see Berberidopsis corallina*
163

CORNELIAN CHERRY, *see Cornus mas*

CORNUS (Dogwood)

Hardy, deciduous shrubs ideal for a low screen or shelter, or an informal hedge. Excellent for a damp situation, but grows in drier places also, and succeeds in sun or shade. The foliage is green or variegated silver and gold; the stems are red, green or golden. Flowers are white to yellowish-green, followed by either whitish, blue or black fruits and autumn tinted foliage. Plant 2–3 ft. apart, October to March. Trim by cutting stems hard back each year in early April, to encourage good young growth for winter colour. Propagate by hard-wood cuttings in October or November.

C. alba (Dogwood)

Brilliant red stems. Height 7–9 ft.
C.a. 'Elegantissima'. Green leaves edged with silver, red stems in winter. Height 8–10 ft.
C.a. 'Sibirica' (Westonbirt Dogwood). Fresh green foliage, sealing-wax red stems in winter. Height 6–9 ft.
C.a. 'Spaethii'. Golden variegated foliage, red stems in winter. Height 5–6 ft.

C. baileyi

Purple-red stems in winter, white berries. Height 8–10 ft.

C. mas (Cornelian Cherry)

Small yellow flowers, freely produced on the naked wood in February and March. Makes a rough hedge some 10 ft. high or may be allowed to run up to 15–20 ft. as a screen.

C. stolonifera 'Flaviramea'

Stems yellow, very effective in winter. Height 4–6 ft.

COROKIA

C. virgata

Evergreen and hardy, except in very severe winters. Small spoon-shaped leaves, on twiggy, slightly zigzagged shoots. Small yellow flowers in May followed by orange-yellow egg-shaped berries. Makes a good ornamental hedge and does not appear to be particular as to soil. Very wind-hardy, good for coastal areas. Plant pot-grown plants 1½ ft. apart in March or April. Trim in late summer. Propagate by hard-wood cuttings in November. Height 4–6 ft.

CORONILLA

C. glauca

Here is a shrub which can hardly rank as a climber or screen plant, but it is such a favourite I must include it. It needs a well-drained soil and protection of a wall. It is evergreen, with pea-shaped yellow flowers which are very fragrant; the glaucous green pinnate foliage will, I know, sometimes be touched by frost even to being denuded in bad winters— if it is killed outright plant another. It blooms in March or April and often through to August. I have known it to bloom in November and December. Plant in spring. Pruning requirements—no regular pruning needed, except to tidy it up after flowering. Propagate half-ripened cuttings with a slight heel attached, in June to July. Height 4–5 ft.

CORYLUS (Hazel)

C. avellana (Common Hazel)

Hardy, deciduous shrub with roundish leaves. Male catkins 1½–2½ in. long, female ones red and small. 'Lambs' tails, a favourite of every child, are too well known to require further description. Hazel is an excellent shrub to plant in a mixed hedge, it is also good on its own, especially when properly laid (for laying of hedges see page 29). Thrives on any type of soil, dry, heavy or chalk, and does not mind shade. Plant 1–2 ft. apart, October to March. Trim in late February or March. Propagate by seed, which should be stratified, seed being finally sown in early spring. Stratification is a process by which hard-coated seeds are softened. To do this, place the seeds in pots or boxes filled with equal quantities of sand and peat, standing them on a bed of ashes besides the north side of a fence, hedge or wall. Here they remain for 6, 12 or 18 months before they are ready for sowing. Height 10–20 ft.
C. maxima 'Purpurea'. Has purple leaves; otherwise as for *C. avellana*.

COTONEASTER

A large genus of evergreen and deciduous shrubs with many species and varieties. Their foliage varies in size and shape, leaves measuring from 1–5 in. in length, mostly dark rather than light green and of a leathery texture, some being covered with white, grey or brown downy felt beneath. Flowers are white or pinkish and borne in clusters of three to twenty, followed by red or orange-red fruits in autumn and winter. The cotoneasters are handsome shrubs at any time of the year. Many of them make superb screens or shelters and several are excellent for hedges. They are not particular about soil and will thrive anywhere, whether in a clay or chalk soil.

As a general recommendation the cotoneasters are best pruned at the end of the winter when berries are starting to spoil, usually between the end of February and the end of March. Propagation can be either by seed or cuttings. Seed should be stratified and sown the following spring. Half-ripened wood cuttings are taken in June or July and inserted in a cold frame or beneath a bell glass. For hedges and screens the following eight would be useful.

C. franchetii

Evergreen, silvery-grey-green foliage, the flowers are white, tinged with rose-pink, followed by a profusion of orange-red berries. Plant 1½ ft. apart, October to March. Height 8–10 ft.

C. frigidus

Deciduous, and makes a fine screen or shelter shrub. Leaves are a dull deep green 3–5 in. long and 1–2 in. wide. Bright red fruits about the size of a pea, borne in large clusters. Plant 2 ft. apart, October to March. Thrives well in town areas, also in cold Sussex clay. Height for screens 25–30 ft.; height for hedges 12–15 ft.

C. lacteus

Evergreen, large oval leathery leaves, dark green above, thick white down beneath, becoming yellow with age. Milky-white flowers in late June and July. Red berries. Plant 1½–2 ft. apart. Height 8–12 ft.

C. microphyllus

Low evergreen shrub of pretty habit. It makes a low hedge or is useful for draping over walls. Small leaves, deep glossy green above, grey and woolly beneath. Scarlet-red berries. Plant October to March. Height 1½–2 ft.

C. rotundifolius

Semi-evergreen, leaves dark glossy green. White flowers, suffused pink, followed by bright scarlet-red fruits which remain until February and are usually left alone by birds. Plant 1½ ft. apart, October to March. Height 4–6 ft.

C. salicifolius

Evergreen, with attractive wrinkled, dark glossy green leaves, glaucous beneath. Bright red berries. Makes a fine tall hedge. The variety *C. s. floccosus* has reddish-brown stems and attractive leathery foliage. Plant 2 ft. apart, October to March. Height 10 ft. for a hedge.

C. simonsii

A semi-evergreen shrub of erect habit. The lozenge-shaped leaves are dark glossy green. Orange-scarlet fruits. The foliage also colours well in autumn. It is a thoroughly hardy shrub and makes a first-rate hedge which can easily be kept to a thickness of 1–1½ ft. and up to 5 ft. in height. Plant 1½ ft. apart, October to March. Height 5–8 ft.

C. wardii

Evergreen, with dark, shining grey-green leaves covered with white felt beneath. Orange-red berries, and beautiful autumn foliage. It has the advantage that birds do not appear to attack the berries. Plant 1½–2 ft. apart, October to March. Height 6–9 ft.

COTTON LAVENDER, *see* SANTOLINA

CRATAEGUS (Hawthorn)

C. oxyacantha (Hawthorn, May or Quickthorn)

Hardy, deciduous shrub or tree which could, I think, be called 'the king of hardy deciduous hedge plants'. I cannot speak too highly of its value both as a garden or farm hedge. Apart from the privet I should say that there are more miles of quickthorn hedge than any other. It has three- to seven-lobed leaves and sweet-scented white flowers in May. Quickthorn has no qualms as to how ruthlessly it is clipped. During the Second World War I saw quickthorn hedges forty years old or more and 10 ft. high cut hard back to within 2 or 3 ft. of ground level, and in a short while rejuvenated. Farm hedges that have become overgrown and out of hand are often 'laid' (see page 29). Quickthorn is an excellent hedge plant to mix with privet, hazel, hornbeam or beech. It will thrive on any soil, chalk or otherwise, and will grow in sun or shade.

Hedges may be planted in single or double rows, though single is more usual. Hedges that are clipped several times during the summer will have a very neat appearance. Best planting sizes are either 1–1½ ft. or 1½–2 ft. high, spaced 9 in.–1 ft. apart for a single row; for a double row, 15 in. apart in the row and 8 in. between the rows.

Cut back newly planted bushes in March or early April, to within 6 to 9 in. of ground level to encourage strong vigorous growth from the base. Hedges can be trimmed from June onwards to the end of the summer. Farm hedges are usually trimmed during the winter months when the foliage is off. Propagation is by seed, which should first be stratified. Collect haws in autumn, stratify in sand and peat, and sow seed 18 months later. Height 5–20 ft.

There are many other thorns which could no doubt be used for hedging purposes, but the only one I have seen used is *Crataegus prunifolia*, which has large, dark, glossy green leaves, turning red and yellow in autumn. It also has formidable spines 1½–3 in. long, and round red fruit. Height 5–20 ft.

CROSS VINE, *see Bignonia capreolata*

CRYPTOMERIA

C. japonica 'Elegans'

An attractive conifer having feathery juvenile foliage which is permanently retained. During the summer foliage is glaucous green, changing in autumn and winter to a rich bronzy colour to rosy red. It has a bushy habit and is usually seen as a specimen tree some 20 ft. high. I have seen only one hedge, this was in Will Ingwersen's garden at East Grinstead. It is not fussy as to soil. The best planting size is 1½–2 ft. high, spaced at 1½ ft. apart; for screens 6–8 ft. apart. Plant in September to October or March to April. Trim in April, or its bushiness at the base may be impaired, so Will Ingwersen tells me, and again in August. It stands up to hard cutting back in April, as and when necessary. Propagate by cuttings in September. Height as a screen 20–30 ft., width 12–16 ft. Height as a hedge 5–6 ft.

CUCURBITA

The cucurbitas, or gourds, are extremely useful and decorative plants where climbers are required to make a quick coverage on a fence, or over a pergola or trellis, What is more, their attractively coloured and weirdly shaped fruits are ideal for indoor decoration during the winter months. They also look well when trained up a tripod of stout stakes or canes strategically placed in a border.

Seed should be sown at the end of April, in peat or clay pots filled with John Innes Seed compost or one of the soilless composts. The seeds should be put in edgeways, pushing the eye-end into the soil. Three seeds should be sown in each pot. Place the pots in an electric propagator with a temperature of 75° F. (24° C.). Germination will take from four to six days, when the pot can be moved into the greenhouse and kept in a temperature of 65° F. (18° C.). At the end of May start to harden them off, for a week to ten days, in a frame, in readiness for planting out in early June. Even then some protection will be needed such as a cloche or 2 lb. jam jars.

Seed can be sown out of doors during the first or second week of May. Prepare a seed bed by adding some coarse sand. The seedlings should be transplanted before the first two true leaves have been made.

Gourds like good rich soil, and a bucket of well-rotted manure or rotted garden compost should be placed in each planting hole. They need an ample supply of moisture but must not be overwatered. Once the plants have made a start they grow rapidly and must therefore be

169

tied to their supports, fairly regularly, stopping the vine when it has reached about 8 ft., unless, of course, you wish to let them ramble at will. As soon as a gourd has set on a lateral, pinch the lateral back to two leaves above the fruit.

The fruits should be cut before the vine is frosted or the gourds may also be damaged.

I have listed below the varieties available from most seedsmen.

Apple Gourd	Creamy-white, attractively striped, smooth-skinned and small.
Chinese Gourd	Very attractive, having small orange-red coloured fruits.
Hercules Club Gourd	Very long fruits.
Japanese Nest Egg	White, ornamental egg-shaped gourds, with a very hard skin.
Orange Gourd	An attractive bright orange, hard-skinned gourd.
Pear Gourd	The pear-shaped gourds are prettily marked green and yellow, often with the top half yellow and the bottom green.
Spoon Gourd	This is a small, hard-skinned, yellow-coloured gourd, 4–5 in. long, fruiting freely on lateral and sub-lateral growths; no stopping is necessary.
Turk's-cap Gourd	In varying colours of green and yellow, small gourds and very decorative.
Warted Gourd	These small verrucose gourds are exceedingly attractive and of various colourings.

Most of these gourds will reach anything from 15–20 ft. in length.

CUPRESSOCYPARIS

C. leylandii (syn. *Cupressus leylandii*) (Leyland Cypress)

Although this hybrid was raised as long ago as 1888, it is still looked upon as something rather new. *C. leylandii* is a hybrid between *Chamaecyparis nootkatensis* and *Cupressus macrocarpa*. In 1911 the cross was reversed, but according to Dallimore and Jackson both hybrids are exactly alike. This conifer was named after Mr. C. J. Leyland of Leighton Hall, Welshpool. In habit it is pyramidal, with the featheriness of *Cupressus macrocarpa* and the colour of *Chamaecyparis nootkatensis*.

One reason that this conifer has not become popular as it might have is that nurserymen have found it slow to propagate, but with the advent of hormone rooting substances and mist propagation this disadvantage has been overcome. It has also been found that certain clones propagate more rapidly than others. The best planting size for hedges is 1½–2½ ft. high, spaced 1½–2 ft. apart, and for screens 6–8 ft. apart, planted between September and October or March and April. Trim in July and August. Propagate by cuttings in April or in September. As there are several clones, some of which root more easily than others, it is therefore wise to obtain a leaflet on the Leyland Cypress published by the Royal Forestry Society. Ultimate height for individual screen trees 50–60 ft. and for hedges 5–8 ft.

CUPRESSUS

C. macrocarpa (Monterey Cypress)

This conifer is a native of California and was introduced in this country as long ago as 1838. The young feathery foliage is at first bright green, but with age it becomes darker and less bright. From the end of the First World War to the outbreak of the Second the macrocarpa hedge was more popular than any because of its rapid growth. Unfortunately, this hedge is not fully hardy except in maritime districts and especially favoured localities; hedges in cold localities may suddenly turn brown, this may be through cold winds or frost and snow damage. Normally, a hedge can be expected to remain in good condition for about ten years, though, sometimes longer. C. macrocarpa has been extensively planted in maritime districts. Most nurseries send out pot-grown plants, though some supply open ground plants. Another fault, apart from its sensitiveness to frost, is its dislike of being clipped back into old wood.

The Monterey cypress does specially well in lighter soils, and grows successfully in chalk or sandy soils. Best planting size is 1½–2 ft. high, spaced at 1½–2 ft. apart, for screens 4–5 ft. apart, and planted in late March or April. Trim during the middle of April, if you have time and patience with secateurs, otherwise with shears. Propagate by seed sown out of doors in April, or, for small quantities, under glass in February and March. Height as a specimen or individual screen tree is 60–80 ft., and grown in this way they are handsome. As clipped hedges they are usually anything from 10–15 ft. high.

C.m. 'Lutea'. A beautiful golden form of the Monterey cypress; where
171

a screen of golden foliage is required this conifer would be hard to equal. Plant young grafted trees 5–6 ft. apart. No trimming is needed. Height 20–25 ft. Trim as for *C. macrocarpa*; also same planting sizes and spacing.

CUPS AND SAUCERS, *see* COBAEA

CURRANT, BUFFALO, *see Ribes odoratum*

CURRANT, FLOWERING, *see Ribes sanguineum*

CYDONIA, JAPONICA, *see* CHAENOMELES

CYPRESS, *see* CHAMAECYPARIS

CYPRESS, DAWN, *see* METASEQUOIA

CYPRESS, LAWSON, *see* CHAMAECYPARIS

CYPRESS, LEYLAND, *see* CUPRESSOCYPARIS

CYPRESS, MONTEREY, *see* CUPRESSUS

CYTISUS (Broom)

This is a deciduous shrub. Our native broom, *C. scoparius*, has yellow pea-shaped flowers in May and June. Although cytisus is deciduous, its fresh green stems give it a kind of evergreen look, even in winter, when its leaves have dropped. The common broom (*C. scoparius*) is probably the most useful as an informal hedge. It is also an ideal plant for clothing a dry bank.

Generally speaking, a light, loamy soil or a sandy soil suits it best. It dislikes lime soils; but when bushes are grafted on laburnum the distaste for lime is overcome. It does not seem to mind heavy clay soils, and at Crawley it thrives in the soil of one-time brick-fields.

As brooms are coarse- or tap-rooted, always choose young pot-grown plants 1–1½ ft. high, spacing them 1½–2 ft. apart. They produce seed very freely, and so annual clipping after flowering is essential or the plants will suffer through exhaustion. However, never prune back into the old wood, as fresh growth from this will be produced slowly or not at all. But annual attention will prevent too much old wood forming. Propagation is by seed sown under glass in February or out of doors in April.

C. 'Burkwoodii'. Flowers with cerise wings and deep maroon keel. Vigorous and bushy. Height 5–7 ft.

C. multiflorus (syn. *C. albus*) (White Spanish Broom)

Slender branchlets, with silky leaflets and white flowers. Height 8 ft. or more.

C. scoparius (Common Broom)

Bright green stems and foliage, yellow flowers. Height 5–6 ft.

C.s. 'Andreanus'. Flowers with crimson wings and yellow keel suffused crimson. Height 6–8 ft.

C.s. 'Firefly'. An improvement on 'Andreanus', similar colour. Height 6–7 ft.

C.s. 'Fulgens'. Clear yellow, suffused orange, with a deep maroon keel. Height 6–7 ft.

Cytisus hybrids. There is today a wide and varied collection of colourful hybrids (only a few are mentioned here), but they are dearer to buy, and for a hedge the common broom is much cheaper.

DAWN REDWOOD, *see* METASEQUOIA

DECUMARIA

D. barbara

A deciduous or semi-evergreen, self-clinging climber, which attaches itself by aerial roots and, like the climbing hydrangea, is ideal for ascending the trunks of trees. It has glossy green foliage, small white, fragrant flowers which are freely produced in June and July. Height up to 30 ft.

D. sinensis

An evergreen with dull green leaves, not so vigorous as *D. barbara*, it also climbs by the aid of aerial roots and has clusters of small white flowers, with a honey-like fragrance, which are freely produced during June. It makes an excellent plant, on an east or west wall, as it does not reach more than 10–15 ft. high. Plant October to December. Pruning, none required. Propagation by half-ripened cuttings taken in August and inserted in sandy soil in a close frame with gentle bottom heat, if possible, or by shoots which can be layered in autumn.

DENDROMECON

D. rigida

This deciduous shrub can hardly be termed a climber, but as its poppy-like flowers are so attractive and it appreciates, in fact needs, the warmth and protection of a wall, I feel its inclusion is to be permitted. It has thick, narrowly ovate leaves of a glaucous hue. In the right situation, by a south wall, it will produce its large golden-yellow poppy-like flowers, 2–3 in. wide, from spring to October. It is suitable for coastal areas. In the centre of each single flower there is a boss of many stamens. Plant in spring from pot-grown plants, in well drained loamy soil. Pruning is rarely necessary, except when a shoot dies or it becomes frosted—then cut it out in spring.

For propagation, take cuttings of well-ripened wood in late summer, making each one three joints long and inserting the cuttings singly in small pots filled with sandy soil, placing the pots in a closed frame with gentle bottom heat; or root cuttings 2 in. long inserted singly in small pots in a sandy compost, in a closed frame with bottom heat in spring. Height 8–15 ft.

DEUTZIA

D. scabra

Hardy deciduous shrub. Its rather harsh or rough leaves are 4 in. long and 2 in. wide, with pink and white star-like flowers. It would make a quick growing informal hedge or screen up to 10 ft., though I have never seen it used for either purpose. I have, however, heard that it is used effectively in Avranches, France. Best planting size is 1½–2 ft. high, spaced 3 ft. apart, in sun or shade, and it grows best in good loamy soil. Prune by thinning out old worn-out branches every two years and trim bushes lightly in summer after flowers fade. Propagate by seed sown in March, or half-ripened wood cuttings in June or July, or hard-wood cuttings in October. Height 8–10 ft.

D.s. 'Plena'. Double, rose-purple blooms. Height 8–12 ft.
D.s. 'Watereri'. Single, white blooms. Height 8 ft.

DIERVILLA, *see* WEIGELA

DIPLOPAPPUS, *see* CASSINIA

DOGWOOD, *see* CORNUS

DOUGLAS FIR, *see* PSEUDOTSUGA

DREGEA, *see* WATTAKAKA

DUTCHMAN'S PIPE, *see Aristolochia macrophylla*

ECCREMOCARPUS

E. scaber (Glory Flower)

A semi-woody, evergreen climber, which attaches itself by a tendril at the ends of the stems. This Chilian beauty is not fully hardy in cold districts, but in the south and west plants will often come through the winter with little damage. Its pinnate leaves have a fern-like grace. The pretty, tubular, orange-scarlet and orange-yellow flowers, each about 1 in. long, are carried on graceful 6–10 in. long racemes bearing 10 to 20

175

blooms. It is best grown against a wall or allowed to scramble through a bush. It is frequently seen as an annual and, as such, seed should be sown in February in gentle heat, potted on and finally planted out of doors in May, when it will start to flower in June, though established plants will, in an early and favourable season, commence to flower in April, and continue until frost comes in the autumn. Eccremocarpus will thrive in any soil except a chalk soil. Pruning should be carried out at the end of February or March when all dead or frosted shoots should be cut back, and one or two shortened so as to encourage new growth lower down. Height 10–12 ft.

ELDER, *see* SAMBUCUS

ELM, *see* ULMUS

ERCILLA

E. volubilis (syn. *Bridgesia spicata*)

This is another evergreen, self-clinging climber, which attaches itself by aerial roots to a wall or tree trunk. It will thrive in any good soil and is wind hardy. Although not spectacular for its dullish-white flowers in March and April it is nevertheless a most useful evergreen, making a formidable tangle of shoots. Plant in autumn or spring. Prune after flowering by careful thinning out. Propagate by cuttings or by layering in August or September. Height 15–20 ft.

ERICA (Heath)

These hardy, evergreen shrubs are the heaths, closely resembling the common heather. Several species and varieties can be used to form low informal hedges and, where flower is not wanted, a low, closely-clipped formal hedge can be grown.

E. arborea (Tree Heath)

Sombre green foliage, and white flowers March to April. Plant young pot-grown plants 1–1½ ft. apart in April to May or September to

176

A pleached lime
screen in summer

The screen in
winter, with its
branches trained
out horizontally

Part of a pleached
lime avenue at
Batemans, Bur-
wash, Sussex

A laurel hedge,
Prunus laurocerasus,
and a Lawson's
cypress screen,
*Chamaecyparis
lawsoniana*

*Rhododendron
ponticum* makes a
good hedge or
screen

A 'fedge' of ivy,
Hedera helix cover-
ing a fence

October. This erica thrives in any good loamy soil, but not in lime soil. It dislikes cold east winds and, therefore, should be planted in a sheltered position. Trim after flowers fade. Propagate by cuttings in August, inserted in sandy soil beneath a bell glass. Height up to 6 ft.

E.a. 'Alpina'. Bright green foliage and white flowers sweetly scented, March to April. Plant young pot-grown plants in April to May or September to October. Trim after flowering. Other remarks as for *E. arborea*, except that *E.a.* 'Alpina' is much hardier.

E. carnea

Dark purplish-pink flowers. This makes a good low hedge 12–15 in. high and will grow on lime soils. Plant 9–12 in. apart April to May or September to October. Most growers of heathers offer a good selection of *E. carnea* cultivars of white, pink and red shades. Height 12–15 in.

E. mediterranea

An erect-growing evergreen shrub, it makes an ideal medium to low hedge, in a sheltered position, and will thrive in most soils, whether loam or limestone. Rich rose-crimson flowers, March to May. Plant 12–15 in. apart, April to May or September to October. Trim after flowering. There are also cultivars of white, pink and red shades. Height 2–4 ft.

E. terminalis (syn. *E. stricta*) (Corsican Heath)

An erect-growing evergreen. The young foliage is light green and the flowers a pale rose colour. It blooms from July well into the autumn. In winter its russet-red seed-heads are equally lovely. The Corsican heath will grow in a chalky soil. Plant 1–1½ ft. apart, April to May or September to October. Trim in early spring before new growth begins. Height 6–9 ft.

E. vagans (Cornish Heath)

This species and its cultivars will make a neat, closely-clipped low hedge or a more informal flowering hedge, the latter being the more decorative. It has pinkish rose-coloured flowers in August and September. Plant 1 ft. apart, April to May or September to October. Trim in early spring, before new growth begins. Height 1½–2 ft.

M   177

Three outstanding cultivars of *E. vagans* are: 'Mrs. D. F. Maxwell', deep cerise flowers, July to October, height 1½ ft.; 'St. Keverne', bright pink flowers, August to September, height 1½ ft., and 'Lyonesse', ivory-white flowers enhanced by pale brown anthers, July to October, height 1½ ft. Plant 12–15 in. apart, April to May or September to October. Trim in early spring before new growth begins.

All the above ericas can be propagated by cuttings taken in August, by inserting them in sandy soil beneath a bell glass, or in a cold frame or cool greenhouse. Layering is also successful at any time of the year except in cold or frosty weather.

ERIOBOTRYA

E. japonica (Loquat)

An evergreen tree or large shrub which will thrive in the open in Cornwall and similar climates, elsewhere it requires the protection of a south or west wall. It will thrive in any soil. Its beauty lies in its foliage, not its flowers. The leaves are 8–10 in. long, rough in texture, being coarsely wrinkled, thick with reddish-brown tomentum (felt) beneath. The upper surface is dark and glossy. Its fragrant, white flowers, which open in autumn, are seldom produced in this country. Plant in spring. Prune in April when required. Propagate by seed in spring, or cuttings of well-ripened wood in August, in a cold frame. Height 10–15 ft.

ESCALLONIA

Hardy or half-hardy evergreen shrubs; probably the most popular evergreen flowering hedge shrub or windbreak there is for planting in coastal areas. Escallonias have beautiful pink and red, small bell-shaped flowers, and dark green, leathery gummy leaves which exude an unforgettable scent, or rather odour, for it always reminds me of the smell of a well-kept piggery. Mr. J. R. B. Evison states in the Royal Horticultural Society's Journal, Vol. LXXIX, page 297, that *E. macrantha* 'is one of the "gummiest" of the genus, which appears to give it immunity from the fiercest and saltiest storms'. Once they are established, escallonias will make fairly rapid growth and form excellent hedges from 6–8 ft. high. As open ground bushes transplant badly obtain pot-grown plants. Best planting size is 1½–2 ft. high, spaced 1–1½ ft. apart. Plant in

September or March to April. They thrive best on a sandy loam and well-drained soils; they also do well on chalk soils, but do not like the rich ones. Trim fairly closely, immediately the blooms fade. Propagate by taking half-ripened cuttings in July and August. Height 4–10 ft.

E. 'Apple Blossom'. Evergreen, with soft pink chalice-shaped flowers from June to July. Height 4–6 ft.

E. 'C. F. Ball'. Evergreen with especially large tubular flowers, a vivid rose-crimson. Height 6–7 ft.

E. 'Donard Seedling'. A vigorous evergreen shrub, with apple-blossom flowers. Height 6–8 ft.

E. 'Ingramii'. Evergreen with large foliage and deep rose-pink flowers. Height 6–8 ft.

E. 'Iveyi'. Evergreen with large shining dark green leaves, white flowers from July to autumn, but only really hardy in favoured districts. Height 8–10 ft.

E. 'Langleyensis'. An old favourite, with rosy-carmine flowers in June and July. Height 8–10 ft.

E. macrantha

Evergreen with large foliage, bright rose-red flowers in June and July. Height 6–10 ft.

E. 'Slieve Donard'. Evergreen, free-flowering, large rose-pink flowers. Height 5–7 ft.

There are several new Donard cultivars which could be used to make informal hedges. Names and varieties can be seen in any good tree and shrub nursery catalogue.

EUCALYPTUS (Gum Tree)

An evergreen tree of great interest. The gum tree has beautiful blue-grey-green foliage, and makes rapid growth, which is an advantage when it is used as a screen or windbreak. The fragrant foliage is stiff in texture. It is an ideal tree to blot out some unsightly object in a very short while. Owing to its rapid growth it is sometimes difficult to anchor young trees, as they will put on as much as 5–6 ft. of growth in one season. They resent root disturbance; therefore, always plant young pot-grown plants and turn them out of the pots as carefully as possible. The ground where eucalyptus are to be grown should be well prepared and a liberal application of decayed compost, rotted manure or peat added at the time of digging. Plant 6 ft. apart in March–April. If a dry season should follow see that the plants do not lack water. To prevent root disturbance stake with strong bamboo canes after planting. Tie with broad raffia or tape so as not to damage the main stem of the tree. In very cold and windy districts give some form of protection in the plant's early life. All thrive best on light well-drained soils, but resent chalk soil. If and when pruning is necessary do this in March–April. Propagate by seeds sown in early spring in pans of light soil in a temperature of 65° F. (18° C.). The two considered most suitable for planting are as follows:

E. dalrympleana

In early growth the adult leaves are often a fiery red. The bark is deciduous and peels, showing a stem beneath like that of silver birch. Height 20–30 ft.

E. gunnii

Young foliage is rounded, and elongated when mature. In October it produces insignificant flowers with attractive pale yellow stamens. The leaves during the summer are coated with a glaucous bloom. This species is considered to be the hardiest of genus. Height 20–30 ft.

EUONYMUS (Spindle-tree)

E. europaeus (Common Spindle-tree)

Hardy, deciduous shrub. It is most decorative in autumn, when its small green leaves turn to a pinkish-crimson, it also has pink fruits which contain orange coloured seeds. This shrub is not used as a farm hedge—in fact it is discouraged because it is the host plant for the bean aphis. However, for an informal hedge where its full beauty is wanted it is ideal, and is equally effective when planted in a mixed hedge. It will make a good hedge up to 6 ft. Best size for planting is 1½–2 ft., spaced 1½ ft. apart. Plant in October to March. Trim in winter after fruit and foliage has fallen, or in early spring before flowering. Thrives in heavy loam, though best colour is obtained on chalk soils. Propagate by seeds sown in March or layers in summer. Height 6–10 ft.

E. fortunei

Two evergreen dwarf spindles are *E.f.* 'Silver Queen' which has oval leaves, with bright silver variegation, and will reach an ultimate height of 2½–3½ ft., and *E.f.* 'Variegatus', which has narrow leaves with silver variation. In autumn the leaves take on a pinkish tinge. They can also be used as ground cover plants. Plant 9 in. apart, October to April. Trim in April or July. Height 2½–3½ ft. *Euonymus fortunei* and its varieties can also be used to clothe walls or banks where plants will reach a height of 20–25 ft. A good example of how vigorous it is can be seen on the sea walls at Black Rock, Brighton, Sussex. Good specimens are also frequently seen trained on house and cottage walls.

E. japonicus

An evergreen shrub hardy in the south and west of England, particularly successful in southern and western coastal areas. Alfred Gaut, in *Seaside Planting of Trees and Shrubs*, states: 'It has also been noted as answering this purpose (as a seaside hedge) well along the eastern coast.' It is undoubtedly the most popular hedge along the southern coast, and it is invaluable for extremely windy areas, as it tolerates sea spray. The leaves are dark glossy green; the flowers are greenish-white followed by smooth globose pinkish fruits, containing seeds with pale orange seedcoats. Unfortunately it does at times suffer from mildew and attacks by the caterpillar of the ermine moth; for remedies see Chapter 4, page 47. There cannot be a less fastidious evergreen hedge, as it thrives on sand on the foreshore, in chalk, peat or good loamy soils, and does not object to industrial areas and smoke. Best planting sizes are 1–1½ ft. or 2 ft. according to one's pocket, spaced at 1½ ft. apart. Plant September or April. Trim once or twice during the summer and, when severe pruning is necessary, in April. Propagation by half-ripened wood cuttings in July, August and September. Height 8–12 ft.

There are also gold and silver variegated varieties. The best are *E.j.* 'Ovatus Aureus', golden, and *E.j.* 'Macrophyllus Albus' (syn. *E.* 'Latifolius Variegatus'), silver variegated variety. Not a fast grower but makes a good hedge. Height 6–8 ft.

EVERGREEN LABURNUM, *see* PIPTANTHUS

EVERGREEN OAK, *see Quercus ilex*

181

EVERLASTING PEA, *see Lathyrus latifolius*

FAGUS (Beech)

F. sylvatica (Common Beech)

A hardy, deciduous tree with oval pointed leaves, of rich to dark glossy green turning a pleasing shade of brown in autumn. When beech is planted as a hedge the leaves mostly persist throughout the autumn and winter, until new leaves are produced in the spring. Beech also makes a useful screen. It thrives on almost any kind of soil, provided it is not too heavy and waterlogged. It does well in a light soil overlying chalk. Its chief merit is as a hedge plant, although when grown as a large forest trees, its grey boles are beautiful. The best hedges are made from young plants, but I have planted larger ones, 4–4½ ft. high. A hedge planted during the Second World War at 4½ ft. high and 1½ ft. apart was, in 1956, 6 ft. high and 2 ft. wide. For a long time this hedge was bare and very thin at the base. The best planting size is anything from 1–3 ft. high, the ideal height is 1½–2 ft. Hedges are planted in single rows at 12–15 in. apart, or in double staggered rows 15 in. apart in the rows and 8 in. apart between the rows. For screens plant 6–8 ft. apart. Plant from October to March. No clipping should be done during the first two years after planting, except for cutting back any extra long shoots; after this time, clip in July or August, though established hedges can be clipped in autumn or winter. Propagate by seed, which should be gathered in November. Sow seeds 1 in. apart and ½ in. deep. Make sure the mast (nut of the beech) is full. Height of hedge 5–10 ft. (Plate 31), and screens 10–18 ft. or more.

F. s. purpurea (Purple Beech). Identical in every respect to *F. sylvatica*, except that the foliage is purple coloured. Hedges of this variety are not so common as those of green beech. Other remarks as for common beech.

FEIJOA

F. sellowiana

An evergreen shrub, rather tender except in the most favoured districts, such as parts of the south and west country. It needs wall protection, and then a south- or south-west facing one. The 1–3 in. dark, grey-green leaves, the undersides of which are covered with a white felt, as are also the flower stalks. The solitary, myrtle-like flowers are borne in the lower leaf axils of the current year's shoots in July; they are red and white with a bunch of rich crimson 1 in. long stamens. Plant in spring. Pruning is undertaken as soon as flowering has finished by taking out unwanted shoots in order to keep the plant sufficiently close to the wall. Propagation, cuttings of half-ripened shoots July to August inserted under glass jar in a greenhouse with heat. Height up to 15 ft.

FICUS

F. pumila (syn. *F. stipulata*)

An evergreen climber attaching itself to walls and trees by its aerial roots. Its habits are similar to ivy, both by the way it clings and its change of foliage, which becomes like a normal fig leaf, when it reaches the top of a high wall or tree. Otherwise the leaves are small and heart-shaped. It seldom fruits in this country. It is not fussy over soil though it dislikes lime. Plant in spring. No regular pruning needed. Propagate by cuttings. Height up to 40 ft.

FIELD MAPLE, *see Acer campestre*

FIR, DOUGLAS, *see* PSEUDOTSUGA

FIR, SPRUCE, *see* PICEA

FIRETHORN, *see* PYRACANTHA

FLAME FLOWER, *see Tropaeolum speciosum*

FORSYTHIA

F. × intermedia

Hardy, deciduous flowering shrub. There are several cultivars of this species: 'Densiflora' fairly compact and free-flowering, 'Lynwood' rich yellow, 'Primulina', soft yellow flowers, 'Spectabilis', the best known and most planted; and 'Vitellina' more upright in habit. All have yellow, bell-shaped flowers and bloom during March and April. Although forsythia is best known as a spring-flowering shrub, it can make an attractive semi-formal hedge. I know a fine example of a forsythia hedge at Crawley, Sussex, planted in 1945, which eleven years later, was over 5 ft. high. For a hedge that needs to be kept narrow as this one does, some form of early support such as a wire fence or cleft chestnut fencing is an advantage.

Best planting size is about 2–3 ft. high, spaced at 1½–2 ft. apart, October to March. When grown as a hedge keep it 2 ft. wide at the base, running it up to 12 or 15 in. at the top; do not allow it to be higher than 6 ft. Forsythias will thrive anywhere and in any soil, but they do not take kindly to shade. Trim annually after flowering by spurring back the young shoots to within two to three buds. Alternatively, hedges can be allowed to grow more informally, when pruning should be less drastic, the aim being to keep the hedge trim and tidy. Propagation for all forsythias is from hard-wood cuttings, in October to November, which can be inserted in a prepared bed out of doors. Height 5–10 ft.

F. ovata

This is a more bushy species with stiffer growth and would make an excellent informal screen between the vegetable and flower garden. Plant as for other forsythias, but do not prune too severely. Height 5–6 ft.

F. suspensa

This is a rambling shrub and best grown against a wall or fence or over a tree stump. Its golden-yellow flowers are freely produced in April, on long, arching wand-like shoots. The flowers are borne two to six blossoms at each joint of the previous summer's growth. It does well on a north wall. Plant October to March. Prune by cutting back the secondary shoots to within one or two buds of the old wood and tying in any shoots where it is necessary. Propagate by hard-wood cuttings, inserted

184

out of doors in October or soft-wood cuttings in June in a closed frame. Height up to 20 ft.

F. s. atrocaulis. Attractive because of the stems which are a blackish-purple. Large, lemon-yellow flowers.

F. s. sieboldii. Very slender stems, its branches being particularly pendent. Excellent on a north or east wall.

FRAXINUS (Ash)

Fraxinus excelsior (Common Ash)

Hardy, deciduous tree of vigorous habit, should not be planted near to buildings as its roots could cause damage. An excellent tree to plant as first line of defence in coastal areas. As it comes into leaf late it is less likely to suffer damage from blistering winds. It thrives on heavy and calcareous soils. Planting size 3–7 ft. spaced at 5–6 ft. apart, thinning them later to 8–10 ft. apart. Propagate from seed sown at the end of October out of doors. Height up to 100 ft.

FREMONTIA, *see* FREMONTODENDRON

FREMONTODENDRON

F. californicum

A semi-evergreen shrub, although introduced from California over 200 years ago, it is not planted as much as it should be, partly because it is not fully hardy, though it will come through most winters with the protection of a south or west wall. It does well in chalk or sandy soils. It has curiously curled, palmate, roughish, dark green leaves, covered with a brownish-white felt beneath. It has no real petals but again, curiously curled sepals, which are waxy and golden yellow, with a centre of fine radiating stamens which unite to form a short column. It blooms from May to July. Plant young pot-grown plants in the spring. No pruning is required except to cut out any dead shoots in the spring. Propagate by seeds which are encouraged to germinate by soaking them in lukewarm water two to three days before sowing them. Height up to 10 ft.

185

FUCHSIA

F. magellanica

Tube and sepals deep red with purplish petals (the corolla). Most of the cultivars of this species are, broadly speaking, hardy deciduous shrubs. It must be remembered that the greenhouse fuchsias are neither hardy nor suitable to plant as hedges. *F. magellanica* flourishes in Cornwall and the West Country, also in Ireland and the Isle of Man. In these areas this species of fuchsia and its varieties are planted extensively as hedges and as wind breaks near the sea coast. Their virtues are long duration of flowering and speed of growth. They make better informal hedges than formal ones, and are ideal for planting as a break between the vegetable and flower garden. A width of at least 3 ft. is needed for them to spread. Plant young pot-grown plants, spacing them $1\frac{1}{2}$–2 ft. apart in late May. Fuchsias should be planted 4 in. below soil level. In winter cover the crowns, after the first frost, with soil or weathered ashes. Prune in spring, cutting plants back lightly or severely. After bad winters they can be cut back to within a few inches of ground level. They will thrive in any good soil, alkaline or otherwise. Propagation is by cuttings taken in August and inserted in a cold frame. Height 4–5 ft.

F. m. conica. Scarlet with dark purple petals. Height 3–5 ft.

F. m. gracilis. Scarlet with purple petals. Very wind hardy. Height 4–5 ft.

F.m. 'Mrs. W. P. Wood'. Pale flesh pink with pure white petals. Height 5–6 ft.

F. 'Riccartonii'. Red with purple petals. This is undoubtedly the hardiest and most extensively planted fuchsia for hedges, particularly in Cornwall. Height 4–8 ft.

FUJI CHERRY, *see Prunus incisa*

FURZE, *see* ULEX

GARRYA

G. elliptica (Tassel Bush)

A hardy, evergreen unisexual shrub, which shows to its best advantage when grown against a wall or fence. This is a case where the male is the most beautiful. The greyish-green catkins are 6–10 in. long, and when brushed against, give off yellowish-green pollen as soft as any face powder. The catkins are produced from November to February or March. The foliage is a dull matt grey-green. I have seen plants flourishing on south and north walls and it will thrive equally well on an east wall, and plants will thrive in any kind of soil. Pot-grown plants transplant better than open ground ones in the autumn or spring. Prune by shortening long secondary shoots in spring after flowering. Propagate by layering in June, or grafting male plants on to *Aucuba japonica* stocks in February, under glass in heat, or by seeds sown in March which will produce male and female plants. Height up to 12 ft.

GAZANIA, CLIMBING, *see* MUTISIA

GEAN, *see Prunus avium*

GLORY FLOWER, *see* ECCREMOCARPUS

GOAT WILLOW, *see Salix caprea*

GOLDEN RAIN, *see Laburnum anagyroides*

GORSE, *see* ULEX

GRAPE, OREGON, *see* MAHONIA

GRISELINIA

G. littoralis

Evergreen shrub, hardy in the milder parts of Britain. It makes a first-class maritime hedge, and it is equally good as a wind shelter on account

187

of its very dense growth. It thrives at Whitby and Scarborough in Yorkshire; it also does well in London, in the Embankment Gardens. It has leathery, oval-shaped leaves, shining yellowish-green and paler beneath. Best planting size is 1½–2 ft. Plant 1½ ft. apart in March or April. Larger specimens will transplant satisfactorily, which is an advantage where wind shelter is urgently needed. It thrives in any soil and will grow under trees. Trim between May and July. Propagate either from half-ripened wood cuttings in July or hard-wood cuttings in October to November. Height: hedges 5–7 ft., screens 7–10 ft. or more, judging by specimens I have seen in Cornwall.

GUELDER ROSE, *see Viburnum opulus*

GUM TREE, *see* EUCALYPTUS

HAWTHORN, *see* CRATAEGUS

HAZEL, *see* CORYLUS

HEATH, *see* ERICA

HEATHER, *see* CALLUNA

HEBE (syn. Veronica)

This is a genus of evergreen shrubs. Some are very hardy, others are not quite so hardy, but all are suitable for maritime districts.
H. 'Alicia Amherst' (syn. 'Veitchii' or 'Royal Purple'). It has deep, royal purple flowers. Height 4–5 ft.
H. 'Autumn Glory'. A very popular cultivar with intense violet flowers from August to October. Height 2 ft.

H. brachysiphon (syn. *H. traversii*)

This hardy evergreen shrub has small pointed dark leaves of a rather dull green, and white flowers with purple-brown anthers; it blooms very freely. Although erect in habit it will, if allowed, make a wide-spreading rounded bush. This is one of the first evergreens I can remember at my home at Lingfield in Surrey, along with the variegated aucuba, box, Portugal and Cherry Laurel. All are worth-while evergreens, though they are often wrongly despised by many. *H. brachysiphon* is particularly frost-hardy and wind-hardy. Best planting size is 1½ ft. high. Trim after flowering, and for hedges that grow out of hand prune hard back in April. Propagate by cuttings in August. Height up to 6 ft.

H. cupressoides

This evergreen shrub resembles a cypress, as its name implies, and is useful as a small compact evergreen hedge. Pale blue flowers in summer. It has bright green lanceolate leaves and variously coloured flowers ranging from white to white tinged with lilac to bluish-purple, and it blooms freely in July and August. It is frost-hardy and specially wind-hardy, and is not fussy as to type of soil it is grown in. Best planting size is 9–12 in. spaced at 1 ft. apart; plant in September or April. Trim in late summer. Propagate by cuttings in July to August, or October. Height 1–3 ft.

H. salicifolia (Willow-leaved Veronica)

An excellent evergreen shrub for the seaside. Choose young plants 1–1½ ft. high, spacing them 1½ ft. apart, and plant September or April. Trim in April. Propagate by cuttings taken in July to August, or October. Height 6–8 ft.

H.s. 'Midsummer Beauty'. This variety has extra long spikes of lavender-coloured flowers, which are pleasantly scented. It is stated to be one of the hardiest of the hebes. Judging from the plant in my own garden it is not only hardy but tough, as I had a plant lying around in a pot for at least three years before it was planted, which stood up to a very hard winter. It was from this plant I received an Award of Merit in 1960. Best planting size is pot-grown plants 1–1½ ft. high, spacing them 15 in. apart and planting in September or April. Trim in April. Propagate from cuttings in August, placed in a cold frame or beneath a bell glass. Height 4–5 ft.

189

HEDERA (Ivy)

H. helix (Common Ivy)

Hardy evergreen, chiefly planted as a climber. Its flowers produce black fruits in autumn. It cannot, in the true sense, be termed a hedge plant, except when used as a 'fedge' (Plate 16). The name is a corruption of fence and hedge invented, I believe, by Will Ingwersen. The first time I saw a fedge was in August 1953, at Batemans, the home of Rudyard Kipling. It consists of wattle hurdles with ivy planted on one or both sides. It makes a very dense, narrow screen or partition, and is ideal where space is limited and little sun available, and is an excellent barrier between two houses. A fedge can be made from either green or variegated ivy. Young pot-grown plants should be used and spaced 1½ ft. apart. Plant October to March. Trim several times in early and late summer; when hard pruning is necessary do this in April. Ivy grown against a wall or fence or on a pergola or archway should be trimmed annually in April. Propagate by cuttings in August and September. Height 3–6 ft.

Ivy is also suitable and effective when grown as a dwarf or low edging at the top of a bank, or trained along railings or balustrades. As ivies do not object to shade and stand up well to smoky atmospheres they are particularly suitable for planting in industrial areas, and will tolerate any soil. There are several species of hedera, the one with the largest number of varieties being the common ivy, *H. helix*, which are excellent for covering walls, fences and old tree trunks. I cannot do better than quote a sentence from the catalogue of Hillier & Sons, Winchester: 'Ivy-covered walls are both dry and warm.' This was certainly the case with an east-facing wall at my home, which was covered with ivy and when it was trimmed dust would fly. Incidentally it was a haven of rest for sparrows. W. J. Bean states in *Trees and Shrubs Hardy in the British Isles*, "As regards its use on buildings it is capable of attaining at least 100 ft. in height."

Ivy does not require tying as it clings by aerial roots. When grown against a tree, once it reaches the top it branches out and bears black berries. At this branching stage, ivies are known as 'tree ivies'.

H. canariensis (Canary Island Ivy)

Its large rounded leaves are bright green in summer changing to a deep bronze and veiled green in winter.
H.c. 'Azorica'. Large leaves of a light matt green.
H.c. 'Variegata' (syn. 'Gloire de Marengo'). This attractive variegated variety has dark green leaves bordered with silvery-grey and white.

H. colchica (syn. *H. amurensis, H. roegnerana*) (Persian Ivy)

Large, handsome, dark green, lustrous leaves often 8 in. long and 4 in. wide. Vigorous grower.
H.c. 'Dentata'. Paler coloured foliage than *H. colchica*, the leaves being slightly toothed.
H.c. 'Dentata Variegata'. One of the most colourful and handsome ivies, having large soft green leaves with pale yellow variegation.

H. helix (Common Ivy)

Ideal for walls, fences or trees. Also excellent as a ground-cover plant. Dark green foliage.
H.h. 'Aureo variegata' (syns. *H.h. angularis aurea, H.h.* 'Chrysophylla'). Suffused soft yellow leaves.
H.h. 'Buttercup' (syn. 'Golden Cloud', 'Russell's Gold'). Rich golden coloured leaves.
H.h. 'Caenwoodiana'. Small dark leaves, divided into narrow lobes with a long central lobe.
H.h. 'Chicago'. Small lobed leaves often splashed with purple.
H.h. 'Cristata'. The pale green leaves are twisted and have crimped edges.
H.h. 'Digitata'. Broad five-lobed leaves.
H.h. 'Gold Heart'. The leaves of this charming variety have a central splash of yellow in each leaf which makes it a most striking small-leafed ivy.
H.h. 'Hibernica' (syn. *H. hibernica*) (Irish Ivy). Handsome, large, bright green leaves 4–5 in. wide. A fast and vigorous climber to cover walls, fences or bare ground.
H.h. 'Marginata' (syn. *H.h.* 'Silver Queen', and *H.h.* 'Argentea Elegans'. Triangular-shaped leaves with creamy-white edges becoming pink-tinged in winter.

H.h. 'Marmorata' (syn. *H. h. discolor*). Small dark green leaves with cream and red mottling.

H. h. poetica (syn. *H. chrysocarpa*) (Italian Ivy). It has shallowly lobed leaves which are bright green. On reaching tree form it will bear yellow berries.

H.h. 'Purpurea'. Its dark green leaves are a handsome bronzy-purple in winter.

H.h. 'Tricolor' (syns. *H. h. elegantissima* and *H. h. marginata rubra*). Small grey-green leaves with a white border, with rosy-red edges in winter.

HEMLOCK FIR, *see* TSUGA

HIBISCUS

H. syriacus (syn. *Althaea syriacus*)

(Sometimes called the bush hollyhock, and in Canada and the U.S.A. the Rose of Sharon). A very hardy, deciduous flowering shrub, erect and stiff-branched, with greyish-white stems and mostly three-lobed, coarsely toothed oak-like leaves. Its large, single and double hollyhock-like blooms of white, red, blue or purple, sometimes striped, are most colourful from about the middle of August to the end of September. I do not think I have ever seen them flower more profusely than I did in the hot dry summers of 1955–9 and 1967, which gave them ideal conditions. They are not rapid growers, but they make a very stiff and substantial hedge. Young plants 1½–2 ft. high are the best size for planting, spaced 1½–2 ft. apart, October to March. They thrive on any soil and almost anywhere except damp soil and shady situations; what suits them best is a hot dry soil. Trim in April; this perhaps will not be required every year. Propagate by half-ripened wood cuttings, taken with a slight heel, in July. Height 8–10 ft. though 6 ft. is sufficient for a hedge.

There are many varieties of *H. syriacus*, both single and double. Here is a list of the best.

Single: 'Coelestis', deep blue; 'Hamabo', pale rose with crimson blotches at the base of each petal; 'Mauve Queen', large mauve flowers; 'Monstrosus', white with maroon centre; 'Snowdrift', large white; 'Woodbridge', vinous red blotched with carmine at the base of each petal.

192

ABOVE: Yew, *Taxus baccata*, used effectively as topiary and a hedge
BELOW LEFT: an old yew hedge after severe pruning
BELOW RIGHT: vigorous growth on a yew hedge before being trimmed

Griselinia littoralis has yellowish-green foliage

Laurustinus, *Viburnum tinus*

Euonymus japonicus macrophyllus has large, shining foliage. It is evergreen and makes a good hedge or screen in coastal areas, town or country

Double: 'Ardens', violet-purple; 'Caeruleus Plenus', purple-blue; 'Duc de Brabant', red; 'Elegantissimus', white with maroon centre; 'Jeanne d'Arc', white with rosy exterior; Leopoldii Plenus, blush-pink, dark centre.

HIMALAYAN HONEYSUCKLE, see LEYCESTERIA

HIPPOPHAE

H. rhamnoides (Sea Buckthorn)

A hardy, dioecious,* deciduous shrub. An outstanding shrub on account of its stiff habit. It has greyish-brown stems and narrow silvery leaves. Its small flowers, which are produced in April, are followed in autumn by orange-coloured berries. But in order to have berries one male must be planted to five or six females. It is not really suited as a formal hedge, but makes a good informal one. It is useful as a wind shelter against sea breezes and is also planted to check shifting sands. Best planting size is 2–3 ft. high, spaced 2–3 ft. apart, October to March. Sea buckthorn will thrive in almost any soil. Trim in late March or early April. Propagation by seed sown in the spring. Height 10–15 ft. or more.

HOLBOELLIA

Two twining evergreens, with luxuriant dark green leathery leaves, made up of three or more radiating leaflets. The flowers are unisexual, having both male and female flowers on the same corymb. They are very fragrant. Their twining stems are fine for covering trees or pergolas, also house walls where a vigorous climber is wanted. It thrives in any soil. Plant October to March. No pruning required. Propagate by half-ripened shoots in spring. Height up to 20 ft.

H. coriacea

A vigorous climber with trifoliate leaves. Male flowering purple, appearing in April, the female ones white, appearing in May. Fleshy purple fruits 2 in. long.

* Male and female flowers on separate plants.

H. latifolia

This needs protection. The male flowers are white and fragrant, and the female flowers are purple, both borne in March. It has more leaflets than *H. coriacea*, and the sausage-shaped fruits are 3 in. long.

HOLLY, *see* ILEX

HOLLY OAK, *see Quercux ilex*

HOLM OAK, *see Quercus ilex*

HONEYSUCKLE, *see* LONICERA

HONEYSUCKLE, HIMALAYAN, *see* LEYCESTERIA

HOP, *see* HUMULUS

HORNBEAM, *see* CARPINUS

HUMULUS (Hop)

H. japonicus (Japanese Hop)

A half-hardy perennial and usually grown as an annual. It is a vigorous twining plant, ideal for covering a trellis, fence or pergola. Light green foliage. Plant out in late May. Propagate by seed sown under glass in April. Height 10–18 ft.
H.j. 'Variegatus'. This is similar to the species, but with prettily marked creamy-white variegated leaves.

194

H. lupulus (Common Hop)

This is the native plant found in our hedgerows. A hardy perennial, very vigorous, and has similar uses to *H. japonicus*. It has greenish-yellow flowers. It is not fussy over soil. Plant in March to April. Propagate by seed in April, or by division. Height up to 15 ft.

H.l. 'Aureus'. This is similar in all respects to the common hop, but has golden foliage.

HYDRANGEA

Hydrangeas are perhaps one of the most accommodating deciduous flowering shrubs, thriving in towns and suburbs as well as near the sea coast, and growing especially well in southern and western counties. They are hardy, though young, early growth is sometimes damaged by late spring frosts. They will grow in full sun, but will do just as well in partial shade. Their colours range from white and pink to red, crimson and varying shades of blue and purple. The white to crimson shades do well in chalk and limestone soils, whereas the blues require an acid, peaty, soil. They flower from July to September. They are ideal for planting on slightly raised banks, beds or borders beside rivers or paths, and are also excellent as an informal hedge between formal and informal parts of the garden. The hydrangea is a thirsty plant, therefore it is a good plan to keep the soil mulched during the summer with leaf soil, bracken, hop manure or even lawn mowings. Before planting see that the ground is dug at least two spits or more. Fortunately hydrangeas move at almost any size. They should be spaced 3 ft. apart and planted between October and March. Pruning of hydrangeas is undertaken during the middle of May, when the old flower heads should be removed and any thin, weak or frosted shoots cut back or entirely removed. Propagate by half-ripened cuttings in May, June and July. A selection of worth while varieties is best obtained from a reliable nurseryman's catalogue; alternatively, consult Michael Haworth-Booth's book, *The Hydrangea*, published by Constable. Height 6–8 ft., and old-established specimens as much in width. There are two climbing hydrangeas, which are ideal for covering trees or walls.

H. anomala

A deciduous climber. Its glossy leaves are curled and its creamy-white flower heads are not as flat as those of *H. petiolaris*.

195

H. hortensia or **H. hortensis**, *see H. macrophylla*

H. macrophylla (syns. *H. hortensia, H. hortensis*)

This hardy, deciduous flowering shrub, has many varieties, varying in shades of pink, red and blue, also white. Height 2½–8 ft.

H. petiolaris

A vigorous, deciduous self-clinging climber, having large flat, white flower heads, up to 9 in. wide in June, which continue well into the summer months. Plant October to March. Pruning, none required. Propagate by half-ripe cuttings in July to August, inserted under a cold frame or large glass jar.

HYPERICUM (St. John's Wort)

Hardy, deciduous and evergreen flowering shrubs, the St. John's worts all bear yellow flowers with large or small bosses of yellow stamens, from June to August. They are best suited to growing as informal hedges rather than formal hedges. *H. patulum* and its varieties are suitable for informal hedges and *H. calycinum* (Rose of Sharon) is ideal for edgings or covering banks. Their cultivation is simple; they like best a well-drained loamy soil and do not object to lime soils. In fact, they will grow anywhere, and in sun or partial shade. Propagation of all the hypericums is by half-ripened wood cuttings in July and August, except *H. calycinum*, which is increased by division in spring.

H. beanii (syn. *H. patulum henryi*)

Golden-yellow saucer-shaped flowers, July to August. Plant 1½ ft. apart. Trim each year in April. Height 3–4 ft.

H. calycinum (Rose of Sharon)

Evergreen, with large single flowers 3–4 in. across, June to August. An ideal plant for edging. Grows equally well in full sun or shade. Does well in chalk soils. Plant 1–1½ ft. apart. Trim each spring with a pair of shears or a sickle. Height 1–2 ft.

H. × inodorum 'Elstead'

A small yellow-flowered variety which later produces clusters of scarlet, pointed fruits. To have a good display of fruits each year cut back severely each March. Height 3–4 ft.

H. patulum 'Gold Cup'

One of the newer varieties and should make an excellent informal screen. Bright yellow cup-shaped flowers are borne on arching sprays, in July and August. Plant 1½ ft. apart. Trim by cutting back last year's growth to its base in April. Height 3–4 ft.

H.p. 'Hidcote'. Another very fine introduction, having large, golden, saucer shaped flowers from July to August. Plant 1½ ft. apart. Trim each year in April. Height 5–7 ft.

H. prolificum

Evergreen, with a dense upright habit, bright yellow flowers, 1 in. across, borne in great profusion. Plant 15–18 in. apart. Trim by cutting back the last year's growth to its base in late March or early April. Height 4–6 ft.

HYSSOP, *see* HYSSOPUS

HYSSOPUS

H. officinalis

A hardy, partially evergreen aromatic bush, hyssop has small, narrowly oval leaves and pale bluish-purple flowers, from midsummer until September. Suitable for a dwarf hedge or edging in a herb garden or similar position. Useful in coastal areas as it stands up to gales. Plant 1 ft. apart in March or April. Trim by cutting back last year's growth in April. It is not particular as to soils, but does best in a light soil and prefers a sunny position. Propagate by half-ripened wood cuttings in June or July. Height 1–2 ft.

ILEX (Holly)

Hardy evergreens, mostly dioecious. There are many varieties and forms of the familiar holly, in green, gold and silver. Some varieties are, however, more suitable for making hedges and screens than others. When holly is grown as a hedge few, if any, berries are produced, but with informal screens this need not be so, provided that male and female bushes are planted, or that a bush of the opposite sex is near by, when berries will be produced. Holly has thick, leathery leaves which are mostly a dark glossy green, except in the case of the gold and silver variegated varieties. It is wind-hardy but will not tolerate severe exposure. It is also an excellent hedge plant for towns and industrial areas. It makes a very close impenetrable hedge on account of its spiny foliage, and will keep out animals and humans more successfully than almost any other hedge. A hedge well cared for will remain clothed down to ground level. (Plate 28.)

Mixed holly hedges are also most effective and decorative, such as beech or hornbeam and holly, blackthorn or sloe (*Prunus spinosa*) and holly; in fact, one could have almost any mixture. In mixed hedges plant one holly to four or five of the other plants. Where expense is no object and in the right setting a green hedge with standard trees of gold or silver at intervals makes a spectacular sight. Holly, on account of its pleasant green, makes a good background for shrubs and herbaceous perennials. Hollies are not fastidious as regards soils and will grow in deep loamy, light sandy or chalk soils; they thrive in full sun or considerable shade.

Before planting, the ground should be dug at least two spits deep and some well-rotted manure added at the time of digging for, if hollies are planted in poor soil conditions in the first place, they can look exceedingly miserable for the first few seasons. During hot dry periods after planting see that the plants are not allowed to become dry at the roots; to prevent this give a thorough soaking, followed by a mulch of compost or rotted manure. Also syringe foliage with clear water in the evening after sunset.

The ideal planting size is $1\frac{1}{2}$–2 ft., or 2–$2\frac{1}{2}$ ft., though hollies can be successfully moved at any height, from 1–5 ft. However, when planting the taller sizes make certain, before purchasing, that they have been transplanted within the last two or three years, for old untransplanted bushes can sometimes be a long time in becoming re-established. Distance to plant is from $1\frac{1}{2}$–$2\frac{1}{2}$ ft. apart, either in late August and September

198

or April and early May. Trim in August or September. When severe cutting back is needed, do this in April. Height 5–20 ft.

In 1908 W. Dallimore states in his book *Holly—Yew and Box*: 'the cost of "Common Hollies" for hedges varies somewhat in different parts of the country, but may be averaged as follows: 1–1½ ft. high, 35s. hundred; 1½–2½ ft. high, 55s. hundred'. In 1939, 1½–2 ft. high, 175s. per hundred was quoted. Here is a present-day quotation from a very reliable nurseryman in 1971: 1½–2 ft., 180s. (£9) per ten; 2–2½ ft., 210s. (£10.50) per ten.

I. × altaclarensis

Large, deep green leaves, purple bark, very vigorous and dense habit. Male.

I. × a. 'Camelliifolia'. Large, dark green camellia-like foliage, often almost spineless, pyramidal in growth and a good berrying form. Female.

I. × a. 'Golden King', leaves margined with bright yellow, contrary to the name, this is a female form.

I. × a. 'Hodginsii'. Large glossy leaves, purple stems. Male. Very good for hedging.

I. × a. 'J. C. van Tol' (syn. *I.* 'Polycarpa'), has very handsome green foliage and is a free-flowering form, female.

I. × a. 'Wilsonii'. Large dark glossy leaves, very spiny, green bark, more compact in habit. Female.

I. aquifolium (Common Holly)

This ranks as one of our finest evergreen hedge plants. The following varieties are all useful hedge shrubs: *I.a.* 'Argenteomarginata', broad-leaved silver holly, female; *I.a.* 'Aureomarginata', leaves margined with gold; *I.a.* 'Bacciflava' (syn. *I.a.* 'Fructuluteo', bright yellow berries, female; *I.a.* 'Golden Queen' (syn. *I.a.* 'Aurea Regina'), leaves margined with bright gold, male.

I.a. 'Silver Queen', leaves margined creamy-white, male. This anomalous naming of the gold and silver kings and queens arose because young trees were named before they had flowered and borne crops of berries.

IPOMOEA, *see* PHARBITIS

ITEA

I. ilicifolia

A handsome, evergreen wall shrub, tender except in favoured localities, such as Devon and Cornwall and the west coast of Scotland, though in mild winters safe enough in other areas. It has large, holly-like leaves, 3 in. long and 2 in. wide, which are a bright glossy green, edged with spiny teeth. The pendulous catkin-like greenish-white, sweetly-scented flowers are borne in August and bloom for a long while. Plant in April. No regular pruning needed, though it may sometimes be necessary to cut out any unwanted shoots in February. Propagate by cuttings of almost mature side shoots, in August and September, inserted in a cold frame. Avoid heavy wet soils. Height 8–10 ft.

IVY, *see* HEDERA

JASMINE, *see* JASMINUM

JASMINE, CHILEAN, *see* MANDEVILLA

JASMINUM (Jasmine)

The two best-known jasmines are *Jasminum nudiflorum*, winter flowering, and *J. officinale*, summer flowering. There are, however, several other species worthy of inclusion beside these two popular climbers. Jasmines are not fussy with regard to soils.

J. beesianum

A deciduous or semi-evergreen, and a semi-climber of rather slender habit. Its small, rose-coloured, fragrant flowers are borne during May and June. These are followed by black fruits in autumn. Prune as necessary after blooms have faded. Height up to 8 ft.

J. nudiflorum (The Chinese Winter-flowering Jasmine)

A deciduous, rambling shrub with a rather loose habit. An ideal choice
200

for an east or north facing wall or fence. It can also be used to carpet banks, if the shoots are pegged down to the ground. Even in the severest winters it will grace its thin angular stems with its yellow blossoms. It is very hardy. Plant from pots from October to March. Prune by cutting back the flowering shoots each year, as soon as blooms have faded. Propagate in November by hard-wood cuttings, 4–7 in. long, with a heel, inserted in a cold frame. Height 12–15 ft.

J. officinale (The Summer-flowering or Common White Jasmine)

This is a magnificent semi-evergreen twining shrub with pure white, delicately scented flowers. It is very hardy and a rapid grower. Flowers from June to September. Plant October to March from pots. Prune in late summer after blooms have faded, when the growths should be well thinned. Alternatively, pruning can be done in the winter. Propagate by half-ripe cuttings 3–5 in. long, in July or August, inserted in a cold frame. Height 10–15 ft.
J. o. 'Affine'. This is similar in all respects to the species except that it has larger flowers, which are prettily tinged with pink on the outside of the petals.
J.o. 'Aureovariegatum'. This requires similar treatment to *J. officinale*, it has attractive variegated creamy-white foliage.

J. polyanthum

A most handsome evergreen, but only suitable outside for the mildest localities. I saw it flowering freely out of doors on a wall at Salcombe in S. Devon in July 1967. It is best suited as a cool-house climber, where there is enough heat to keep out the frost. This spring-flowering beauty bears large panicles of wax-like flowers which are white inside and pale pink without and are richly fragrant. Prune after flowering. And to obtain the maximum amount of bloom pinch out the tips of the young side shoots (when a few inches long) throughout the summer—until September. Propagate by taking half-ripe cuttings, inserted in a propagating case in a greenhouse in June or July. Blooms March to May. Height up to 20 ft.

J. primulinum

This deciduous jasmine is often very nearly evergreen. It is also only suitable for the mildest localities and, therefore, requires similar treatment and conditions to *J. polyanthum*. It flowers from March to May, bearing semi-double, bright yellow flowers, but unfortunately it is scentless. It is a vigorous climber. Height up to 12 ft.

J. × stephanense

A deciduous hybrid, also vigorous, hardy, flowering through June and July, when it bears fragrant pale pink flowers which are followed by black berries. It likes full sun. Propagate either from half-ripe cuttings in July or hard-wood cuttings in the autumn. Height up to 20 ft.

JEW'S MALLOW, *see* KERRIA

JUNIPER, *see* JUNIPERUS

JUNIPERUS (Juniper)

J. communis (Common Juniper)

This hardy native conifer, with small needle-like glaucous leaves, is a slow-growing tree, but is very hardy and is excellent on chalk soils but is happy in any kind of soil; it makes a good wind-resister. Best planting size is 15–18 in., and not higher than 2–3 ft. Space them 2 ft. apart and plant in September or April. Trim when needed in late summer. Propagate by seed sown in March; it often remains dormant for 12 months after sowing. In view of this delay it is wiser to stratify the seed for 18 months before sowing, when germination will be speeded up. Height 6–10 ft.

J.c. 'Hibernica' (Irish Juniper). This fastigiate or pyramidal juniper has attractive feathery bluish-grey foliage, and although it does not make a thick hedge it is ideal where a narrow, formal one is required. Best planting size is 1½–2 ft., spaced 15–18 in. apart; plant in September or April. If trimming is needed, do it during late summer. Propagate by cuttings taken in late September. Height 6–12 ft.

J. virginiana (Red or Pencil Cedar)

Another juniper of tall pyramidal habit and with glaucous grey-green foliage. It is quick growing and does best in well-drained, loamy soils; it will, however, grow in any good soil and it is hardy. Best planting size is 1½–2 ft., spaced 2–3 ft. apart. Plant during September or April. Trim in late summer. Propagate from seed sown in March out of doors; it should be stratified for 18 months before sowing. Height as specimen trees 40–50 ft. Hedges 6–8 ft.

KADSURA

K. japonica

A rare evergreen twining climber from Japan, belonging to the magnolia family, and requiring similar soil conditions, preferably an acid soil as also loved by rhododendrons. Its small cream-coloured cup-shaped flowers, which are produced singly in the axils of the leaves in June, are later followed by clusters of scarlet berries. The leaves also turn red in autumn. It needs the protection of a wall as it is not fully hardy in the open. Height 10–12 ft.
K.j. 'Variegata'. An attractive form with a broad, creamy-white margin to the leaves. Plant in April. Propagate by half-ripe cuttings inserted in a warm propagating case in July. Height 10–12 ft.

KERRIA (Jew's Mallow)

K. japonica (syn. *Corchorus japonicus*) (Jew's Mallow)

Hardy, deciduous shrub with bright green foliage and stems. Bears yellow, single, buttercup-shaped flowers at the end of the previous year's shoots in April and May. There is also a form with creamy-white margins to its leaves, *K.j.* Variegata. It makes an informal hedge or low screen. Best size to plant is 1½–2 ft. high, spaced at 1½ ft. apart, October to March. Thrives in any soil and does not object to partial shade. For hedges trim after flowers fade, and for screens cut out as much old flowering wood as possible. Propagate either by division in spring, or hard-wood cuttings October to November. Height 4–6 ft.
K.j. 'Pleniflora' (Double Jew's Mallow). A deciduous shrub bearing bright green, bamboo-like shoots which are attractive during the winter months. The foliage also gives its share of autumn colour when the leaves change to a light shade of yellow. From mid-April to June it

203

produces many pompon-like double yellow flowers. It also looks well when trained against a wall or fence. Suitable provision must be given to which it can be tied, such as wires, trellis, wire netting or one of the modern supports of rigid wire covered with plastic. Best planting size is 2–3 ft. high, spaced 1½ ft. apart. Trim after flowers fade by cutting out as much old flowering wood as possible. Propagation as for *K. japonica*. Where semi-formal hedges are sought, give a light trimming after flowers have faded. Height 6–8 ft.

KOWHAI, *see* SOPHORA

LABURNUM

L. alpinum (Scotch Laburnum)

This handsome, deciduous tree has deep green trifoliate leaves, not as downy beneath as those of *L. anagyroides*, but its many golden-yellow flowers are carried on pendulous racemes 10–15 in. long. It is a superior species to the common laburnum. Height 20–25 ft.

L. anagyroides (syn. *L. vulgare*) (Common Laburnum)

It is also known as Golden Rain in Germany and Golden Chain in the United States. Laburnum is probably one of our most popular garden trees. It is deciduous, with trifoliate leaves, green and downy beneath; its golden-yellow flowers are borne on pendulous racemes 6–10 in. long; it blooms from the end of May, and well into June. Not fussy over soils. As a tree it will reach a height of 30–35 ft.

L. × watereri. A hybrid between *L. alpinum* and *L. anagyroides*, and very similar to the next, *L.* 'Vossii', except that it has very glossy foliage, and the golden-yellow flowers are borne on long, slender racemes. It blooms in June. Height 30–35 ft.

L. 'Vossii'. Another hybrid between *L. alpinum* and *L. anagyroides*, and is similar in all respects to its parents except that its profusion of golden-yellow flowers are produced on extra long racemes. It blooms from late May into June. Height 30–35 ft.

Although laburnums are usually seen growing either as trees or bushes they are extremely beautiful when trained over a pergola or trellis, particularly the type of tunnel trellis, which at one time was so popular, and over which were trained cordon or espalier fruit trees. My first recollection of seeing laburnums trained in this way was at Hever Castle, Kent, and I understand they were trained to form a tunnel at West Dean, Sussex, and recently an alley way of laburnums can be seen in the Tudor Garden behind Kew Palace at the Royal Botanic Gardens, Kew, Surrey. Plant them any time from October to March; bushes are best for the purpose 4–6 ft. high, and planted 9 ft. apart and the rows 11 ft. Young standards can be used but they will be more costly. Prune in the early stages, at the end of April to early May. When established prune after flowering by spurring back young shoots where they are not wanted to form extension growth. Propagate by seed for *L. alpinus* and *L. anagyroides*; *L.* × *watereri* and *L.* × *w.* 'Vossii' by grafting on to young stock of *Cytisus scoparius*, or by hard-wood cuttings 9–12 in. long, inserted out of doors from late November to December.

LABURNUM, EVERGREEN, *see* PIPTANTHUS

LAD'S LOVE, *see* ARTEMISIA

LAPAGERIA

L. rosea (The Chilean Bellflower)

This lovely, evergreen twiner is, unfortunately, only hardy out of doors in the more favoured localities of the south and western parts of the British Isles. In less favoured areas it requires the protection of a cool greenhouse. Out of doors a warm, sunny position should be chosen where it will receive some shade during the hottest part of the day. A peat and rotted leafmould mixture added to the soil suits it best. It needs an ample supply of moisture, and the soil should never be allowed to dry out. The glorious, rosy-crimson, faintly spotted, water-lily-like bells, which are 2 in. wide and 3 in. long, are produced singly or several together at the ends of short shoots from mid-June to early October. It has leathery, dark green foliage. Plant in spring. Prune only when required in the autumn after the flowers have finished. Propagate by layering strong shoots in spring or autumn. When grown under glass in a large pot or border provide a porous soil of coarse peat and loam, plus a fair quantity of broken brick together with some rotted cow manure and bonemeal. During the summer keep a check on mealy bug, scale insects and aphids by syringing regularly. Height 15–20 ft.

L. r. albiflora is a variety with pure white flowers.

LARCH, *see* LARIX

LARDIZABALA

L. biternata

A handsome twining, evergreen climber of vigorous habit, but only suitable for favoured parts like the south and west, and needs to be planted on a wall. Elsewhere it requires the protection of a cool green-house. A sandy loam and peat soil suits it best, and well drained. The chocolate, purple and white unisexual flowers are borne in the axils of the leaves—the female flowers are solitary and the male flowers are in drooping racemes. The blooms are usually followed by sausage-shaped, edible, sweet pulpy fruits. Propagation is by seed sown in heat in a greenhouse or frame in spring, or by half-ripe cuttings in June–July, inserted in a propagating frame. Height 20 ft.

LARIX (Larch)

L. decidua (syn. *L. europaea*) (Common Larch)

The fresh green of larch is one of our loveliest spring delights. As a hedge larch has little use, although Will Ingwersen, the well-known nursery and plantsman, once saw a fine hedge of the European and Japanese larch in Bavaria. It does, however, make an ideal screen or windbreak, even though it is deciduous. It is excellent for mixing with conifers such as pine and spruce. *L. decidua* is good on chalk or sandy soils. *L. kaempferi* (syn. *L. leptolepis*) (Japanese larch) is more suited to heavier soils; this species is distinguished by its reddish twigs. Either species will make an effective screen, but the Japanese larch is faster growing than the common larch. Best planting size is 2–3 ft. high, spaced at 4 ft. apart, eventually thinned to 8 ft. For an effective wind-break, a double row is best, 4 ft. apart. Propagate by seed, which should be gathered as soon as ripe, stored in bags in a cool, dry shed and sown in March out of doors. Height 80 ft.

L. kaempferi (syn. *L. leptolepis*) (Japanese Larch), *see L. decidua*

LATHYRUS

Undoubtedly the best-known species of this genus is *Lathyrus odoratus*, the sweet pea, perhaps the most popular of all annual climbers, of which today there are many beautiful colours available. A close second to this species would be *L. latifolius*, the everlasting pea.

L. grandiflorus

A hardy climbing perennial with large, rosy-crimson flowers, shading to purple and produced in pairs, sometimes threes, from June to August. Cultivation as for *L. latifolius*. Some twiggy support is necessary. Height 5 ft.

L. latifolius (Everlasting Pea)

This hardy climbing perennial has for a long time been a popular cottage garden and railway embankment plant where, in both situations, it flourishes exceedingly well. It can either be trained up pea sticks, wire netting or any similar type of support, or allowed to ramble over a bank, as it does freely beside many railway lines. Although it is looked upon as a plant that will grow anywhere or anyhow, it does appreciate ground which is deeply dug and well enriched with manure or some good humus. It can be had in various colours from rosy-pink to reddish-purple to white, and it blooms from July to August. The flowers are produced in sprays arranged in pairs on the end of stiff stems which are ideal for cutting. Plant October–November, March–April. This plant dislikes being moved and it may therefore take a year or two to settle down. Prune in October or November by cutting back to the ground. A handful or two of bonemeal in the spring will be beneficial, plus an occasional feed of liquid manure in the summer. Water freely in dry weather. Topdress with manure or some well-rotted garden compost in March. Propagation by seed sown in March in John Innes Seed Compost, in pots in a cold frame, or by division of roots in March or April. Another method is to cut the thong-like roots into 3 in. lengths as root cuttings in late autumn or winter, inserting the cuttings in pots or boxes of a sandy cutting compost, and placing them in a frame. Also, cuttings of young shoots can be taken in April. Height 8–10 ft. Some good varieties are: *L. l. albus*, white; *L.l.a.* 'Snow Queen'; *L.l.a.* 'White Pearl'; and *L. l. roseus*, bright rose.

L. pubescens (Downy Everlasting Pea)

This is of a more sub-shrubby nature than a climber and not quite as hardy as *L. latifolius*. However, its pale lilac to violet-blue flowers are produced in dense racemes of clusters from June to August, and the protection of a wall is necessary. Cultivation is as for *L. latifolius*. Height 3–5 ft.

L. rotundifolius (Persian Everlasting Pea)

A hardy perennial with rosy-pink flowers freely produced in large clusters, 4–5 in. long, from June to August. Cultivation as for *L. latifolius*.

All the species of lathyrus can be used to make useful and attractive summer hedges; they will, of course, require some form of support, such as pea sticks, wire netting or rope netting.

LAUREL, BAY, *see* LAURUS

LAUREL, CHERRY, *see Prunus laurocerasus*

LAUREL, MAGNOLIA, *see* MAGNOLIA

LAUREL, PORTUGAL, *see Prunus lusitanica*

LAURUS

L. nobilis (Sweet Bay or Bay Laurel)

An aromatic evergreen shrub. The foliage is dark glossy green 3–5 in. long and 1–1½ in. wide. The flowers are yellowish-green, male and female being borne on different trees. Dried leaves are used for flavouring milk puddings, fish stews and so on. This attractive evergreen is

Cupressus macro-carpa 'Lutea' in Jersey. It has golden-coloured foliage

Cryptomeria japonica 'Elegans' has attractive, feathery foliage

Leyland cypress, *Cupressocyparis leylandii*, makes a fast growing hedge or screen

ABOVE LEFT: grown informally, *Cotoneaster lacteus* produces red berries
ABOVE RIGHT: sweet bay is equally good as a hedge, like this one at Mount Stewart, Northern Ireland
BELOW: a fine screen of sweet bay, *Laurus nobilis*, at Chichester, Sussex

excellent for a tall hedge or screen and thrives well by the sea, provided it has a first-line defence.

Bay laurel in its young state is a trifle tender, but as it grows to maturity it becomes hardier; should plants ever be severely damaged by frost, they usually grow again. A large specimen I saw at Woking in March 1956, had come through unscathed after a month's severe weather. Best planting size is 1–1½ ft. high and spaced 1½–2 ft. apart, in September or April. It thrives best in a well-drained, loamy soil, though it will tolerate any type of soil. Trim two or three times during the summer with secateurs. When hard pruning is required do this at the end of April. Propagation by cuttings of firm growth 4–5 in. long, taken during August to October and inserted in sandy soil in a cold frame. Height 20–40 ft.

LAURUSTINUS, *see Viburnum tinus*

LAVANDULA (Lavender)

Lavender is probably one of our most popular herbs. It is an evergreen, low-growing bushy aromatic shrub, of which there are many varieties. From July to August it produces sweetly-scented flowers, varying from a pale bluey-mauve to purple, at the end of long wiry stems. The grey-green, narrow foliage and branches are equally fragrant. Their height varies from 1–4 ft. It is ideal for low hedges, flanking paths and lawns or planted on the top of low retaining walls. Lavender grows best in a well-drained, well-limed, light soil. Before planting, the ground should have a generous application of well-rotted farmyard manure or some other form of humus such as hop manure. If good healthy hedges are to be maintained a mulch of well-rotted farmyard manure, hop manure or good garden compost should be given each autumn, and lightly forked in. In spring give a dressing of a general fertilizer such as National Growmore at 4 oz. per sq. yd. A well-kept lavender hedge is of great beauty, but an ill-kept one is awful. One-year-old plants are the best size to plant, the tall-growing ones being spaced 2–2½ ft. apart, and the dwarf ones 1 ft. apart. The best planting time is in the spring, early March to early April, according to the season. It is advisable to puddle in the plants. Lavender can also be planted from late September to the end of October, but in a severe winter following autumn planting there may be losses.

Lavender flowers required for drying should be gathered by cutting the stems about mid-July. Trim lavender hedges by clipping with shears in March or early April. Propagate by heel or nodal cuttings or ripened wood 2–3 in. long inserted in sandy soil in a cold frame in August. Pieces may be torn off old plants in spring and inserted without preparation in a cold frame or a prepared bed out of doors.

L. spica (English lavender)

Grey-green foliage, pale lavender-blue flowers, July to August, plant 2½ ft. apart. Height 3–4 ft.

L.s. 'Folgate'. Grey foliage, soft lavender flowers. July. Plant 1 ft. apart. Height 1–1½ ft.

L.s. 'Grappenhall'. Large blue flowers. Plant 2½ ft. apart. Height 3 ft.

L.s. 'Munstead'. Deep purple flowers. Plant 2½ ft. apart. Height 1 ft.

L.s. 'Hidcote' (syn. 'Nana Atropurpurea'). Silvery foliage, deep purple-blue, dwarf and very compact, flowers in July. Plant 1 ft. apart. Height 1–1½ ft.

L.s. 'Twickel Purple'. Rich purple blooms in July on extra long flower spikes, semi-dwarf and bushy. Plant 2 ft. apart. Height 2–3 ft.

L.s. 'Vera' (Dutch lavender). Broad silver foliage, soft lavender, July to August. Plant 2 ft. apart. Height 2½–3 ft.

LAVENDER, *see* LAVANDULA

LAWSON CYPRESS, *see Chamaecyparis lawsoniana*

LEMON VERBENA, *see* LIPPIA

LEYCESTERIA

L. formosa

The Himalayan Honeysuckle is a hardy deciduous shrub with hollow bamboo-like green stems with a glaucous bloom, and large deep green leaves. It bears pinkish-white pendant flowers surrounded by purplish-red bracts from June to September, followed by clusters of reddish-purple berries in autumn. Not a formal hedge plant, but ideal as an informal screen; excellent for draughty or shady places. Best planting size 1½–2 ft. high, spaced at 2½ ft. apart. Thrives in any soil, in full sun or partial shade. Trim in March and occasionally cut out oldest shoots to ground level, and cut back all dead or frosted growth to live wood. Propagate by hardwood cuttings in October to November, inserted in a prepared bed out of doors. Height 6–8 ft.

LEYLAND CYPRESS, *see Cupressocyparis leylandii*

LIGUSTRUM (Privet)

Hardy, deciduous, semi-evergreen shrubs. There can be no shrub more freely planted in Britain than privet, except perhaps quickthorn. Privet is frequently maligned—in fact, unnecessary harsh words are often uttered about it—yet there could not be a better tempered and more tolerant plant. It will thrive in town or country and in any soil, including lime. But, like many good things, it must not entirely lack attention. The deep green oval leaves of *Ligustrum ovalifolium* (Oval-leaved Privet) look fresh when well cared for as do those of the golden form, *L.o.* 'Aureum'. For general cultivation of privet see *L. ovalifolium.*

L. delavayanum (syn. *L. ionandrum*)

Evergreen, small dark glossy green leaves, making a flat branching bush similar in habit to a cotoneaster. Useful as a compact hedge, plant 1 ft. apart. Height 8–10 ft.

L. ovalifolium (Oval-leaved Privet)

The privet most used. Semi-evergreen; miles of it have been planted up and down the country, especially on housing estates. Best planting size is 1–2 ft. high, spaced at 1 ft. apart for single rows which are usually planted, or 15–18 in. apart in double rows with 8 in. between the rows. Plant October to March. After planting cut young hedges back to within 9–12 in. of ground level. Mixed hedges of privet and quickthorn are also very successful. Plant one privet to three or four quickthorn, spacing them as for privet. Trim at least twice a year, in May and September. Hedges that are growing freely can have several clippings

211

throughout the summer. Over-grown hedges can be severely pruned in March–April. Height from 2–10 ft.

L. ovalifolium 'Aureum' (syn. *L. o. aureo-marginatum*, and *L. o. aureo-variegatum*) (Golden Privet)

It is semi-evergreen. The leaves of golden privet vary in accordance with their age. New young foliage is at first a rich golden-yellow, but as it matures each leaf becomes green in the centre leaving a narrow or broad edging of golden-yellow. Therefore, hedges that are regularly trimmed throughout the summer will remain fairly constantly a rich golden yellow. It makes a very bright hedge, though occasionally golden shoots revert to green and these should be removed immediately with a pair of secateurs. Although it will reach a height of 10–12 ft., hedges of not more than 6 ft. are better—in fact, the best are usually about 4 ft. high. Plant as described for *L. ovalifolium*. Height 4–6 ft.

L. vulgare (Common Privet)

Hardy, deciduous shrub, which, however, often retains its leaves for a long while through winter, when its jet black berries show off to advantage. It is not so neat in habit of growth as *L. ovalifolium*. It is very tough and will grow in any soil and under almost any condition, sun or shade, but owing to its lax and springy habit it is rather difficult to trim. Plant 1 ft. apart. Height 6–10 ft.

LILAC, *see* SYRINGA

LIME, *see* TILIA

LIPPIA

L. citriodora (syn. *Aloysia citriodora*) (The Lemon or Sweet-scented Verbena)

A not fully hardy shrub, but worth while planting where a south or west wall is available, to which it can be trained and tied. It is, however, only suitable in the more favoured localities, such as Devon and the south-west. When on holiday near Kingsbridge, S. Devon, in October 1966, I saw a number of plants in cottage gardens, and on each occasion I could not resist pinching a leaf or rubbing my hand through the leaves to enjoy the fresh lemon scent given off by the foliage. The leaves are narrow, 3–4 in. long, pale green and roughish to touch. Its fragrance never fails to thrill me. The pale purplish-blue flowers are insignificant. It is as well not to grow too lusciously, as this tends to make them tender and more liable to frost damage. Plant in spring from pots. Prune in March, cutting back all shoots within an inch or two of the main stems, and this will keep the plant nice and bushy against the wall. Propagation by half-ripe cuttings in June–July, inserted in sandy soil in pots in a cold frame. Height 6–10 ft.

LOBSTER CLAW, *see* CLIANTHUS

LONICERA (Honeysuckle, Woodbine)

The genus *Lonicera*, the honeysuckle, is a large one which includes climbers as well as some species of a shrubby nature which are suitable for hedges—these are evergreen, whereas the climbers are deciduous and evergreen or semi-evergreen.

Many are sweetly scented, and nothing is more breath-taking than to have a whiff of honeysuckle on a warm summer's evening. Some are very vigorous and require keeping in check by pruning. In planting a honeysuckle it is as well to bear in mind the conditions that they thrive under and enjoy in nature. Like the clematis they appreciate shade at their roots with their tops and flowers in the sun and a moist, rich, loamy soil. Older specimens need a topdressing of well decayed farmyard manure or something equivalent. It is, I think, why one sometimes hears of and sees plants growing indifferently; they are dry and starved, added to the fact of being attacked by aphids, which these days can be kept at bay by a good insecticide. If growth is too vigorous this can cause lack of flower, and this I have experienced in my own garden. To check vigorous growth apply sulphate of potash at $\frac{1}{2}$ oz. per sq. yd. in the spring. As climbing honeysuckles are usually pot grown, they can be planted at almost any time, though autumn and spring are best. Pruning should be done after flowering when their growths may be thinned and old or weak shoots removed, if necessary down to ground level. Young and vigorous new shoots should be tied to some kind of support. Propagation is by half-ripened cuttings of the current year's growth, 4 in.

long with a heel, taken in June–July–August, inserted in sandy compost in a frame with gentle heat, or hard-wood cuttings 9 in. long and inserted in a prepared bed out of doors in October.

L. × americana

Hybrid between *L. caprifolium* and *L. etrusca*. This deciduous, vigorous honeysuckle has white flowers which become pale and later deep yellow to apricot within, and tinged purple without. The flowers are freely produced and richly fragrant, in June and July. Height up to 30 ft.

L. × brownii (*L. sempervirens* × *L. hirsuta*) (Scarlet Trumpet Honey-suckle)

A deciduous to semi-evergreen of moderate vigour but scentless, having glowing orange-scarlet flowers in June and again in September. It enjoys semi-shade.

L. caprifolium (Early Cream Honeysuckle)

A deciduous, free-flowering honeysuckle, bearing creamy-white, fragrant blooms, produced in the axils of the terminal stems, which are clasped by glaucous foliage. Height to 20 ft.

L. ciliosa (The Western Trumpet Honeysuckle)

This beautiful deciduous twining plant is almost fully hardy, and well worth a sheltered, semi-shady place in the garden where it can show off its yellow to orange-scarlet flowers in June. Its young leaves are covered with soft hairs.

L. etrusca

A semi-evergreen, vigorous mediterranean species, with large clusters of cream flowers on opening, deepening to yellow in June and July, very fragrant. A little slow at flowering when young.

L. × heckrotii (*L. americana* × *L. sempervirens*)

A deciduous hybrid with oblong leaves, $1\frac{1}{2}$ in. long, which are glaucous beneath. The upper pairs are usually united. It is a striking plant,

214

though not as vigorous as some. It has orange-yellow flowers within, pink outside, which are fragrant and freely-produced, from June onwards.

L. japonica

This vigorous evergreen, though sometimes semi-evergreen, will easily reach a height of 10–30 ft. Its fragrant creamy-white flowers blushed purple and borne in pairs in the leaf axils, are freely produced from June onwards.

L.j. 'Aureoreticulata'. The glory of this honeysuckle is its prettily netted golden-yellow variegated foliage, which in autumn changes to gold and bronze. It too, has fragrant white to creamy flowers, but these are not an outstanding feature.

L. j. halliana. This is one of my favourites and is, like the species, a rampant climber, bearing an abundance of sweetly scented white flowers which pale off to a creamy-yellow. It blooms from June to October. On account of its vigorous growth plants may be pruned each spring, when all shoots can be cut back to last year's growth.

L. nitida (Chinese Honeysuckle)

Evergreen shrub with small, box-like leaves, of a pleasing dark glossy green. Although introduced over 125 years ago, its popularity has come in the last 30 to 40 years, and up to a point it has vied for pride of place with oval privet. It is not quite as hardy as privet and after severe winters hedges often have a sorry brown or singed look about them. Unkempt hedges will soon become bare and bony at the base. But hedges that have grown out of hand, if not too old, can be cut hard back in April, and as a rule respond when cut to within as little as 9 in. of the ground. It makes a useful seaside hedge. Hedges are best grown in a wedge form, narrower at the top than at the base. Best planting size is 1–1½ ft. As *L. nitida* is of a wiry habit, a framework of wire netting as a support is very beneficial. Space them 12 in. apart when planting, October to April, and in March or April cut them back after planting to 9–12 in. Trim two or three times, when established, throughout the summer. Propagate by taking hard-wood cuttings in March. Height 4–4½ ft. (Plate 28.)

L.n. 'Baggessen's Gold'. This is by no means a common plant, more the pity. Its raiser, Mr. Niels Baggessen of Pembury, near Tunbridge Wells, gave me a plant for my garden during the Second World War, before it was introduced. It is a rich golden shade and is as suited to hedge work as *L. nitida*. In fact, all other remarks are the same as for this species. Height 4–4½ ft.

L. n. Fertilis. Evergreen and of stiffer growth and more upright in habit than *L. nitida*. Very free fruiting; otherwise similar to *L. nitida*. Height 4–4½ ft.

L. periclymenum (The Woodbine or Common Honeysuckle)

Although this deciduous native climber of our hedgerows is commonly known—at least to country folk—it is nevertheless worthy of garden space. Its sweet scent, once inhaled, will never be forgotten. The yellowish-white and red flowers are followed in autumn by red berries which are equally attractive. It blooms from June to September. Height 20 ft.

L.p. 'Belgica' (Early Dutch Honeysuckle). A deciduous climber of a rather bushy habit. The tubular flowers are flushed red-purple on the outside, fading yellowish within. Its stems are purplish. It is very free-flowering during May and June, and again in late summer.

L.p. 'Serotina' (Late Dutch Honeysuckle). Similar to *L.p.* 'Belgica' though stronger growing and later flowering. The flowers are dark purplish-red outside, which become paler with age. The lips inside are creamy-white, later changing to yellow. It blooms from late June–early July until September and October.

L. sempervirens (The Trumpet Honeysuckle)

This handsome, evergreen climber was introduced from the United States in 1656. It is, however, a little less hardy than some and is, therefore, more at home in south or western climates. In colder areas it must have the protection of a wall or fence. The foliage is a rich green above and bluish beneath. Its unscented flowers are orange-scarlet and yellowish-white within. It blooms from early June to late September.

L. × tellmanniana

A hybrid between *L. tragophylla* and *L. sempervirens*, and introduced in 1927, so as plants go it is a comparative newcomer among honeysuckles. It is a strong grower and it received an Award of Merit in 1931. The long slender-tubed, unscented flowers are an orange-yellow, which in the bud state are tipped with a bronze-red. The flowers are borne in June

216

and July in terminal heads of six to twelve, each bloom as much as 2 in. long and 1 in. wide across the lips. The large leaves, 2–3½ in. long, are united in the upper pair. It enjoys a rich, loamy soil, where it can have its roots and lower branches in the shade. It does well on a north aspect.

L. tragophylla

This deciduous climbing shrub was the first honeysuckle to receive an Award of Garden Merit in 1928. Its large, scentless, bright yellow flowers are often over 3 in. in length and 1 in. wide at the tips. The flowers are borne in clusters of 10 to 20 in June and July. The glaucous leaves are also large, below the flowers they are united. The flowers are followed by bright red berries in autumn. Like *L.* × *tellmanniana*, it prefers shade for its roots and lower branches. Again a north wall and rich, loamy, moist soil suits it best.

LOQUAT, *see* ERIOBOTRYA

LYCIUM

L. chinense (Chinese Box-thorn)

Hardy deciduous scandent shrub, vigorous and quick growing. It has grey spine-tipped stems and greyish foliage, purplish flowers in summer, followed by orange, or orange-red, egg-shaped pendant fruits. It is a good seaside shrub and very wind-hardy. Best used as an informal hedge or screen. It is also a useful subject to plant at the top of a bank or old wall and allowed to hang over. Best planting size is 2–3 ft. high, spaced 15–18 in. apart. Plant October to March. Thrives in any soil, but prefers a dry well-drained soil. Trim by cutting it hard back in March. Propagate by seed or hard-wood cuttings in autumn. Height 8 ft.

MAGNOLIA

M. grandiflora (Laurel Magnolia, Bull Bay)

This is, undoubtedly, one of our most handsome evergreen wall shrubs. The leaves are leathery, glossy dark green above, and covered with a

217

thick reddy-brown felt beneath. They are oblong to oval and 6–10 in. long, 3–9 in. wide. Their magnificent creamy-white globular flowers are very large being as much as 8–12 in. across when fully developed. The thick petals are richly fragrant; the flowers, which open like tulips, are produced in batches from July to October. It is a shrub for the south and west, not the north. They should be sheltered from the north and north-east winds. A south or south-west position suits them best. Fortunately *M. grandiflora* and its varieties tolerate lime, in fact, they flourish as well as they do on other soils. Should they, by any chance, show signs of chlorosis this can soon be put right by applying Sequestrene. Also an annual mulch of good leaf soil or peat plus a little rotted farmyard manure will benefit their health. I have found the foliage excellent for flower arrangements, particularly for church flower decorations. Plant in spring, using pot-grown plants. Prune as and when required in April. Propagate by seed, layering in early spring or air layering in June. Height 30–40 ft.

M.g. 'Ferruginea'. Glossy dark green leaves, richly felted with a rusty-brown beneath. They are rounder in shape. The white flowers are produced at an earlier age than *M. grandiflora*.

M.g. 'Goliath'. Larger flowers and leaves and also blooms at an earlier age.

M.g. 'Exmouth' (syn. 'Lanceolata'). Large glossy green oval leaves and white globular flowers which are produced throughout the summer.

M. × soulangiana

Although this deciduous species is usually looked upon as a large shrub to be grown in the open, it does, however, make an excellent wall shrub, and so do some of its cultivars. The white flowers, which are stained purple, are freely produced from mid-April to mid-May. By growing it on a wall there is less likelihood of frost damage. Choose a south or west wall. As it is not a climber it will need support to which it can be trained and tied. By planting a clematis at the foot of *M. soulangiana* the wall will have a further flush of flowers to extend its use. Plant in the spring, just before leaf bud burst, in ground well enriched with leaf-mould or peat and well rotted farmyard manure. Prune after flowering, when required, which will be late spring or early summer. A type of spur pruning is necessary if the plant is not to get out of hand. Height 20–30 ft.

M. × *s.* 'Alba'. White scented flowers, rather more upright in growth.

M. × *s.* 'Alexandrina'. White, with a purple flush at the base.

MAHONIA

M. aquifolium (syn. *Berberis aquifolium*) (Oregon Grape)

Hardy, evergreen shrub. It has large pinnate leaves of a dark glossy green, sometimes tinged with brown, turning a purplish-crimson in autumn and winter. Golden-yellow flowers in March to April, and in favourable seasons earlier. It makes a slow growing informal hedge and spreads by underground suckers. Best planting size is 15–18 in. high, spaced 1½–2 ft. apart. Plant October to April. Thrives in any soil, lime included. Little attention is needed, as a rule, and it is sufficient to cut back or reduce any long straggling shoots. If a formal hedge is required, then clip it each year in April. Propagate by seed or division of suckers in spring. Height 3–4 ft. (Plate 21.)

M. pinnata (syn. *M. fascicularis*)

Hardy, evergreen shrub similar in many respects to *M. aquifolium*, except that the leaflets often number thirteen to a leaf, and that individual leaflets are longer and narrower. Foliage is glossy and grey-green, turning red or purplish in autumn and winter. Other remarks as for *M. aquifolium*. Height 6–9 ft.

M. 'Undulata'

A hardy evergreen with glossy green, crenulated foliage. Its bright yellow flowers are freely produced from March to April. It is more erect in habit and very bushy. Other remarks as for *M. aquifolium*. Height 6–9 ft. Propagate by layering in early spring.

MANDEVILLA

M. suaveolens (Chilean Jasmine)

This attractive deciduous twining shrub is nothing like as well known or popular as it should be, partly as it is a little on the tender side, though if given a sheltered and warm south or west wall it will well repay its keep. An acid soil or sandy loam suits it best. It gains its common name from the richly fragrant white funnel-shaped flowers, five to six are borne on slender stems in the axils of the opposite leaves, during the summer months. It has remarkable seed pods, 12–16 in. long

219

and as thick as a pencil, which are produced in pairs. Some protection is advisable in winter except in very favoured areas. Plant in spring. Propagate by cuttings, choosing half-ripened shoots in July inserted in a sandy compost placed beneath a bell glass or large glass jar. Height 12 ft.

MAPLE, *see* ACER

MAPLE, NORWAY, *see Acer platanoides*

MENISPERMUM

M. canadense (Moonseed)

A vigorous deciduous twining plant of a semi-woody nature, its greenish-yellow flowers in June and July are inconspicuous, but its crescent-shaped seeds, which look like bunches of blackcurrants, are attractive in the autumn. The large heart-shaped leaves look like those of ivy. It makes strong suckering roots. On account of its spreading habit it should only be planted where it can spread itself; choose an acid or light clay soil. Plant in spring. Prune by cutting it back to the ground in winter. Propagate by the division of the underground suckering roots. Height 12–15 ft.

METASEQUOIA

M. glyptostroboides (Dawn Redwood)

This ancient deciduous conifer is a recent introduction to this country; it was found living in China. The first mention of it here was by Lord Aberconway in his Presidential Report at the Royal Horticultural Society's Hall, London, on 17th February 1948. Since then many young trees have been distributed throughout the British Isles. In many respects *Metasequoia glyptostroboides* is similar to the swamp cypress, *Taxodium distichum*. In habit it is upright and pyramidal, with enchanting soft green feathery foliage in spring and summer, turning a tawny pink in autumn. It is quick growing. Another reference to this conifer appeared in the R.H.S. Journal, Vol. LXXVIII (February 1953), where Mr. E. Armitage stated that a seedling about 6 in. high, which was planted in the autumn of 1949, had in three years made a shapely pyramidal tree 6 ft. high and 3 ft. wide at the base.

At the Royal Botanic Gardens, Kew, the late Sydney Pearce, when Assistant Curator, had young trees planted in between sapling birches 10 ft. apart to form a screen; I first saw them on 1st January 1968, and they looked in excellent condition, all feathered to the ground. On the same visit I also saw another of Sydney's ideas, an experimental hedge of metasequoia planted in 1957, the 3 ft. high plants being spaced 2 ft. apart. The best planting times are October to December or March to April. From what I saw the young trees were standing up to hard clipping, the hedge in 1958 being 4 ft. high, and I can see no reason why metasequoia should not make a useful, fast-growing and attractive hedge. I have seen the screen and hedge many times since 1958 and in May 1968 both were well established. Trim hedges three or four times a year, between spring and late summer. If an informal hedge is needed, then once only in late July. Propagate either by seed or cuttings in September, inserted in a propagating case with a temperature of 65°–70° F. (18°–21° C.) As this tree is a recent introduction, references on propagation may be helpful (see R.H.S. Journal, Vol. LXXIII, page 334, and Vol. LXXV, page 359). Height of a fully grown tree is 115 ft. I should think that hedges could be grown up to 10 ft. high.

MEXICAN ORANGE BLOSSOM, *see* CHOISYA

MILE-A-MINUTE PLANT, *see* POLYGONUM

MOCK ORANGE, *see* PHILADELPHUS

MONTEREY CYPRESS, *see* CUPRESSUS

MOONSEED, *see* MENISPERMUM

MORNING GLORY, *see Pharbitis purpurea*

MOUNTAIN ASH, *see* SORBUS

MUEHLENBECKIA

M. complexa

This curious deciduous climber, a native of New Zealand, is perhaps more interesting than beautiful, but it is a useful twining plant. Its slender wiry stems are excellent for covering an old tree stump or for scrambling through a derelict shrub. It can also be used to cover a stack pipe or to form a 'fedge' when allowed to scramble through wire netting. The small leaves are fiddle shaped, the flowers greenish-white. It is best in well-drained sandy soil, though it will grow in any kind of soil. Plant any time from October to March. No trimming is necessary. Propagate by inserting cuttings of young shoots in sandy soil in a cold frame during late summer.

MUTISIA (Climbing Gazania)

A genus of evergreen, South American climbers, the climbing gazanias support themselves by tendrils. Their daisy-like flowers are in varying shades of pink orange and red. To me they have always had a rather untidy appearance, though their flowers are quite brilliant. My first encounter with a mutisia was when a student at the Royal Botanic Gardens, Kew. Through my ignorance, I cut almost to the ground *M. decurrens*, a very special plant of Mr. G. W. Robinson who was the Assistant Curator in charge of the Herbaceous and Rock Garden Department in 1936. But (to me) it looked so untidy scrambling over a rather indifferent looking pine. Its needs are a good, moist peaty soil, well-drained but not too dry nor too wet, it likes its roots in the shade, but where the shoots can scramble through a shrub. Slugs enjoy the young new shoots, so a little slug bait spread around in the spring will be an advantage. Plant in spring. Prune as and when required, in spring. Propagate by seeds, though cuttings are best, using half-ripened shoots inserted in a sandy compost in a propagating frame in July to August.

M. decurrens

Orange-scarlet or vermillion gazania-like flowers up to 4 in. across, with a central cluster of yellow disk florets. June to August. Height up to 10 ft.

M. ilicifolia

Has holly-shaped leaves, flowers 2–3 in. wide with pinkish-mauve ray florets and a central disk of yellow, 1 in. wide. The flower heads are borne singly and are almost stalkless. Height 15 ft.

M. oligodon

This species was introduced by H. F. Comber from Chile in 1927. It is a beautiful plant with clear pink flowers about 3 in. across. It is hardy in the milder areas. Height 3 ft.

MYROBOLAN PLUM, *see Prunus cerasifera*

MYRTLE, *see* MYRTUS

MYRTUS

M. communis (Common Myrtle)

Evergreen, hardy only in the more favoured districts in the south and west. Has small, dark, glossy green leaves, fragrant when crushed. White flowers in July and August, each flower being filled with a boss of stamens. Best planting size is 1½ ft. high (pot-grown plants) spaced at 2–3 ft. apart. Plant in March or April. Trim in April. Light, sandy, well-drained soils are best; it also grows on chalk soils. Propagate by heel cuttings of half-ripened wood in July. Height 8–10 ft. As a hedge it is best kept at 4–5 ft.

M. ugni (Chilean Guava)

Evergreen, ovate leathery leaves, pinky-white drooping flowers. Makes a useful low hedge 3–6 ft. high, stands wind well.

NASTURTIUM, *see* TROPAEOLUM

NORWAY MAPLE, *see Acer platanoides*

NORWAY SPRUCE, *see Picea abies*

NOTHOFAGUS

N. obliqua (Roble Beech)

A deciduous tree, a native of Chile. The leaves are smooth dark green above, pale green and rather glaucous beneath. This is a faster growing tree than our common beech and it makes an excellent hedge plant. Best planting size is $1\frac{1}{2}$–2 ft. high, spaced at 1–$1\frac{1}{2}$ ft. apart and planted from November to March. It thrives in most soils. Trim in August. Propagate by seed. Height as a screen tree up to 10–25 ft.; as hedge 5–10 ft.

NUTTALLIA, *see* OSMORONIA

OAK, *see* QUERCUS

OAK, EVERGREEN, *see Quercus ilex*

OAK, HOLLY, *see Quercus ilex*

OAK, HOLM, *see Quercus ilex*

OAK, TURKEY, *see Quercus cerris*

ABOVE: evergreen *Berberis stenophylla* has yellow flowers
BELOW LEFT: *Mahonia aquifolium* has golden-yellow flowers, and holly-like foliage which colours in autumn
BELOW RIGHT: *Forsythia intermedia* 'Spectabilis', with its bright yellow flowers, makes a useful screen to this shed

A majestic group of Lawson cypresses, the tallest one is *Chamaecyparis lawsoniana* 'Pottenii' (centre) and (centre left) a golden form

OLD MAN'S BEARD, *see Clematis vitalba*

OLEARIA

Evergreen flowering shrubs hardy in the milder counties, except *Olearia × haastii* which is hardy anywhere. The wind-hardy olearias are ideal shrubs to plant in coastal areas where winds are a menace to newly-planted shrubs, but again, they are only suitable in the milder counties. The other well-known one is *O. macrodonta*. However, W. Arnold-Forster in his book *Shrubs for the Milder Counties*, recommends the species *O. albida*, which he says is 'one of the half-dozen best shrubs for wind-shelter in exposed coastal gardens'.

'*O. ilicifolia*', he says, 'resembles macrodonta, but has long narrow leaves: very wind-hardy, and is pleasantly musk scented.' He goes on to say that: '*O. traversii* is one of the most valuable plants for wind shelter, and is very fast growing.' He also says that 'it grows in any soil including sand', and 'plants from cuttings will form a hedge 6 ft. high in two years'. Although I have no personal knowledge of these olearias, apart from *O. × haastii* and *O. macrodonta*, they are, undoubtedly, essential in parts of Cornwall if any other shrub or plant is to be grown with success.

Choose young pot-grown plants, spacing them 2 ft. apart. Plant in September to October or March to April. Trim young bushes in March, and older ones in April, where harder cutting is required. Propagate by seed or cuttings.

O. × haastii

Hardy evergreen bushy shrub of rounded habit and is the best known of the olearias. It is sometimes despised on account of its dull appearance, but it makes up for this as it is extremely hardy, and wind-resistant. I saw it thriving at Dudley in the Midlands along with *Senecio greyi*. It also thrives in our cold Sussex clay soil. In July and August it produces a profusion of white and yellow fluffy flower heads. Height 6–8 ft.

O. macrodonta

An evergreen with holly-like leaves, dark glossy, grey-green above with a silvery-white felt beneath. In June it produces large flowerheads with white ray florets, and a few reddish disk florets; the flowers are scented. This species of olearia does well as a hedge shrub at Fleetwood, Lancs. Height 10–15 ft.

ORANGE, MOCK, *see* PHILADELPHUS

ORANGE BLOSSOM, MEXICAN, *see* CHOISYA

OREGON GRAPE, *see Mahonia aquifolium*

OSMANTHUS

O. delavayi (syn. *Siphonosmanthus delavayi*)

Evergreen shrub with small box-like leaves and sweetly-scented pure white tubular flowers, freely produced in April. This attractive shrub is slow growing in the colder parts of the country, but in more favoured localities, such as the south-west and west, it quickly makes a low hedge. According to the late Mr. J. Coutts of Kew there is a fine hedge in South Wales. Best planting size is 1–1½ ft. high, spaced at 1 ft. apart, and planted in April or early May. It thrives in most soils, including chalk. Trim in late April or early May after flowering. Propagate by half-ripened wood cuttings from side shoots with a heel, insert under a bell glass in a greenhouse with bottom heat, in mid-June. This handsome evergreen with its sweetly-scented flowers also makes an excellent wall or fence shrub. A fine specimen used to grow on the stables, facing south, when J. Cheal and Sons Ltd. were at Crawley. In the Midlands and northern areas wall protection is most necessary. It will grow from 7–10 ft. high, but hedges of 4–5 ft. are best.

O. heterophyllus (syn. *O. aquifolium, O. ilicifolius*)

An evergreen shrub of dense bushy habit, bearing dark green, glossy, holly-like leaves, paler beneath. Fragrant white flowers produced in September and October. An excellent town shrub, which can make a large hedge and provide a good dark background to other plants. It grows in any soil, in sun or shade, and thrives near the coast. Best planting size is 1½–2 ft. high, spaced 2–2½ ft. apart, though larger specimens move satisfactorily. Plant September, March or April. Trim at the end of April or in early May. Propagate by cuttings of almost ripened wood taken with a heel 3–5 in. long in September to October, inserted in a cold frame. Height 8–10 ft.

O. h. 'Purpureus'

Young leaves are of a blackish-purple shade. It is a particularly hardy variety, and in other respects the same as for *H. heterophyllus*.

OSMAREA

O. burkwoodii

A hardy evergreen with dark green box-like foliage with a vigorous upright habit of growth. This evergreen is a cross between *Osmanthus delavayi* and *Phillyrea decora*. In flower it is similar to *Osmanthus delavayi* but not so sweetly scented, though it has a pleasant fragrance. It flowers in May. It was first shown at the Royal Horticultural Society on 9th March 1937; it is surprising that it is still so little known as a hedge plant. Although it costs more than *Lonicera nitida*, it is much hardier and makes a good hedge up to 5–6 ft. It will grow satisfactorily in any soil. Best planting size is 1½–2 ft. high, spaced 15–21 in. apart, and planted from October to March. Trim after flowering or, if hard cutting is necessary, do this in April. Propagate by half-ripened wood cuttings in May to June, inserted in a close case with medium bottom heat. I have not seen *O. burkwoodii* trained against a wall or fence, but see no reason why it should not be treated in the same way as one of its parents *Osmanthus delavayi*. Height 9–12 ft.

OSMARONIA

O. cerasiformis (syn. *Nuttallia cerasiformis*) (Oso Berry)

Hardy, deciduous, flowering shrub. Narrow lance-shaped leaves, green above, grey below. Its green and white almond-scented bell-shaped blossoms are freely borne at the end of March. Male and female flowers are usually on different bushes; therefore, its plum-like purple fruits are not produced unless both sexes are planted. This shrub is suitable only for an informal hedge, as it makes a dense thicket several feet through, so an area of at least 3 ft. wide is needed. It does well in all soils except chalk. Best planting size is 2–3 ft. high, cut down in spring, spaced 2 ft. apart. Plant October to February. Trim lightly after flowering. Remove unwanted sucker growth from time to time in spring; such suckers can be used to form new plants. Height 6–8 ft.

OSO BERRY, *see* OSMARONIA

PARROT'S BILL, *see* CLIANTHUS

PARTHENOCISSUS

The genus *Parthenocissus* contains the true Virginia creepers which have been at various times known under such generic names as *Ampelopsis*, *Cissus*, *Psedera*, *Quinaria* and *Vitis*, and which botanist is right, I do not know, but for my part I am sticking, at the moment, to *Parthenocissus*. These useful climbers thrive in any soil. The genus *Vitis* (the grape) is dealt with on page 301.

P. henryana (syn. *Vitis henryana*)

This beautiful, deciduous, Chinese creeper, has forked tendrils ending in pads which cling satisfactorily to flat surfaces, though I have heard of cases where it almost refuses to cling. The leaves are made up of three to five leaflets of a dark velvety green, which are enhanced by a silvery-white and pinkish-purple on the main veins. In autumn the variegated foliage turns a brilliant warm red. It requires the protection of a wall and will flourish on a west or north aspect. Plant from pot-grown plants in autumn or spring. No regular pruning is required. Propagate from cuttings of semi-mature wood 4–6 in. long, inserted singly in sandy compost in small pots, placed in a propagating case, with a little bottom heat, in early autumn.

P. himalayana (syn. *Vitis himalayana*)

This deciduous self-clinging Himalayan 'Virginia creeper' has extra large leaves composed of three leaflets, two of which are obliquely shaped, being wider on one side of the mid-rib than the other. They are dark green, changing to a rich crimson in autumn. After a good summer they will produce small, deep blue grapes. Other remarks as for *V. henryana*.

P. inserta (syn. *Vitis vitacea*)

This deciduous plant is the common Virginia creeper of town gardens, but it is not the true one—which is *P. quinquefolia*. Its main difference is that it has no pads by which it can cling to walls; it must, therefore, have some support around which it can twine its tendrils. It is an excellent climber to clamber among trees or over a pergola. This handsome vine has good autumn colour when the foliage turns red. Other remarks as for *P. henryana*.

P. quinquefolia (syns. *Vitis quinquefolia* and *V. hederacea*) (Virginia Creeper)

This vigorous, deciduous climber is the true Virginia creeper, clinging by means of a disk at the end of each tendril. The leaves are composed of five leaflets, occasionally three, which are bright green, changing in autumn to a brilliant orange and scarlet. It is ideal for growing up lofty trees or high walls. I have seen fine examples on both, on one occasion up a Scots Pine and on another up a Lawson cypress. The latter looked like an enormous scarlet cone of fire. Plant pot-grown plants in autumn or spring. No regular pruning. Propagate from cuttings of half-ripened shoots 3 in. long, inserted in sandy soil in a warm propagating frame, during July.

P. thomsonii (syn. *Vitis thomsonii*)

An attractive deciduous slender climber, having compound leaves of five leaflets, which are slightly downy, as are the leaf stalks also. When young, the leaf-stalks, leaves and shoots are a bright claret-purple, later becoming a greenish-purple, gradually turning to a deep reddish-purple and finally in autumn to a brilliant crimson-scarlet. Other remarks as for *P. henryana*.

P. tricuspidata 'Veitchii' (syns. *Ampelopsis veitchii* and *Vitis inconstans*)

This deciduous, vigorous climber has for over a century been our most popular coverer of walls. It was introduced from China and Japan in 1862. It is self-clinging, attaching itself by sticky disks at the end of the

229

tendrils. The foliage varies in its formation, being shallowly or coarsely toothed, slightly lobed or not at all; there are three distinct leaflets, each deeply three lobed. The last is usually seen on old mature plants. Its foliage is large and coarse, dark green, but in autumn it can hardly be surpassed for the richness of its red and crimson colourings. Propagate by soft summer cuttings, inserted singly in small pots filled with a sandy-peaty compost, in a propagating frame.

P.t.v. Beverley Brook. This is a small-leaved variety introduced by Jackmans Nurseries Ltd., Woking, Surrey. It is self clinging, and has good autumn colouring but is much less rampant than the species.

PASSIFLORA

P. caerulea (Passion Flower)

A vigorous evergreen climber, though in some localities and in bad winters it becomes deciduous. It needs support, to which it will cling by tendrils. The leaves are palmate, being five- to seven-lobed and 4–7 in. wide, dark green. It is a remarkable flower made up of five sepals and five petals of a blue-white colour, and in the centre there is a 'corona' of purplish stamens and pistil. There is an interesting story attached to the flower as follows:

The ten petals and sepals represent the ten disciples, leaving out Judas and Doubting Thomas. The corona represents the crown of thorns; the five stamens the wounds, and the three stigmas the nails. The hand-like leaves represent the hand of the tormentors of Jesus and the tendrils the whip with which He was scourged.

The passion flower blooms from June to September, and the flowers are followed by orange coloured fruits, the size of a bantam's egg. Plants need the protection of a south or west wall. In less favoured districts it will be necessary to protect the base of the plant by bracken or straw and sacking or polythene. Plant pot-grown plants in spring. They prefer poor soil to rich and flower better when their root run is restricted. They do not like chalk soils. However, a little encouragement is helpful in the first place. Prune in February by cutting back secondary branches to within several buds of the base, and at the same time tie in new young shoots to take their place. Propagate by heel or nodal cuttings 4–6 in. long inserted in a sandy soil in a closed propagating frame or under a glass jar in July. Height 30–40 ft. *P.c.* 'Constance Elliott' is a white flowered variety.

PASSION FLOWER, *see* PASSIFLORA

PEA TREE, *see* CARAGANA

PERIPLOCA

P. graeca (Silk Vine)

A deciduous, vigorous, hardy twining shrub, little known although introduced as long ago as 1597. It has ovate to lanceolate opposite leaves,
3–4 in. long. In July and August, loose clusters of 8–12 star-shaped
flowers are produced, greenish-yellow outside and brownish-red inside,
each flower 1 in. wide. They have a rich velvety appearance. The seed
vessels are interesting, produced in usually united pairs, cylindrical in
shape, about 5 in. long and ¼ in. wide. At the end of each seed vessel
there is a tuft of silky hairs 1¼ in. long, which accounts for its common
name 'Silk Vine'. It is more suitable for pergolas and trees rather than
walls on account of its vigorous habit. It is not fussy as to soil. Plant in
spring from pots. Pruning is not required. Propagate by division of the
rootstock in spring, or half-ripe cuttings in July, inserted in sandy soil
in a cold frame or under a large glass jar; or by layering ripened shoots
in October. Height 30 ft.

PERNETTYA

P. mucronata

A hardy evergreen and one of our most decorative dwarf berried shrubs.
It has dark green, glossy leaves which are prickly and tightly packed on
wiry reddish stems. The nodding, cylindrical white flowers are produced
in May, singly in the leaf axils, followed by globose berries varying in
colour from pure white to pink, lilac, purple-crimson and red. Their
berries are very useful for indoor decoration. It is an ideal shrub to form
a low hedge or border and associates happily in the heather garden. It
tolerates sun or partial shade, and needs a lime-free soil; it objects to too
dry a situation. With *P. mucronata* it is necessary to plant one male to

four or five female bushes, otherwise berries will not be produced, because the plants are dioecious. However, there are hermaphrodite forms, in which both sexes are on the same plant. Pernettya is a shrub that soon gets going in the right soil and quickly increases by suckers. Plant young bushes 12–15 in. high, spacing them 12–15 in. apart, October to April. Trim—no regular clipping is needed, though extra long shoots can be reduced in length immediately after flowering. Propagate by seeds or suckers, or cuttings in August and September. Height 2–4 ft.

P.m. 'Alba'. White berries.

P.m. 'Bell's Seedling'. A hermaphrodite form, with crimson-red fruits September to March. No separate male bush is needed to effect pollination.

P.m. 'Davis's Hybrids'. A hermaphrodite form, with large berries in many colours. No separate male bush is needed to effect pollination.

P.m. 'Donard Pink'. Large, pink fruits.

P.m. 'Donard White'. Large, pure white fruits.

P.m. 'Lilacina'. Lilac fruits.

P. m. mascula. Useful to plant as a pollinator.

PEROVSKIA

P. atriplicifolia

Deciduous semi-woody plant, with upright branches covered with a white down. The plant has a sage-like odour, with coarsely-toothed, grey-green leaves and violet-blue flowers produced in profusion during August and September. This will not make a hedge in the true sense, but is useful as an attractive summer screen or barrier. A fine example of such a screen can be seen on the left as one enters the Royal Horticultural Society's garden at Wisley, Surrey, planted along the top of the wall in front of the Curator's house. Best size for planting is young pot-grown plants, spacing them 12–15 in. apart. It does best in a loamy soil, in a hot dry situation, and should be given the sunniest position possible. Does well in lime soils. Prune each year in late March to April by cutting it back to the base of the previous year's growth. Propagate by half-ripened wood cuttings in July. Height 3–5 ft.

PHARBITIS

P. purpurea (syns. *Convolvulus purpurea, C. major* and *Ipomoea purpurea*) (Morning Glory)

This half-hardy annual twiner is frequently seen growing in a conservatory or greenhouse; it can, however, be grown out of doors during the summer months, on a warm sunny wall, fence or border. The striking blue convolvulus flowers are freely produced throughout the summer, until cut down by frost. It will grow in any type of soil other than a limy soil. Plant from pots in late May or early June. Propagate from seed sown $\frac{1}{8}$ in. deep, in a temperature of 65° F. (18° C.) in March. Height 10 ft.

PHILADELPHUS (Mock Orange)

The mock orange—erroneously called syringa which is the botanical name of lilac—is perhaps one of our most loved summer flowering, hardy, deciduous shrubs. The pineapple-like scent of its flowers during June and July, once appreciated, will never be forgotten. This is not a shrub to make a formal hedge, but is ideal for an informal flowering hedge or screen: in fact it is excellent where a summer screen is wanted. It is not fussy as to soil or situation, and appears to thrive under town and back garden conditions. Best planting size is from 2–4 ft. spaced at 3 ft. apart for most, small growing varieties at $1\frac{1}{2}$–2 ft. apart, in October to March. After planting, cut bushes back to within 1–2 ft. of ground level so as to induce plenty of basal growth. Prune after flowering by cutting back old flowering growths on which there are no new shoots, and from time to time remove entirely some of the very oldest shoots. Propagate by half-ripened wood cuttings in June to July or hard-wood cuttings in autumn. Height varies from 4–12 ft.

P. 'Burfordensis'

A dense upright branching variety, which is apt to become bare at the base of the main shoots if not checked by pruning. It has large, single, white goblet-shaped scented blossoms. Plant 3 ft. apart. Height 8–10 ft.

P. coronarius (Common Mock Orange or Syringa)

Vigorous grower with cream-coloured flowers, sweetly scented. Plant 3–4 ft. apart. Height up to 12 ft.

P. × lemoinei 'Erectus'

Has close, upright, wiry stemmed growth, is small leaved and very sweetly scented. Makes a good close hedge. Plant 1½–2 ft. apart. Height 3–4 ft.

P. 'Manteau d'Hermine'

Bushy grower, dwarf in habit, with sweetly scented, double white flowers. Plant 1½ ft. apart. Height 3½–4 ft.

P. microphyllus

A dense shrub, with wiry twiggy growth, bearing very fragrant, pine-apple scented, pure white flowers in June. Plant 1½ ft. apart. Height 2½–3 ft.

Apart from those I have mentioned, there are a number of other varieties with single and double flowers which could be used to make attractive informal hedges and screens.

PHILLYREA

P. angustifolia

Hardy, evergreen shrub, closely related to osmanthus. It has narrow leaves 1–1½ in. long and fragrant, dull white flowers in May and June, followed by blue-black fruit. It is dense in habit and stands hard clipping, and for this reason it should be planted much more frequently than it is. Best planting size is young plants about 1½–2 ft. high. Space 1½–2 ft. apart. Plant September or April. Will thrive in any soil, in sun or shade. Trim in April. Propagate by half-ripened wood cuttings in August. Height up to 10 ft.

P. decora

Hardy, evergreen shrub, with dark glossy green leaves being longer and wider than those of *P. angustifolia*. It has white flowers in April. Other remarks as for *P. angustifolia*. Height 5–10 ft.

PHYLLOSTACHYS, *see* BAMBOO

PICEA (Spruce)

P. abies (Common or Norway Spruce)

A hardy conifer; in habit it is tapering and pyramidal, and its densely clothed branches bear short needles or leaves of a deep, glossy green. Although spruce is more frequently planted as a screen, it can be used as a hedge. Spruce does not like dry, sandy soils, nor is it a success as a sea-coast tree, but it thrives in cool, moist soils. When spruce is planted as a hedge choose transplanted seedlings 2–3 ft. high, spacing them 1½–2 ft. apart. Plant in September to October, or March to April. Trim by removing very long branches and stop back all other shoots. Propagation is by seed. For screen planting, choose plants 2–3 ft. high and space them 4–8 ft. apart; finally every other tree should be removed when necessary. Their rate of growth is approximately: 10 years, 10 ft.; 18 years, 25 ft.; 30 years, 50 ft., 80 years, 100 ft.

P. glauca (syn. *P. alba*) (White Spruce)

This is particularly hardy and is a first-rate shelter tree, similar in most respects to *P. abies*, except that the leaves are a greyer green. It has the advantage that it will thrive on windswept dunes and by the sea. Best planting size is 2–3 ft. high, spaced 4–8 ft. apart; as with *P. abies* remove every other one. Plant September to October, or March to April. Eventual height 60–100 ft.

P. mariana (syn. *P. nigra*) (Black Spruce)

A spruce with glaucous-blue leaves which is suitable where a lower screen is needed. Plant and treat as for other spruces. Eventual height 20–30 ft.

P. omorika (Serbian Spruce)

This spruce has a slender trunk, and its branches are of a fine pyramidal habit. The leaves or needles are dark glossy green above and greyish beneath. It is an ideal conifer for towns and does particularly well in the London area, where it keeps well furnished. A useful screen tree. Plant September to October, or March to April. Space trees 6–8 ft. apart. Height 60–80 ft.

P. sitchensis (Sitka Spruce)

In many ways this is similar to *P. omorika*, except that it is more upright in habit and its leaves are arranged all round the branchlets. The leaves are green above, silvery beneath and prickly. This conifer thrives in moist land and under peaty, heathery conditions. It is also wind-firm. A useful screen tree. Plant September to October, or March to April. Space trees 6–8 ft. apart. Height 80–100 ft.

PILEOSTEGIA

P. viburnoides

A hardy, evergreen self-clinging shrub, which attaches itself by its aerial roots, like ivy or the climbing hydrangea, *H. petiolaris*. This native of China, Japan and India, introduced 60 years ago (1908), is indeed an accommodating climber as it clambers equally well over a tree stump or a tree or up a wall, and will thrive on a north wall, though it prefers the comfort of a south or west one. It needs a well-drained loamy soil. The 4–6 in. long, dark green, leathery foliage makes an attractive background for the 3–5 in. wide panicles of creamy-white flowers which are produced during July, August and September. Plant pot-grown plants in spring. No pruning is required. Propagate from half-ripened cuttings in July inserted in sandy soil in a propagating frame in a greenhouse, or by ripened shoots in September, also inserted in a greenhouse. Height 15–20 ft.

PINE, *see* PINUS

PINUS (Pine)

Undoubtedly the best known and most planted of all the pines is *P.*

sylvestris (Scots Pine). It is frequently planted as a screen or wind-break. It has, however, the unfortunate habit of losing its lower branches, which means that all its screening virtues are at the top and not where they are wanted; nevertheless, the pines play a worthy part as screen and shelter trees. Pines can be found growing on all types of soil. All pines resent disturbance, therefore always plant young trees 1–1½ ft. high or 1½–2 ft.—no higher, as nothing will be gained from taller plants. For screens and windbreaks double rows are best. At first space them 3 ft. apart, later thinning them out to 6–9 ft.; I have seen them thinned to 12 ft. apart. The distance varies in accordance with the species, the number of rows and the type of screen or windbreak that is needed. Where several rows are planted, space the outer row at 6 ft. apart; this ensures better root development of the main line of defence. Thinning can take place when trees are 8–10 ft. high. Plant in September or April. No trimming will be needed. Propagation is by seed. (The heights given at the end of each species refer to old mature trees.)

P. mugo (syn. *P. montana*) (Mountain Pine)

This pine is much smaller in stature than the others, but it has different virtues to its credit. It thrives on almost all soils, including rocky ones, and in the driest situations, standing up to exposure and drought exceedingly well, but it is of little use by the sea. Height up to 15 ft.

P. muricata (Bishop's Pine)

A tough-looking conifer. Its cones sit on its branches as though they had been glued on, and remain thus for a considerable time. It has dark green foliage. It stands up to wind, particularly salt winds and sea sprays. When visiting Guernsey in 1957 I noticed several fine specimens. It grows in most soils but not chalk. Height 50 ft.

P. nigra (syn. *P. n. austriaca*) (Austrian Pine)

Not quite such a fine pine as the Corsican. It has dark green foliage, but loses its bottom branches as it gets older. It is wind-hardy and well suited to exposed situations, and thrives on poor chalky soils. Plant young trees when they are 1 ft. high. Height 80–100 ft.

P. n. maritima (syns. *P. calabrica* and *P. laricio*) (Corsican Pine). This is a very hardy pine, with handsome, dark green foliage. It has the merit of

237

holding its branches well down to the ground. It is an excellent wind resister; thrives in almost any soil and does exceptionally well in sandy soil. Unfortunately it is a bad transplanter and, therefore, small plants about 1 ft. high are best. Height 80–100 ft.

P. pinaster (Cluster or Maritime Pine)

This pine is not one to plant where protection low down is needed, as its branches are mostly at the top. Its dark green needles are 4–8 in. long. Its chief virtue is that it is particularly useful in sandy soils and exposed maritime districts—hence one of its common names. This species is much planted at Bournemouth. Height 80–100 ft.

P. radiata (syn. *P. insignis*) (Monterey Pine)

A pine which is given a richness of colour by its grassy-green foliage. Its needles, which are 2–5 in. long, are very soft and pliable. The Monterey pine is fast growing and thrives best in mild maritime districts; it is also wind-hardy. Dry soils which are deep and rich seem to suit it. Height 80–100 ft.

P. sylvestris (Scots Pine)

The doyen of pines. How often one has seen a lone pine and admired its singular beauty, its reddish-brown trunk, with several stub-like branches capped by small grey-green needles and small brown cones! This is a very wind-hardy tree; it succeeds inland and in coastal areas, but does not stand salt or sea spray. When contorted by the wind it becomes more charming than ever. The Scots pine can be planted as a rough farm hedge or screen at 2 ft. apart. It is excellent for screens where protection low down is not wanted. It thrives on most soils but does best on light, gravelly loam. Height 80–100 ft. (Plate 26.)

PIPTANTHUS

P. laburnifolius (syns. *P. nepalensis* and *Thermopsis laburnifolia*) (Evergreen Laburnum)

Not a climbing shrub in the true sense but a useful evergreen wall shrub, though deciduous during severe winters. It has trifoliate leaves, and bright yellow, pea-shaped flowers resembling those of the laburnum. The flowers are closely packed, being in erect clusters 2–3 in. long and produced in May. It enjoys the protection of a south or west wall or fence. It grows well in most soils except chalk soils. Plant in spring—pot-grown plants. Prune in February, when old, worn out wood should be cut out and long shoots shortened by about half their length; other shoots should be retied securely. Propagate by seeds sown in March, or take cuttings of half-ripened shoots in July or August, inserting them in a sandy compost in a warm propagating case. Height 8–12 ft.

PITTOSPORUM

This attractive evergreen tree is suitable only for hedges and screens in the milder counties; in coastal areas they will make good hedges or screens from 15–20 ft. high, though for a normal garden hedge 5–12 ft. high is sufficient. The foliage is grey-green and leathery in texture, and the flowers, which are often dark chocolate-purple, white or creamy-yellow, are sweetly fragrant. Pittosporum will grow in a good loamy well-drained soil, and also in sand or chalk soils. The best example I know growing in chalk is the tall hedge of *P. tenuifolium* in the late Sir Frederick Stern's garden at Highdown near Goring-by-Sea, Sussex, though a well-grown hedge at Warnham Court, Horsham, Sussex, succumbed to the frost of 1962–3 winter. Pittosporums do not transplant easily, therefore young pot-grown plants 1½–2 ft. high are of the best planting size, planted 2 ft. apart in September or April. Trim in April with a pair of secateurs. Propagate by cuttings of half-ripened wood in June to July, inserted in a close case, with bottom heat. Mist propagation is useful for striking pittosporum cuttings. When seed is available sow in March or April under glass. Height 10–20 ft.

P. buchananii

Thinnish leaves, dark glossy green, dark purple flowers in April. It is hardy in the south and west areas and by the sea. It is erect in habit. Height 10–20 ft.

P. ralphii

Similar to *P. buchananii*, except that its leaves are downy and it does not grow so tall. It has dark crimson flowers. According to the late J. Coutts, this is the hardiest of the genus. Height 8–15 ft.

239

P. tenuifolium (syn. *P. mayi*)

This is the most commonly planted pittosporum. The young wood is almost black, the wavy leaves are pale shining green. The chocolate-purple, honey-scented flowers appear in May. The cultivar 'Silver Queen' has attractive grey-green foliage. Height 10–20 ft.

PLEACHING LIMES, *see* TILIA

PODOCARPUS

P. andinus (syn. *Prumnopitys elegans*)

This conifer is a native of the Andes of Chile and is in many respects similar to yew. In the arboretum nursery at Kew there is a hedge of this conifer some 3–4 ft. high and 2 ft. wide; it is perhaps not outstanding but is interesting as something different from the usual hedge. It can be grown on any type of soil. Plant young bushes 1½–2 ft. apart. Trim in August or September. Cut the sides fairly severely, or else the width will increase at the expense of height. Propagate by seed or cuttings, in July, inserted in a heated close case. Height as a hedge 5–6 ft., as a tree up to 10 ft.

POLYGONUM

P. baldschuanicum (Russian Vine or Mile-a-Minute Plant)

This vigorous and fast growing deciduous twiner is appropriately named the Mile-a-Minute Plant on account of its very rapid growth. It will, in fact, grow as much as 15 ft. in a season. It has pale, bright green arrow-head-shaped leaves, 2–4 in. long. Although its creamy-white, slightly tinged pink, flowers are small, each loose panicle is so large that when a well-established plant is in full bloom it is a sight to behold from July to October. When grown against a wall or fence it must have some form of support around which it can twine. It makes an ideal plant to cover an old tree stump or, climb a tree, deciduous or evergreen. In London after the Second World War, I noticed several shored-up buildings covered by *P. baldschuanicum*. It is not fussy with regard to soil. Plant in autumn or spring, pot-grown plants. I have known cases where it has

ABOVE LEFT: the opalescent blue foliage of *Ruta graveolens* 'Jackman's Blue', a variety of rue

ABOVE RIGHT: *Senecio greyi* has yellow flowers and striking, silvery-grey foliage

BELOW: sweet-scented rosemary, *Rosmarinus officinalis*, makes a neat informal hedge

A hedge-bank of *Hydrangea macrophylla* at Rosewarne, Camborne, Cornwall

An informal rose hedge of 'Zéphirine Drouhin', at the Northern Horticultural Society's Garden at Harlow Car, Harrogate; the cerise-pink flowers are raspberry scented

The hybrid musk rose 'Penelope' has pale pink and salmon shaded, fragrant flowers

taken a little while to establish plants, though usually it romps away. Pruning is only necessary when plants are grown where space is limited, such as on walls or fences or over a shed. In such cases, prune in the autumn after flowering or in February when growths should be shortened and tied in. Propagate by heel cuttings of half-ripened shoots in July or August, inserted in a frame with gentle heat; or by hard-wood cuttings in the autumn.

POMEGRANATE, *see* PUNICA

PONCIRUS

P. trifoliata (syns. *Aegle sepiaria, Citrus trifoliata* and *Limonia trifoliata*)
Hardy, deciduous citrus-like shrub, with formidable spines. It has dark green angular branches and trifoliate leaves. In May and June it produces large, pure white, sweetly-scented blossoms which are followed by small fruits, orange in shape and colour. Best planting size is young pot-grown plants 1–1½ ft. high, spaced at 2 ft. apart and planted in October to March. Thrives best in moderately rich loamy soil, in a sunny position. Although poncirus responds well to close clipping it should be spared unnecessary trimming if flowers and fruits are wanted. Any clipping needed should be undertaken after flowers fade. Propagate by seed. Height 8–12 ft.

POPLAR, *see* POPULUS

POPULUS (Poplar)

Hardy, deciduous tree of vigorous habit, the poplar is much used where fast growing screens are wanted. In fact, there can hardly be any tree more frequently planted as a screen than *Populus nigra* 'Italica', the Lombardy poplar. Fortunately, poplars are not fastidious as to soil and can be grown almost anywhere. They are, perhaps, at their best when growing in a moist loam, but they grow equally well in sandy, gravel or chalk soils, provided such soils are not too dry.

Although the poplar is the most common screen tree, many unfavourable remarks have been written and spoken about it, because of its far-reaching roots, which can, and sometimes do, penetrate drains, and cause cracking of garden and house walls, etc. In the latter case it is not the roots that actually cause the damage but the soil in which the trees are growing. In particular the shrinkable clays are the worst offenders; for in very dry weather the roots extract moisture from the soil in order that the tree can exist, and in consequence the soil becomes leached of moisture. When eventually rain does come, the soil expands and causes the brickwork to crack. In view of this, caution should be exercised before planting poplars near to buildings, and especially in respect of your neighbours' property. The results of such damage and its legal consequences are explained in Chapter 5 (page 77). I cannot do better than quote the advice given by A. D. C. le Sueur in his book *Hedges, Shelterbelts and Screens* (Country Life): 'While it is impossible to lay down definite distances they should certainly not be planted within 20 to 30 yards of houses or drainage installations.' From these measurements one can safely plant a row of Lombardy poplars at the end of a normal suburban garden, provided the dividing boundary is at least 30 yd. away from buildings on the opposite side or sides, and as many such gardens are placed back to back it is normally safe. As I have said, poplars are fast growing, but fortunately their height can be kept in reasonable check by pruning, and one frequently sees rows of pollarded Lombardy poplars, particularly on the boundaries of playing fields.

Poplar wood is brittle and during storms there is a tendency for branches to snap. When this happens they should be cut off cleanly.

Generally speaking, the fastigiate or pyramidal growing forms are more suitable for the smaller garden than the wider spreading kinds.

Although poplars are hardy trees they are liable to attacks of bacterial canker which causes unsightly swellings in older trees and occasionally in younger ones; they also suffer from die back. The only remedy is to cut out the offending portions wherever possible.

Best planting size for poplars is from 8–12 ft.; planting distances vary according to the purpose for which the trees are required. Lombardy poplars can, therefore, be spaced from 5–15 ft. apart, but the most satisfactory distance is from 8–10 ft. apart. The more spreading kinds such as *P. alba* will need the full 15 ft. or more, again according to site, conditions, and requirements. It must not be thought, because poplars are vigorous and fast growing and will thrive in almost any soil, that it does not require initial preparation; a moderate dressing of rotted manure or some other form of humus will be invaluable in giving them a fair start.

242

Poplars should be pruned during the winter months, after the foliage is off, and before the sap begins to rise; just before or just after Christmas is a good time. Propagate by hard-wood cuttings 12 in. long in November to December; these root easily when inserted in a prepared bed out of doors.

There are many species of poplars to choose from, but the following list will be sufficient for the average garden, and for that matter for farm, park or roadside planting. In the last case the Lombardy poplar can look very effective when planted on either side of a roadway. When considering heights of the respective poplars, always remember that they are fast growing and can easily be reduced in height when necessary, or young trees replanted.

P. alba (Abele or White Poplar)

Very hardy and especially useful for seaside planting, being resistant to salt winds, and even growing on windswept cliffs where trees will take the form of scrubby bushes. The young shoots and undersides of the leaves of this poplar are covered with a thick white wool. Height 80–100 ft.

P.a. 'Pyramidalis' (syn. *P.a.* 'Bolleana' (Bolle's Poplar). This resembles the Lombardy poplar in habit; like *P. alba*, it has white wool on the undersides of the leaves. It makes a useful street tree. Height 70 ft.

P. × berolinensis (Berlin Poplar)

Another very hardy poplar, again similar in habit to the Lombardy poplar. It is compact in habit and has dark green dense foliage. According to the Forestry Commission Bulletin, No. 19, on poplars: 'It appears to be canker-resistant and should be valuable for street planting.' In North America, it is, I understand, used for windbreaks. Height 60–80 ft.

P. nigra 'Italica' (Lombardy Poplar)

Hardy and the most popular of all poplars for windbreaks, screens and shelters. Its fastigiate or pyramidal habit is almost too well known to need more description, being so often seen standing as sentinels against the skyline. Height will reach 100 ft.

P. 'Robusta'. Hardy, fast-growing poplar of semi-pyramidal habit, making a handsome tree. The young leaves are reddish. Height 80–100 ft.

243

P. trichocarpa (Black Cottonwood or Western Balsam Poplar)

This hardy poplar is very vigorous in growth and as a screen or wind-break should be used only in a garden of some size, and certainly not in a small one. Where room is available plant it by all means, if only for its wonderful balsam-scented leaves. Even its winter buds are coated with a balsamic gum. Its leaves are some 8–10 in. long and half as wide, dark green above, white and net veined beneath. Height 100 ft. or more.

PORTUGAL LAUREL, *see Prunus lusitanica*

POTENTILLA

P. fruticosa (Shrubby Cinquefoil)

Hardy, deciduous low-growing shrub of bushy habit, suitable for a low hedge up to 4 ft. high. Its strawberry-like blossoms are in varying shades of yellow and are produced from June to August. It is a native of the north of England. It grows as well by the sea as in inland areas and grows best in a good loamy soil, but it will grow in any soil, including chalk soils.

Best planting size is young plants 1–1½ ft. high, spaced at 1–1½ ft. apart, planted October to March. Trim in March. Propagate by cuttings of half-ripened wood of the current year, in late summer.

P. f. farreri. Golden-yellow flowers, May–September. Height 2–3 ft.

P.f. 'Farrer's White'. Pure white flowers, June to September. Height 3–4 ft.

P. f. grandiflora 'Jackman's Variety'. Brilliant yellow flowers June to September. Height 3–4 ft.

P.f. 'Katherine Dykes'. Lemon-yellow flowers May to October. Height 5 ft.

P. f. 'Vilmoriniana'. Creamy-white flowers, silvery-grey foliage, July to October. Height 4–5 ft.

PRIVET, *see* LIGUSTRUM

PRUMNOPITYS, *see* PODOCARPUS

PRUNUS

P. avium (Wild or Common Cherry, or Gean)

This hardy deciduous tree fills the air with the almond scent from its white flowers in April, and enriches the copses, woods and hedgerows in autumn with its tints of brown, red and crimson foliage. It has small blackish-red cherries which are usually bitter. It is hardy by the sea. It will grow in almost any soil, though it prefers rich deep loam over a chalk subsoil. An ideal tree to plant in a spinney or belt of mixed trees for shelter. Often trees are rather upright in habit. Plant young trees 9–12 ft. apart, October to March. Propagate by seed. Height up to 60 ft.

P. cerasifera (Myrobalan or Cherry Plum)

A deciduous spiny tree producing many small pure white blossoms at the end of March and early April. When allowed to grow informally it produces small red fruits during the summer. It is fast growing and makes a strong hedge, and is particularly useful to plant in heavy clay soils, where it grows exceedingly well. Fortunately it does not like very dry soils. It grows in lime soils and does well by the sea. Generally speaking it can be treated in a very similar manner to hawthorn or quickthorn.

Best planting size is about 3–4 ft. high, spaced at 1½–2 ft. apart and planted during October to March. With newly-planted hedges the bushes should be cut back to within 1 ft. of ground level to prevent a gappy bottom at the hedge. Trim during July or August. Where over-grown and neglected hedges require severe cutting back, this is best done during December. Propagate by hard-wood cuttings during the winter. Height up to 20 ft.

P. c. blireana. It has wine-red leaves and very double pink flowers. It makes a pretty hedge and is best trimmed immediately after flowering. Trim it so as to encourage it to form a rounded top. Plant 1 ft. apart. Height up to 15 ft.

P.c. 'E. M. Myrobalan B'. A cultivar recently introduced and known under the varietal name 'Greenglow', having shiny green leaves and white flowers. It makes vigorous growth and its colour and habit are good. This, with *P.c.* 'Pissardii' (*P.c.* 'Atropurpurea') makes a flamboyant effect when planted at the rate of one 'Greenglow' to two 'Pissardii'. Height up to 15 ft., but hedges are best kept at 5–6 ft.

245

P.c. 'Pissardii' (syn. *P.c.* 'Atropurpurea') and *P.c.* 'Nigra'. These can both be used to form a very attractive hedge with purple or dark purple leaves, bearing whitish-pink and deeper pink blossoms respectively at the end of March to early April. The first hedge of *P.c.* 'Pissardii' I saw was at Droitwich, Worcestershire in 1945. It makes a most decorative hedge during the summer with its striking purple-coloured foliage. Plant *P.c.* 'Pissardii' 2 ft. apart and *P.c.* 'Nigra' 1½ ft. apart. Other remarks as for *P. cerasifera*. Height up to 20 ft.

P.c. 'Rosea' (Sloepink). A pink-flowered form of the sloe, which makes a neat formal hedge. It has bright bronze leaves turning to bronze-brown when older which remain on the hedge until December. It blooms in late March to early April. Trim immediately after flowering. Plant 1½ ft. apart. Height 3–4 ft.

P. 'Cistena' ('Crimson Dwarf'). An attractive prunus with deep crimson foliage. As it will never grow too tall or large it is an ideal hedge for the small garden. It has single, large white flowers, as much as ½ in. wide, with purple centres. It flowers on the young wood. Although growth is vigorous, hedges are best kept to a height of 2–4 ft. Trim immediately after flowering. Plant 1 ft. apart. Height 5–7 ft.

P. incisa (The Fuji Cherry)

This Japanese cherry makes an excellent internal low, flowering hedge; one of its great attributes is that it does not resent the knife, and can therefore be kept neat and trim. It has single white flowers which, on opening, have a tinge of pink. Very free flowering. A fine example of a hedge can be seen at The Grange, Benenden, Kent, that famous garden of cherries belonging to Captain Collingwood Ingram. Trim immediately after flowering. Plant 1½ ft. apart. Height 5–7 ft.

P. laurocerasus (Common or Cherry Laurel)

Hardy evergreen with large leathery bright to dark green leaves. This shrub is often despised as being a Victorian legacy because of the closely cropped bushes found in station yards or approaches. Such accusations are quite unjustified, for a well-groomed boundary hedge of laurel can make a deal of difference to any garden. It also makes a first-class wind screen and an ideal background to a tennis court. It is a useful shrub for planting as a screen beneath large trees, where it can be allowed to grow more or less informally. It thrives in almost any type of soil, including chalk soils. Best planting sizes are from 1½–3 ft. high, planted at 1½–2 ft. apart in September to October, or March to April. Trim where time and labour allows with secateurs in April or July. Shears are not to be recommended, as they slash the large leaves in half and make them look ugly. I must admit, however, that I have used shears on established hedges on many occasions; and a neighbour cuts his laurel hedge with an electric hedge-trimmer most successfully. Propagate by hard-wood cuttings in October. Height 5–20 ft. (Plate 16.)

P.l. 'Caucasica'. Long, dark green foliage about 3 in. wide. Height 5–20 ft.

P.l. 'Rotundifolia'. The leaves are of a lighter shade of green, and half as broad as they are long. Height 5–20 ft.

P.l. 'Schipkaensis'. An exceptionally hardy laurel with dark green, narrow leaves, suitable for a smaller hedge. Plant 1½ ft. apart. Height 3–5 ft.

P. lusitanica (Portugal Laurel)

Handsome evergreen with dark, glossy, bay-like leaves and long racemes of white flowers in June followed by dark purple fruits when grown informally. When properly cared for it makes a neat and close hedge. Best planting size is 1½–3 ft. high, though slightly larger plants can be moved satisfactorily. Plant September to October, or March to April and space them 1½–2 ft. apart. Trim with secateurs in April or July, though shears can be used. Height 10–20 ft.

P. spinosa (Blackthorn or Sloe)

A hardy, deciduous, thorny shrub, mostly planted as a farm hedge. In March it is covered with small pure white flowers. It has the objectionable feature of sending up innumerable suckers, which would be a considerable nuisance in a garden. It will tolerate very windy sites and is especially useful in coastal areas. Best planting size is 1½–2 ft. high, spaced 1 ft. apart and planted in October to March. Trim any time during the winter months. Propagate by seed or suckers. Height up to 15 ft.

P. triloba (syns. *P. t. multiplex* and *P. t. flore pleno*)

This dwarf deciduous tree or bush which belongs to the almond section, is all too often spoken of and written about as *P. simplex*, the flowers of which are pinkish-white and single, whereas those of *P. t. multiplex* are a delicate rose-pink and double. Last year's shoots are covered with a mass of 1½ in. wide, pompon blooms, which are borne singly or in pairs at each bud from the end of March to the end of April. Although this prunus is often grown as a bush, it looks and flowers more profusely when grown against a south wall where it should be trained out in a fan-wise fashion. It does, of course, need some form of support to which it can be tied, such as wires or trellis. Plant October to March. Prune immediately after flowering, usually May, by cutting back all shoots that have flowered to within two or three buds of the old wood. Propagate by budding on to stocks of Brompton or St. Julian in late July or early August. Height 9–12 ft. high and as much or more wide.

PSEUDOTSUGA

P. menziesii (syns. *Pseudotsgua douglasii* and *P. taxifolia* (Douglas Fir)

This is not a hedge plant but a fast-growing screen tree. According to Alfred Gaut, in *Seaside Planting of Trees and Shrubs*: 'It grows when sheltered near the sea in Yorkshire,' I know from experience that it grows well in Sussex and likes a moist soil, but not chalk. Its leaves are grass-green with a glaucous sheen, it has reddish-brown, pointed buds. Best planting size is 3–4 ft. high, spacing them at 4–5 ft. apart and removing every other tree as soon as they begin to touch. Plant in September or April. Propagate by seed. Height 100–150 ft.

PUNICA

P. granatum (Pomegranate)

A deciduous flowering shrub; provided it is given the protection of a warm south or west wall, it will produce its scarlet-red, crumpled flowers of five to seven petals, each bloom being 1–1½ in. wide. Its flowers are borne singly, though are sometimes in pairs at the ends of several short shoots from June to September. In favourable summers deep yellow, orange-shaped fruits may be produced, but they seldom ripen. Punicas grow well in all soils except chalk soils. Plant March to April, choosing pot-grown plants. Prune by removing weak or thin growth, and thin out crowded shoots in February, also cut back any very long ones. Propagate by half-ripened cuttings inserted in sandy-peaty compost in a closed propagating frame with medium bottom heat. Height 15 ft. *P. g.* 'Flore Pleno' has double red flowers, in all other respects see *P. granatum.*

PURSLANE, TREE, *see Atriplex halimus*

PYRACANTHA (Firethorn)

These hardy evergreen flowering and berrying shrubs, commonly known as the firethorns, make useful informal or semi-formal hedges, where berries are required. With formal hedges berries will be few, if any. Pyracantha has thorns and small dark green glossy leaves, and white hawthorn-like flowers in May and June, followed by orange, red or yellow berries in autumn. It is an ideal shrub for towns and industrial areas. It does not appear fussy as to soil, as plants can be seen on heavy, light and chalk soils. Always plant young pot-grown plants; the best size is 1½–2 ft. high, spaced 1½–2 ft. apart, planted in September to October, or April. Trim in April where possible with secateurs. Propagate by seed, or half-ripened wood cuttings in July and August, or hard-wood cuttings in autumn. Height 8–15 ft. Pyracanthas are usually seen adorning walls or fences where they will provide a sheet of white flowers in May and June, followed by a crop of brightly coloured berries in autumn and winter, against a background of dark green evergreen foliage. Other remarks for planting and propagation as for hedges. Pruning, however, entails shortening the longest side shoots when required in April. Where space is limited, slightly more severe pruning will be necessary, but this will, to some extent, reduce the crop of berries.

P. atalantioides (syn. *P. gibbsii*)

Tall growing, upright and of vigorous habit, with large oval leaves and crimson-scarlet berries. Very hardy. Will reach 15 ft. in height, though for a hedge 8–10 ft. is enough.
P.a. 'Aurea'. Rich golden-yellow berries, otherwise similar in all respects to *P. atalantioides.*

P. coccinea

Coral-red berries. Height 8–15 ft.

P.c. 'Lalandei'. Orange-red berries; the most popular of all the pyracanthas. Vigorous and upright in habit. Up to 14 ft. high, but a hedge of 8 ft. or less is sufficient.

P. rogersiana

Reddish-orange berries, small leaves, 8–10 ft. high. A hedge of 5–6 ft. is sufficient.
P.r. 'Flava'. Bright yellow berries; remarks as for *P. rogersiana*.
P. 'Watereri'. Red berries, dense twiggy habit 8–10 ft. high, therefore a hedge of 5–6 ft. high is sufficient.

QUERCUS (Oak)

A hardy, deciduous tree, though there are evergreen forms. Normally one thinks of oaks as trees with massive trunks and limbs; one might assume that to have them as shelter belts of moderate proportions was quite out of the question, and they would be even less suitable as a hedge. But one can see gnarled and wind-blown specimens of small stature which are often clipped to form a hedge.

Q. cerris (Turkey Oak)

This oak is so called on account of its mossy-cupped acorns, which look like Turks' caps. According to the late J. Coutts in *Hedges and Screens*: 'There is a good hedge of this oak in the county of Surrey.' It is a vigorous tree and is excellent for planting in chalky soils and maritime areas. It is, however, not fastidious over soils. It has long, dark lustrous green leaves which are very coarsely toothed. Although deciduous, it often retains its leaves well through the winter. Best planting size is 1½–2 ft. high, spaced at 3–4 ft. apart, October to March. Trim in late summer. Propagate by seed. Height in windswept areas 25–30 ft., a specimen tree 100 ft.

Q. ilex (Evergreen, Holly or Holm Oak)

This dark, evergreen-leaved, sombre looking oak is probably the most planted of any for oak hedges. It is a very heavily foliaged tree. The leaves vary in size and shape, but are normally 1½–3 in. long and ½–1 in. wide. It does exceedingly well on poor, sandy and gravelly soils and on chalk soils. It is very hardy and flourishes on the sea coast and wind-swept cliff tops. In April it starts to shed its leaves, just before the new growth commences. It transplants badly, so always plant small pot-grown plants, preferably 1½–2 ft. high. Space them 1½–2 ft. apart. Plant in September, April or early May. Trim in April. Propagate by seed. Height for a hedge 15–20 ft., for a screen up to 30 ft.

Q. robur (syn. *Q. pedunculata*) (Common Oak)

Hardy, deciduous tree, suitable for planting in a mixed hedge of holly, quickthorn, hazel, hornbeam or beech. When so treated it will keep its leaf well throughout the winter. I once knew of a fine bush oak some 5 ft. high which was a veritable thicket owing to consistent clipping. In other respects treat as *Q. cerris*. Height for hedges 5–10 ft., for screens 20–60 ft.

QUICKTHORN, *see* CRATAEGUS

QUINCE, JAPANESE, *see* CHAENOMELES

RHODODENDRON

R. luteum (syn. *Azalea pontica*) (Pontic Azalea)

This is a very old shrub; according to John Street, 'We first hear of *Rhododendron luteum* (syn. *Azalea pontica*) in 410 B.C. after one of Xenophon's battles in the famous retreat of the Ten Thousand.' This shrub is undoubtedly very handsome as a flowering deciduous hedge. In May and June it has yellow, honeysuckle-like flowers which are very fragrant; in autumn the leaves are richly coloured in varying shades of red and crimson. It makes a good informal hedge. Azaleas, like other ericaceous subjects, dislike lime or chalk and prefer the lighter, loamy soils to the heavy cold clay soils.

They make an ideal hedge to plant between the formal and informal garden; they need room to spread. Heavier soils should have leafmould, peat, hop manure or well-decayed farmyard manure added to improve the texture of the soil. Plant young bushes 1½–2 ft. high, spacing them 2–3 ft. apart, from October to April. Trim March to April. Propagate by seed or layering. Height 6–8 ft.

R. japonicum (syn. *Azalea mollis*)

This species and its varieties are similar to *R. luteum*, but can be had in yellow, orange, salmon, pink and red. Height 4–8 ft.

R. japonicum × **sinensis** (syn. *Azalea mollis* × *sinensis*)

These hybrids are equally colourful, but both these and *R. japonicum* varieties are far more expensive than the Pontic azalea. Cultivation for *R. japonicum* and *R. japonicum* × *sinensis* is the same as for *R. luteum*. Height 4–8 ft.

R. ponticum (Common Rhododendron)

A hardy, evergreen, flowering shrub or small tree. Perhaps one of our most outstanding large-leaved evergreens, which will thrive anywhere and in almost any soil, except lime. In Crawley, Sussex, they flourish in the moist and sometimes heavy clay as well as they do in the lighter sandy soils of Ascot in Berkshire and the acid peaty soils of Woking in Surrey or Bournemouth in Hampshire. The dark glossy green leaves, 4–8 in. long and 1–1½ in. wide, look attractive at any season of the year; and in June informal hedges or screens produce many trusses of purplish-pink flowers. This handsome evergreen was introduced in 1763; it is an adaptable shrub, tolerating shade or half-shade and smoky industrial cities. It makes good draught-proof screens and is very wind-hardy. Unlike many shrubs it transplants equally well when young or old, age being an advantage where immediate shelter or screening is required. Although semi-formal hedges or screens do produce flowers, it is equally suitable as a formal hedge and stands regular clipping exceedingly well.

For a young hedge the suitable planting sizes are 1½–2 ft. or 2–2½ ft. spaced 1½–2 ft. apart. Where larger plants are used, space at 3–4 ft. apart. Plant September to October or March to April. Trim in April or directly after flowering, when all faded flower heads should be removed by pinching them out with thumb and finger. The rhododendron does not object to hard pruning. Hedges can be as low as 3–4 ft. or as high as 6–10 ft. Propagate by seed sown in heat in January. Height 8–15 ft. (Plate 16.)

R. 'Praecox'. Dark glossy green foliage, rosy-purple flowers from February to April. It is a compact evergreen shrub. A famous hedge of *R.* 'Praecox' is at the Edinburgh Botanic Gardens. Height 2–4 ft.

R. Hardy Hybrids. These can be used for screening purposes and treated in a similar way to *R. ponticum*, but unless seedlings of named varieties can be purchased, and young plants at that, it is an expensive way of planting a screen. Height 8–15 ft.

RHYNCOSPERMUM, *see* TRACHELOSPERMUM

RIBES (Currant)

The majority of ribes are deciduous, though there are evergreen species. The flowering currant *R. sanguineum* is perhaps one of our most colourful spring flowering shrubs and not fussy over soils which applies to the genus *Ribes* generally.

R. laurifolium

This interesting evergreen flowering currant has leathery, dark green laurel-like leaves, oval to ovate in shape and up to 5 in. long, which are coarsely toothed. The female flowers are greenish-yellow, each about $\frac{1}{3}$ in. wide and borne on drooping racemes 1–2 in. long, carrying up to 12 flowers in February. The flowers are unisexual, the male ones being the most outstanding. It needs the protection of a wall, where it can be trained and tied. Plant, March to April or September to October. Pruning is seldom required except to keep the plant in shape. Propagate by cuttings of half-ripened shoots inserted in sandy soil in a propagating case, in July or August. Height 4–6 ft.

R. odoratum (syn. *R. aureum*) (Buffalo Currant)

Hardy, deciduous flowering shrub with pale green, three-lobed leaves, which are richly coloured in late summer and autumn. In April it produces bright golden-yellow, specially-scented flowers. Best planting size is young plants 2–3 ft. high, spaced 1–1½ ft. apart. Plant October to March. Trim immediately after flowering. Propagate by hard-wood cuttings in autumn. Height 5–8 ft.

R. sanguineum (Flowering Currant)

A hardy, deciduous shrub. Its three-to-five-lobed green leaves are 2–4 in. wide, less in length. In April it produces deep rosy-red flowers which hang down in racemes 2–4 in. long. It is a great pity that *R. sanguineum* and its varieties are not planted a great deal more as hedges and screens. In a previous garden I had a short hedge 9 ft. high and 2 ft. wide which flowered regularly every spring. During the summer it made an excellent screen from my next-door neighbour. Best planting size is 2–3 ft. high, spaced 1½ ft. apart, October to March. Trim after flowering, and give a further light trim over with a pair of secateurs in late summer. Propagate by hard-wood cuttings in autumn. Height 8–10 ft. (Plate 30.)

R.s. 'Pulborough Scarlet'. One of the finest flowering currants, having rich crimson-red flowers. This variety was a chance seedling that appeared in a bed of yews at Cheal's Nursery at Pulborough, Sussex, in 1930, and was picked out by Mr. Daniel Chantler; the original bush was still thriving in 1945. Height 9–10 ft. All other remarks as for *R. sanguineum*.

R. speciosum (Fuchsia-flowered Gooseberry)

A deciduous spiny shrub having small gooseberry-like foliage and pendulous, scarlet, fuchsia-like tubular flowers, each flower being ½ in. long. They are borne in clusters of two to four. Wall protection is necessary and it certainly looks best when grown in this way. Other remarks as for *R. laurifolium*. Height 10–12 ft.

ROBLE BEECH, *see Nothofagus obliqua*

ROCK ROSE, *see* CISTUS

ROSA (Rose)

The rose must undoubtedly be the most popular and most planted shrub that is grown in the British Isles. It has so many uses, being adaptable for small or large gardens. It is ideal as a climbing plant, where it can be grown against a wall, fence, or trellis, or up a tree. Many species and varieties, especially the shrub and floribunda roses, are ideal for planting as hedges, both formally and informally. Purely for convenience's sake I have divided this section on roses into two parts, namely climbers and ramblers, and hedges, giving their colours, heights and time of flowering, together with their respective pruning requirements. With regard to soil, roses can be grown on all types of soil. On pages 111–12, 118–19 can be found tables of climbers and hedge roses.

CLIMBING AND RAMBLING ROSES

When one comes to consider climbing and rambling roses, it is almost impossible to do justice to this section of our 'queen of flowers' in just a few pages, especially when it is realized that a book entirely devoted to them has been written by that great authority Graham Stuart Thomas, *Climbing Roses Old and New*, so my notes on cultivation and selection of varieties and species will be no more than a guide to some of the best of them that are suitable for growing against walls and fences, over trees, arches or pergolas, and so on. There are, indeed, plenty to choose from, both for individual tastes and individual needs. All, however, require some kind of support; even if they are to grow up a tree, some form of training will be necessary at first.

Climbing roses are truly beautiful when correctly chosen for walls of houses; and when planted in conjunction with a clematis, the two together can create a beautiful display for many months.

Climbing and rambling roses are many and varied, in vigour and type of flower; they may be single, semi-double or double; they vary in length of flowering-time, and they may be hybrid tea roses, wichuraianas, perpetuals, floribundas or one of the many species. The Royal National Rose Society classifies them into four main groups.

Group 1   The true ramblers, which consist of hybrids of *Rosa wichuraiana* such as 'Dorothy Perkins', 'Excelsa' and 'François Juranville'.

Group 2   Those which belong to this group are those such as 'Paul's Scarlet', 'Albertine' (my favourite), 'Chaplin's Pink' and 'Albéric Barbier'.

Groups 3   These include the hybrid teas and other large flowered
and 4   varieties such as 'Mme Caroline Testout', 'Mme Butterfly', 'Etoile de Hollande' and 'Ena Harkness'. Also in this group is another of my favourites, 'Zéphirine Drouhin', a Bourbon climber.

SUPPORTING MATERIALS

Old apple trees are ideal hosts for the more vigorous climbers or ramblers. Trellis, arbors and pergolas all make excellent forms of support. On the walls of my own house the roses are supported by plastic covered galvanized wire, which is in a pleasant shade of green. There are, however, many other similar covered wires available on the market. Then there is wooden trellis, or galvanized wire which can be fixed by wall nails and strainers; or nails and small strips of lead, but I do not much favour this method. The use of a plastic strap, or a strip of lead or leather nailed to the wall is preferable. When planting against walls, see that the supports are fixed before planting.

Arches can be made out of bricks, stone, wood—rustic or formal iron, which may be galvanized-iron wire or plastic-coated wire.

Fences and fencing. These can be boarded or open, rustic or formal and made of wood, or chain-link plastic coated or galvanized.

Pergola, of brick, stone, Netlon, or wood, rustic or formal.

Pillars, of brick, stone or wood.

Sheds, wooden or brick.

Trees, and tree trunks alive or dead.

Walls, garden or house.

Wires, fixed by wall nails, with or without strainers.

Cultivation

This is, indeed, the most vital point when preparing to plant either rambler or climber, and in particular when the rose is to be planted near to a wall or fence where it could suffer seriously from lack of moisture. There is nothing better than to bastard trench the ground, i.e. double dig it; this is fully explained on page 24. Should the subsoil be clay, such as it is in my garden at Crawley, Sussex, then fork in hydrated lime at the rate of 3 lb. per sq. yd. This will help to break up the subsoil further, as well as being manually broken up with the fork. However, if your soil is chalky, gravelly, light or sandy, then do not apply the lime.

In the top layer of soil work in any organic humus-forming material that is available, such as leafmould, or well-rotted garden compost. At the same time also give a good sprinkling of bonemeal. It is advisable to do this preparation several weeks beforehand as this allows time for the soil to settle before actual planting.

Although moisture is an essential, drainage is equally important, and where the ground is waterlogged or poorly drained some form of drainage must be applied, such as land drains, clinkers or brushwood like heather laid in trenches; any of these will drain surplus water away. On the other hand, very dry ground should be well soaked, followed by a mulch of farmyard manure, lawn mowings or material from the compost heap.

256

A fine screen of the deciduous dawn redwood *Metasequoia glyptostroboides*

The author trimming a metasequoia hedge. In autumn the light green foliage changes to a rich pinky-brown

ABOVE: a screen in winter of Norway maple, *Acer platanoides*, backed by common laurel

BELOW: Scots pines, *Pinus sylvestris*, used as a wind break to an orchard

Give an annual feed of bonemeal in the autumn, and a rose or well balanced fertilizer in spring, plus a mulch of well-rotted manure or some form of humus. Today there are also foliar feeds which can be applied in accordance with the maker's instructions, and specially prepared rose fertilizers, such as Tonks.

PLANTING

When planting climbers or ramblers against a wall, fence or tree, bear in mind that the soil at the roots of plants in such situations can become exceedingly dry. It is, therefore, essential to give each climber a really good start by incorporating a liberal supply of humus such as well-rotted cow manure, rotted garden compost or leafmould. Also see that the ground is well dug, particularly necessary where the beds or borders are not much more than 12–18 in. wide, as mine are. This good initial preparation will be handsomely repaid. Do not plant tight against the wall, but about 6–9 in. away, as this allows a little more ease when training the shoots to the support. Certainly when planting against trees keep the plant 3–5 ft. away from the trunk, training the young shoots up a cane angled against the trunk. This will enable the roots of the plant to obtain sufficient moisture for their needs.

Plant only when the ground is in a suitable condition, that is, it should be neither too wet, nor too dry, and certainly not when snow or frost is on or in the ground. Set the plants at the same depth as they were in the nursery.

At the time of planting apply the mixture as recommended by the Royal National Rose Society, which is a double handful of meat and bonemeal to a 3-gal. pailful of peat; alternatively raw bonemeal can be used. First, work into the soil of the planting hole two good handfuls of the 'planting mixture'. Secondly, make a small mound of soil on which to rest the roots, which should be well spread out. Thirdly, give the roots a good covering of the planting mixture. Finally, replace the soil, the fine soil first, firming it lightly as the remainder is filled in, by firming first with the hands and finishing off with the feet, treading from the outside into the middle. If the ground is wet or heavy, do not overdo the treading.

PRUNING

Perhaps the pruning of rambler and climbers is not as controversial as that of bush roses; however, there are certain rules which, if followed, will give the best results.

There are four main groups:

Group 1   This includes the true ramblers which are all the hybrids of *Rosa wichuraiana*, such as 'Dorothy Perkins' and 'François Juranville'.

Group 2   The larger flowered ramblers like 'Albertine', 'Chaplin's Pink' and 'Paul's Scarlet'.

Groups 3 and 4   These are the true climbers, all the hybrid teas, other large flowered types and pillar roses, also Bourbons like 'Zéphirine Drouhin'.

Time of pruning
Groups 1 and 2   As soon as the flowers have finished, in early autumn or as soon as convenient after this; after all, the week-end gardener cannot always do everything according to the book.
Groups 3 and 4   These are pruned in late autumn or during the winter, again when most convenient.

Method of pruning
Group 1   The main object is to cut away, in early autumn, all the previous year's growth that has just finished flowering, cutting the shoots back to the ground. The growths which have grown during the summer are retained; these are not pruned but tied in carefully. It is these growths which will provide next year's flowers. Should there be insufficient new growths, which can happen in very dry seasons, then some of the older growths may have to be retained, and when this occurs prune back the laterals to two or three buds.

Group 2   With these, new growths are usually less in number than in Group 1, and more often than not, the new growths will be produced higher up on the old stems. In view of this there is a tendency with the older plants to become bare of new growth nearer the base of the plant, and it is, therefore, necessary from time to time to cut back one or two of the older stems to within 12–18 in. of ground level, always cutting them back to a sound bud. All other old wood higher up should be pruned by cutting it back to a point where new growths have started. In cases where a new leading shoot has not formed, then remove the old wood entirely. Do not prune the leading shoots, simply tie them in

258

carefully. Finally, cut back all shorter laterals to within 2–3 in. of the older wood. With ramblers, such as 'Albéric Barbier', 'Helenae', 'Kiftsgate', 'Longicuspis' and 'Wedding Day', growing through trees very little pruning will be necessary, in fact, in many cases well nigh impossible. However occasionally an old growth may need to be cut back as already recommended in Group 2.

Group 3 The pruning of the hybrid teas and other climbers in this group is much less drastic than that of the two former groups. Only the very old and exhausted wood should be cut out. All new growths are left unpruned unless they are damaged. All healthy laterals are cut back to within two or three buds of the older wood from which they spring. Do not, however, prune newly planted climbers in this group during their first year.

Group 4 With pillar roses and the less vigorous climbers all that is necessary is to cut out all dead, old or worn-out wood so that the plants are kept in good shape. Again, no pruning should be given during their first year after planting.

CULTIVARS

'Albéric Barbier'. Rambler. Almost evergreen, with rich green shiny foliage. Its pure yellow buds open into large, double creamy-white flowers, in large clusters. Vigorous and scented. Height 20 ft. Group 2.

'Albertine.' Rambler. Reddish, copper-pink buds, opening to rich copper-salmon-pink. Large double flowers, richly fragrant. Height 15 ft. Group 2.

'Allen Chandler.' Large-flowered climber of hybrid tea type. The semi-double blooms are a vivid scarlet, each flower being 3–4 in. across and borne in clusters. Fragrant. Height up to 30 ft. Group 4.

'Aloha.' Large flowered climber. Deep, glowing rose-pink, double blooms. Free flowering, perpetual. Richly fragrant, flowers well in autumn. Height 6 ft. Group 4.

'American Pillar.' Rambler. Large single bright rose flowers with a white centre, in huge clusters. Vigorous grower, rich glossy foliage. Height 20–25 ft. Blooms in July. Group 2.

'Casino.' Climbing hybrid tea type. Deep yellow buds, opening to a soft yellow, dark green glossy foliage, free flowering in summer and autumn, richly scented. Vigorous grower. Group 3.

'Chaplin's Pink Climber.' Climber. Warm pink, with golden stamens. Large semi-double flowers in large clusters. Vigorous, very hardy, fragrant. Summer flowering. Group 2.

'Clair Martin.' Climber or shrub rose. Large flowers, semi-double, clear pink with orange stamens very freely borne, vigorous and good foliage. Height up to 8 ft. Group 4.

'Copenhagen.' Climbing hybrid tea. Rich scarlet, large well-shaped pointed double blooms, very sweetly scented. A semi-climber, recurrent flowering. Height 8–10 ft. Group 4.

'Coral Dawn.' Large flowered climber. Large, double, pink flowers, in small clusters, scented, repeat flowering, a climber or pillar rose, fairly vigorous. Height up to 10 ft. Group 4.

'Crimson Conquest.' Climber, semi-double flowers, deep scarlet, fragrant; blooms in July. Group 2.

'Crimson Shower.' Rambler. Small, semi-double, crimson flowers, vigorous and long flowering July to mid-September. Group 1.

'Danse du Feu.' Large flowered climber. Brilliant orange-scarlet, double flowers, free flowering, perpetual. Height 7–8 ft. Group 4.

'Dorothy Perkins.' Rambler. Rich rose-pink, small double flowers, borne in large clusters. Vigorous, free flowering in July. Even though it mildews badly, many gardeners still like to grow this charming old variety. Height 18 ft. Group 1.

'Dortmund.' Kordesii climber. Large, single flowers, red with white eye, showy, free and recurrent blooming. Vigorous. Height up to 8 ft. Group 4.

'Elegance.' Large flowered climber. Deep gold shading to cream at the edges, vigorous, double blooms June to July, sometimes repeats later, slightly scented, hardy in the north. Group 4.

'Emily Gray.' Rambler. Coppery-yellow, semi-double flowers; the almost evergreen, shiny foliage is attractively red-tinted when young. It also has red stems. A beautiful rose. Group 2, but prune very lightly or it will be shy blooming.

'Ena Harkness, Climbing.' Large flowered climber. Bright crimson-scarlet, well formed, large full flowers, free blooming, well into autumn, fragrant. Group 3.

'Etoile de Hollande, Climbing.' Large flowered climber. The deep crimson red blooms of this famous hybrid tea are sweetly fragrant. It is vigorous and free flowering. Group 3.

'Excelsa.' Rambler. Large clusters of double bright rosy-crimson flowers; thick glossy foliage. Late blooming. Height 18 ft. Group 1.

filipes 'Kiftsgate'. This magnificent climber can transform a tree, such as an old apple tree, into a beautiful spectacle, through its clouds of hundreds of creamy-white, fragrant flowers, each 1½ in. wide, with orange-yellow stamens. It has small red hips in autumn. July. Height up to 30 ft. Group 2.

'François Juranville.' Rambler. Large double, deep fawn-pink flowers in clusters, sweetly scented, attractive red stems and glossy foliage. June flowering. Height 18 ft. Group 1.

'Golden Dawn, Climbing.' Large flowered climber. Pale buff-yellow, full flowers, very fragrant, fairly vigorous, summer flowering. Height about 8 ft. Group 3.

'Golden Showers.' Large flowered climber. The long pointed golden-yellow buds, open to hybrid-tea type clusters of semi-double blooms of clear golden-yellow, later paling to lemon; perpetual flowering, fragrant and moderately vigorous. Height 6–8 ft. Group 4.

'Goldilocks, Climbing.' Climber. Large clusters of rich yellow, small, double flowers paling to cream. Very free flowering, fragrant, moderately vigorous. Group 4.

'Gruss an Teplitz.' Chinensis shrub rose. Darkish crimson, very fragrant, recurrent flowering. Vigorous growth, height up to 8 ft. Little pruning required apart from removing old and worn out growths.

'Guinée.' Large flowered climber. Dark velvety scarlet, hybrid tea type blooms, large and very fragrant, dark red foliage, moderately vigorous. Height 8–10 ft. Group 4.

'Hamburger Phoenix.' Kordesii climber. Clusters of large, semi-double, rich scarlet-crimson flowers, deep green glossy foliage. Vigorous. Height 9 ft. Group 4.

'Handel.' Climber. The hybrid-tea sized flowers have an ivory base, with a suffusion of deep carmine on the edges of the petals. Perpetual flowering. Little pruning required. Height 8–12 ft.

'Helenae.' Rambler. Large heads of creamy-white flowers, richly fragrant; ideal for scrambling through trees. Height 15–20 ft. Group 2.

'High Noon.' Semi-climber. Bright canary-yellow, semi-double flowers, freely produced, recurrent flowering, fragrant. Height 6–12 ft. Group 4.

'Hugh Dickson.' Semi-climber. Hybrid-tea type, perpetual. Bright scarlet-crimson, free flowering, very richly scented, vigorous. Height up to 10 ft. Light pruning required; from time to time cut out old wood.

'Lady Hillingdon, Climbing.' Large flowered climber. Deep apricot-yellow to pale orange, medium-sized, semi-double flowers, very free flowering and vigorous, delicate tea scent. Height up to 20 ft. Group 3.

'Lady Sylvia, Climbing.' Large flowered climber. Perfect shape and colouring, flowers light pink with yellow base, hybrid-tea type blooms, very richly scented and very vigorous. It has few thorns and long stems. Height 20 ft. Group 3.

'Leverkeusen.' Kordesii climber. Large semi-double flowers, light yellow blooms on long sprays. Recurrent summer and autumn flowering, dark shiny foliage, vigorous. Height up to 10 ft. Group 4.

'Longicuspis.' Rambler. Masses of single white flowers with a banana-like fragrance. A vigorous grower and ideal for scrambling through trees. Height 20 ft. Group 2.

'Maigold.' Climber. Large semi-double, deep buff-yellow flowers with golden stamens, repeat flowering, vigorous, richly scented. Height 10–15 ft. Group 4.

'Meg.' Large flowered climber. Large clusters of single or semi-double flowers apricot-pink shading to yellow with centres of golden stamens. Vigorous and fragrant. Height 10–12 ft. Group 4.

'Mermaid.' Bracteata climber. Large single, soft, canary-yellow blooms, with evergreen or deciduous foliage, vigorous, sprawling climber. Perpetual flowering from June to October, a truly handsome rose. It dislikes transplanting and pot-grown plants are best, fragrant. Height 25–30 ft. The only pruning it requires is to cut out dead wood and keep the remainder tied within its space.

'Minnehaha.' Rambler. Large clusters of deep pink small, double flowers, glossy foliage, very vigorous. Height 15 ft. Group 1.

'Mme Alfred Carrière.' Noisettiana Climber. Very large semi-double flowers pale creamy-pink, fading to blush-white, very vigorous, free flowering rather intermittently. Height 20 ft. Group 4.

'Mme Caroline Testout, Climbing.' Large flowered climber. Warm silvery-pink double blooms, very free flowering and very vigorous, flowers in summer and again in autumn. Height 20 ft. Group 3.

'Mme Edouard Herriot, Climbing.' Large flowered climber. Orange-salmon flowers in June, often blooms again later in the summer. Moderately vigorous. Height 12–15 ft. Group 4.

'Mme Grégoire Staechelin.' Large flowered climber. The coral-pink, hybrid-tea type blooms are splashed with carmine on the outside, late May to early July. A truly beautiful rose, richly scented, very vigorous and free of mildew. Large dark glossy foliage, which remains almost throughout the winter. Although I have it on a west wall it also does well on a north wall. Height 20 ft. Group 3.

'Mrs. Sam McGredy, Climbing.' Hybrid-tea type, deep orange, coppery-pink flowers with coppery-red shadings, in May, dark mahogany shaded foliage, fragrant. Recurrent blooms in autumn. Height 15–18 ft. Group 3.

'New Dawn'. Rambler. Clusters of small silvery-pink double flowers, freely produced throughout the summer and early autumn, sweetly scented. Perpetual flowering. Height 20 ft. Group 2.

'Parade.' Large flowered climber. Large double flowers in small clusters of carmine-crimson, richly fragrant, perpetual flowering, vigorous, grows anywhere, even on a north-facing wall. Height 10–12 ft. Group 4.

'Parkdirektor Riggers.' Kordesii climber. Clusters of semi-double velvety crimson blooms, very free flowering and recurrent, dark green glossy foliage, vigorous. Height 12–15 ft. Group 3.

'Paul's Lemon Pillar.' Large flowered climber. Large well formed double blooms of pale lemon-yellow paling to white with a touch of primrose-green in the centre, fragrant, a beautiful rose flowering once in the summer. Height up to 20 ft. Group 4.

'Paul's Scarlet Climber.' Climber. Small clusters of semi-double, medium-sized, bright crimson-scarlet blooms. Little scent, an excellent pillar rose. Height up to 20 ft. Group 2.

'Pink Perpetué.' Kordesii climber. This beautiful repeat flowering climber has clusters of good sized double blooms of clear pink with carmine-pink reverse. Height up to 15 ft. Group 3.

'Purity.' Rambler. Semi-double pure white blooms, summer flowering

263

only, attractive glossy foliage, sweetly scented, very vigorous. Height 12 ft. Group 2.

'Réveil Dijonnais.' Climber. Large semi-double, bright carmine flowers with golden centre, in small clusters, rich glossy green foliage, fragrant, free summer flowering, and intermittently later, moderately vigorous. Height 6–8 ft. Group 4.

'Ritter von Barmstede.' Kordesii climber. Clusters of fully double, deep rose-pink flowers, glossy foliage, disease resistant. Repeat flowering. Height 10 ft. Group 4.

'Royal Gold.' Large flowered climber. The beautiful, brilliant yellow, shapely hybrid-tea blooms are borne singly or in small clusters, re-current flowering and vigorous. In severe frosts shoots have a tendency to die back. Height 8–10 ft. Group 4.

'Sanders' White.' Rambler. Large clusters of pure white, double flowers, very fragrant and vigorous, late summer flowering. Height 12–15 ft. Group 1.

'Shot Silk, Climbing.' Large flowered climber. A beautiful rose, with carmine-orange-salmon-pink blooms, sweetly scented, vigorous, re-current flowering. Height 8–12 ft. Group 3.

'Soldier Boy.' Large flowered climber. Brilliant scarlet-crimson single blooms with yellow stamens, perpetual flowering, moderately vigorous. Height 8–10 ft. Group 4.

'Veilchenblau.' Rambler. Large clusters of small semi-double flowers of warm violet-blue, streaked with white, free flowering in July. Very vigorous, sweetly fragrant. Height 12 ft. Group 2.

'Violette.' Rambler. Large clusters of deep violet to crimson-purple flowers. Free flowering, moderately vigorous, thornless. Height up to 15 ft. Group 2.

'Wedding Day.' Rambler. Large trusses of flowers, yellow in bud open-ing to creamy-white, with bright orange stamens, very fragrant. Rich glossy green foliage. Height up to 35 ft. Group 2.

'Zéphirine Drouhin.' Bourbon climber. Exquisite semi-double blooms of bright carmine-pink, richly scented, a rose with a real old-fashioned fragrance, thornless. Free flowering June to July, afterwards inter-mittently throughout the summer. Height 10–15 ft. Group 4.

'Zweibrucken.' Kordesii shrub. Large clusters of fully double deep crimson blooms, leathery foliage, moderately vigorous, free and perpetual flowering, fragrant. Height 8–10 ft. Group 4.

HEDGES—ROSE SPECIES, SHRUBS AND FLORIBUNDAS

The hardy shrub roses in recent years have become more popular, not only as shrubs in the border, but also as hedges; they are for the most part free-flowering, and many are free-fruiting and extremely colourful. In height they range from between 3–5 ft. up to 8–9 ft. Floribunda roses are equally popular for hedges.

The shrub roses are not especially fastidious as to soil, and they will thrive even in poor sandy or stony soils, and in chalk soils. This has been well proved in the late Sir Frederick Stern's Garden at Highdown, Goring-by-Sea, Sussex—they will also thrive on moderately heavy soil, provided it is well prepared beforehand. But whatever the soil, initial preparation is essential. The ground should be deeply dug two spits deep (unless very light soil), and enriched with well-rotted farmyard manure or good garden compost. A mulch of similar material or some other form of humus, such as peat, leaf-soil, sawdust, hop manure or lawn mowings, applied in early spring, will be found most beneficial: and in dry weather it will help to conserve moisture. Plant young bushes, spacing the low and medium-sized ones 2–3 ft. apart and the taller and more vigorous growing ones 4–5 ft. apart. Plant from November to March.

Trimming—or perhaps pruning is a better word—should be carried out among the species and shrub roses in March, when old spent wood can be removed and the hedge generally tidied up. With the Bourbons, Chinas, hybrid musks and rugosas, remove spent flowers, cutting back the top 6 in. or more from June onwards, to encourage more bloom, and remove old worn out wood in March or August. The albas, gallicas and spinosissimas are pruned immediately after flowering has finished.

Since the Second World War the floribunda rose has become immensely popular, not only as a bedding rose but also as a very attractive and floriferous hedge rose. When choosing a floribunda rose for a hedge, one of the more vigorous varieties is best. Do not plant more than one variety, or the general appearance will be impaired and the rate of growth will be uneven. As with all roses, plant maiden bushes, spacing them either in a single row or double staggered rows about 15 in. apart. Plant from November to March. Trim in February to March. In the first year prune the bushes hard back to within 6–9 in. of soil level; this will then encourage plenty of bushy growth at the base. In subsequent years trim the hedge to keep it tidy and of uniform height. Propagation is by budding or by cuttings. Height approximately 3–4 ft. and sometimes 6 ft.

'Agnes' (*R. rugosa* type). Very double flower, rich apricot with creamy-yellow colourings, parsley-green foliage, deliciously fragrant. Height 5–6 ft.

'Alba maxima.' The Jacobite rose or great double white. Double, blush tinted opening to creamy-white, deliciously scented. Height 6 ft.

'Ama.' Floribunda. Semi-double, rich scarlet-crimson, beautifully shaped flowers which weather well, borne in large trusses. Vigorous.

'Belle de Crecy.' Gallica. Very free flowering, exquisitely formed double flowers of rich soft rose, changing finally to lilac-purple and Parma violet, richly fragrant. Height 3–4 ft.

'Belle Poitevine.' Rugosa. Flat, semi-double, soft mallow-pink flowers, but only a few hips. If clipped from the end of May to end of October plenty of fragrant blooms will be produced. Will grow 5 ft. wide. Height 5 ft.

'Blanc Double de Coubert.' Rugosa. The cupped flowers of this very beautiful pure white rose has deliciously scented semi-double blooms, but few hips. It reaches a width of 5 ft. and height of 6 ft.

'Bloomfield Abundance.' Chinensis shrub. Similar in shape and colouring to 'Cecile Brunner', flesh-pink, double flowers, neat foliage, almost thornless and almost always in flower. Height 5–6 ft.

'Bonn.' Shrub, large semi-double flowers, coral-red to orange-scarlet, light green foliage. Large round hips, slight musk fragrance. Height 5–6 ft.

'Buff Beauty.' Bourbon. Large clusters of fully double flowers, warm apricot-yellow, perpetual flowering, delicious tea scent, handsome foliage. June to September. Height 4 ft.

'Capitaine John Ingram.' Moss. Full petalled rosette shaped flowers of dark crimson-maroon having a velvety sheen, dark foliage, midsummer. Height 4–5 ft.

'Celestial' (syn. 'Celeste'). Alba shrub. Exquisitely formed semi-double flowers warm pink opening to shell-pink against grey-green foliage, well-shaped buds and hips, fragrant. Height 5–6 ft.

266

'Charles de Mills.' Gallica shrub. A most lovely rose having beautifully creased and curled petals, the 3–4 in. wide blooms varying from cerise-crimson to a dark plum-purple, richly scented. Said to be immune to black spot. Height 3–4 ft.

'Chinatown.' Shrub. Large flowers, deep golden-yellow, edged cherry, shading to a creamy-pink with age. Free flowering, slight fragrance, perpetual flowering, vigorous. Requires light pruning.

'Commandant Beaurepaire.' Strong grower with fresh green foliage, nearly double bright crimson flowers, striped and splashed with pink, mauve, purple, maroon and scarlet, in June and July, and sometimes in the autumn. Height 5 ft.

'Cornelia.' Hybrid musk. Double flowers rich coppery-apricot, flushed pink when open, delicious scent, perpetual flowering, June to October. Height 5–6 ft.

'Dorothy Wheatcroft.' Shrub. Small, semi-double flowers borne in large clusters orient-red to orange-scarlet, erect, vigorous and bushy; the bright green foliage is very disease resistant. Slightly fragrant.

eglanteria, see rubiginosa.

'Elmshorn.' Shrub. Fully double, flowers of light to dark crimson, small, about 1 in. wide, borne in large clusters; the wrinkled foliage is light green. Vigorous and excellent as an informal hedge. Little scent. Blooms almost perpetually up to November. Height 5 ft.

'Felicia.' Hybrid musk. Large double flowers, silvery-pink to salmon-pink, shaded yellow, very richly scented, perpetual flowering, June to September. Height 4–5 ft.

'Fellemberg.' Chinensis shrub. Large clusters of small flowers, bright rosy-pink to crimson-pink, repeat flowering, attractive foliage. Height up to 8 ft.

'Frau Dagmar Hastrup' (syn. 'Frau Dagmar Hartopp'). Rugosa shrub. This exquisite rose has single flowers of clear flesh-pink, with creamy coloured stamens, followed in the autumn by large rich crimson hips. Continuous flowering. Height 4 ft.

'Frensham'. Floribunda. Large trusses of deep scarlet-crimson, semi-double flowers, rich and beautiful foliage, very free flowering. A first-class rose and a vigorous grower. Height 4–4½ ft.

gallica versicolor, see 'Rosa Mundi'.

'Heidelberg.' Floribunda shrub. Large double flowers, each 4 in. wide, of crimson-scarlet, a little paler on reverse. Vigorous and perpetual flowering. Scented. Height 5–6 ft.

'Hermosa.' Chinensis shrub. Small shapely double flowers, a warm blush to lilac-pink. Very free blooming and excellent for a dwarf hedge. Height 3 ft.

'Highlight.' Floribunda. Large double flowers, bright orange-scarlet, huge trusses, vigorous and upright, slightly scented. Height about 4 ft.

'Iceberg.' Floribunda. This superb rose has flowers which are at first flushed pink, opening later to a greenish-white. Very vigorous, fragrant, and blooms well into the late autumn. Height 4–5 ft.

'Kassel.' Floribunda shrub. Large, semi-double flowers with varying colourings of cinnabar-red and cherry-red, richer in colour than Bonn. The huge clusters produce an abundance of bloom, which is slightly fragrant and recurrent. Very vigorous. Height 4 ft.

'Kathleen Ferrier.' Floribunda shrub. Semi-double, deep salmon-pink with lighter shadings, borne in small clusters. Deep green glossy foliage; fragrant and free flowering. Needs to be lightly pruned. Height 5 ft.

'Kathleen Harrop.' Bourbon. A lovely thornless rose, a 'sport' of my favourite Zéphirine Drouhin, though less vigorous. The very sweetly scented blooms are a clear pink with a light crimson reverse. Height up to 7 ft.

'Korona.' Floribunda. Large trusses of semi-double flowers, $2\frac{1}{2}$ in. across; on opening, they are a bright flame-scarlet, fading to deep salmon, slightly fragrant, free and perpetual flowering, vigorous, an outstanding rose. Height 3–4 ft.

'Lavender Lassie.' Shrub. Huge clusters of lavender-pink flowers, 3 in. wide blooms, very free flowering, richly fragrant, upright growth and moderately vigorous. Height 4–5 ft.

'Lilli Marlene.' Floribunda. Large, shapely clusters of $3\frac{1}{2}$ in. wide, fully double flowers, of rich scarlet-red; compact, bushy habit, slightly fragrant. Height 4 ft.

'Louise Odier.' Bourbon shrub. It has beautiful camellia shaped blooms of rich pink, shaded lilac. Perpetual flowering, deliciously scented, vigorous, in fact, a superb rose. Height 5–6 ft.

'Lübeck.' Floribunda shrub. Very full blooms of orange-red, slightly fragrant, free flowering, an excellent hedge shrub, vigorous and tall.

'Madame Isaac Pereire.' Bourbon shrub. Fully double, quartered flowers of a warm purplish-crimson having a paler reverse; the large richly scented blooms have the aroma of ripe raspberries. It is a vigorous grower with handsome foliage, and a recurrent flower. Height 7–8 ft.

'Maiden's Blush, Great Alba.' Shrub. A lovely old rose, its full globular flowers of warm pink are exquisitely fragrant. Vigorous, midsummer flowering. Height 5–6 ft.

'Masquerade.' Floribunda. A magnificent rose, with handsome foliage; its flowers at first are yellow in bud, gradually becoming salmon-pink to flame, and when fully open are a deep flame-red. All these colours will be on the bush at the same time, making a most remarkable and colourful hedge. The flowers are freely produced. Height 3–4 ft.

maxima, see Alba Maxima

'Nypel's Perfection.' Chinensis shrub. Semi-double flowers of rich rose-pink enriched with golden tints. Its foliage and habit are both charming. Very hardy, it makes an ideal hedge in the north and in colder areas. Height 4–5 ft.

'Old Blush.' The common monthly rose. Chinensis shrub. The crimson tinted buds open to medium sized blooms of soft silvery-pink with deeper shades. The fragrant blooms are borne in small clusters. Fairly vigorous, free and perpetual flowering. Height 3–4 ft.

'Penelope.' Hybrid musk shrub. Large semi-double blooms, shell-pink. Very fragrant and perpetual flowering. June to September. Height 5–6 ft.

'Prosperity.' Hybrid musk shrub. Double flowers, pale creamy-pink, shaded salmon, richly fragrant. Sturdy bushy habit, dark glossy foliage and red stems. June to September. Height 6–8 ft.

'Queen Elizabeth.' Floribunda-hybrid-tea type, or the first 'grandiflora' rose. A vigorous, upright grower. Medium sized flowers of rich glowing clear pink, borne singly and in small clusters, free flowering, rich green foliage. Slightly fragrant. Height 5–6 ft.

'Rosa Mundi' (syn. *R. gallica versicolor*). A most enchanting rose, its crimson flowers are splashed and striped with blush-white. It makes a compact bush and a superb hedge. I remember seeing a fine example at Chatsworth, Derbyshire. Height 4 ft.

'Rosemary Rose.' Floribunda. A fascinating rose with an old-world look about the blooms. The rosette-like flowers are frilled, and fully double, a rich currant-red and enhanced by dark red foliage, sweetly scented. Inclined to mildew. Height 3–4 ft.

'Roseraie de L'Hay.' Rugosa shrub. An irresistible rose, with apple-green foliage which sets off the beautiful, velvety textured crimson-purple double blooms, richly scented and perpetual flowering. Height up to 6 ft.

rubiginosa (syn. *R. eglanteria*). The sweet briar, or Eglantine. Its greatest virtue is its richly aromatic foliage—which I first remember enjoying when a schoolboy, at Oxted, Surrey—especially after a shower of rain on a warm summer's day. It has single pink wild roses, followed in autumn by oval red hips. Deliciously fragrant. Height up to 8 ft. Trim each spring by removing all twiggy growth and shortening all strong shoots by two-thirds their length. Height up to 8 ft.

rugosa. A first-class hedge rose, bearing in July large, floppy deep rose-pink single flowers, with a delicious fragrance, followed in autumn by large red hips. The deep, rich green foliage turns to yellow and orange colourings in autumn. It suckers freely and thrives in any soil. The first rose species I can remember from my earliest childhood. Height 5–7 ft.

'Saarbrucken.' Shrub. Large trusses of semi-double, scarlet flowers, a strong upright grower, free flowering. Height 4–5 ft.

'Sarah van Fleet.' Rugosa shrub. Semi-double, clear light pink, fragrant flowers, free and perpetual flowering. June to October. Height 5–6 ft.

'Scabrosa.' Rugosa shrub. Where large handsome flowers and hips are wanted, this is the variety to grow. Its single, soft rosy magenta blooms are 4–5 in. wide and its hips $1\frac{1}{2}$ in. across. It also has excellent foliage. Width 5 ft., height 4 ft.

'Schneezwerg.' Rugosa shrub. Semi-double, pure white, rosette-shaped blooms, followed by scarlet hips. It makes a compact bush, continuous flowering from May to October. Height 4–5 ft.

'Stanwell Perpetual.' Spinosissima shrub. Double, flesh-pink blooms fading to white. It makes a low, twiggy, bushy hedge. Perpetual flowering from June to August. Height 4–5 ft.

'Tuscany Superb.' Gallica. Large, semi-double flowers, the dark buds opening to a velvety maroon. A vigorous rose. Height 4 ft.

'Wilhelm.' Shrub. Large, loose clusters of semi-double, rich scarlet-crimson blooms, free and perpetual flowering, slightly fragrant. Makes an excellent hedge. Height up to 6 ft.

'Will Scarlet.' Shrub. This is a 'sport' of Wilhelm; the semi-double, medium-sized blooms are a bright scarlet, almost a 'hunting pink', with white, more fragrant than its parent. Fairly vigorous. Height 5–6 ft.

ROSEMARY, *see* ROSMARINUS

ROSE OF SHARON, *see* HYPERICUM CALYCINUM

ROSMARINUS

R. officinalis (Rosemary)

An evergreen aromatic shrub with narrow leaves, dark glossy above, white felted beneath, and fragrant when crushed. It is probably, next to lavender, our most popular scented-leaved shrub. From mid-April to mid-May many small blue-mauve flowers are produced in the leaf axils of the previous year's shoots. It makes an ideal hedge up to 3 ft. or a little more, and does best in a light, well-drained warm soil, though it will tolerate most soils. Best planting size is 1–1½ ft. high, spaced 12–15 in. apart. It can be planted in September or early October, but is best planted from mid-April to the end of April. Trim after flowering, but do not cut back into old wood; if hard cutting has to be undertaken do so in April. Propagate by half-ripened wood cuttings inserted in sandy soil in a cold frame in early August. Height 6–7 ft.

ROWAN, *see* SORBUS

RUBUS

This is a large genus with many species, and among them are several brambles which are useful and attractive ornamental climbers. Their beauty lies either in the foliage or the colour of their stems, though in some the fruits are equally attractive. They are easily cultivated, thriving in good loamy soil, preferably one with a fairly retentive nature for best results; they will, however, grow in most soils. They are useful for training up a post or wigwam of posts, trellis, walls or fences. Plant from mid-October to mid-November or in March. Prune by cutting out the old growths and tying in the new ones. Propagation by tip layering the shoots during the summer, or by dividing plants in the spring.

R. flagelliflorus

An evergreen, climbing shrub with graceful, slender, prickly stems covered with whitish felt. Small white flowers are followed by black edible berries. A useful climber for a trellis, archway or pillar. Height 5–6 ft.

R. henryi

An evergreen rambler with slender stems and three-lobed leaves which are finely toothed and white-felted beneath. Pink flowers in racemes of six to ten in June, followed by black, shining berries. Height up to 20 ft. *R. h. bambusarum*. Similar to *R. henryi* in most respects, except that the leaves are of three distinct leaflets. Height up to 15 ft.

R. lambertianus

A semi-evergreen, rambling shrub, glossy, green leaves and white flowers in June–July, followed by small red berries. Height 6 ft.

R. phoenicolasius (Japanese Wineberry)

This deciduous, vigorously growing bramble has biennial stems, which are attractively and densely covered with reddish, gland-tipped bristles and a few slender prickles. In June and July the pink flowers, which are produced in terminal racemes, are also covered with glandular hairs. They are followed by large crimson-red, sweet, juicy berries. It is ideal for growing against a wall or fence or over a pergola. Height 8–10 ft.

R. tricolor

This attractive, semi-evergreen is a prostrate ground coverer rather than a climber, with bristly stems and heart-shaped foliage 3–4 in. long, dark green above with a whitish-felt covering beneath. Its 1 in. wide, white flowers in July are followed by pleasantly flavoured red berries.

272

Chamaecyparis lawsoniana 'Fraseri' as a screen or wind break

A well-trimmed hedge or wind break of *Tsuga heterophylla*

Double hedges of holly, *Ilex aquifolium*, common laurel, and Austrian pines, *Pinus nigra*, provide wind and noise barriers

An impenetrable
hedge of holly, *Ilex
aquifolium*

A battlement-like
hedge of box,
Buxus sempervirens,
caps this old Cots-
wold stone wall

An example of a
trimmed and un-
trimmed *Lonicera
nitida* hedge, in
Crawley New
Town, Sussex

RUE, *see* RUTA

RUSCUS

R. aculeatus (Butcher's Broom)

A hardy, evergreen, dwarf shrub, a native of Britain; I have found it growing in the New Forest in Hampshire, and also at Pulborough, Sussex. It has ovate, spine-tipped, dark green leaves, slightly glossy on both sides. It is dioecious, i.e. male and female flowers are on different plants; when male and female plants are present red berries are produced in the centre of the leaf. This armed shrub will make only a low hedge, but has the advantage of growing in dense shade. It is not fussy with regard to soil. Plant October to March, spacing the plants 1 ft. apart. Trim by cutting out oldest stems in spring. Propagate by division of suckers in spring. It may also be increased by seed; collect it as soon as ripe, store in bags filled with dry sand and sow in the following year in early spring. Height 1½–3 ft.

RUSSIAN VINE, *see* POLYGONUM

RUTA

R. graveolens (Common Rue)

An evergreen shrub, of a half-woody nature, seldom more than 2½ ft. high. Glaucous green leaves, and dull yellow flowers June to August. Makes a suitable informal low hedge to a herb garden. Plant young plants in March, 12–15 in. apart. It is not particular as to soil. Trim in April. Propagate by seed or cuttings. Height 2–2½ ft.
R.g. 'Jackman's Blue'. This is a striking variety of the common rue with opalescent blue foliage. The dull yellow flowers are produced from the end of June to August. For hedges it is as well to keep the flower spikes removed. Other remarks as for *R. graveolens*. Height 2–2½ ft.

ST. JOHN'S WORT, *see* HYPERICUM

SALIX (Willow)

The willows are hardy, deciduous trees and are best used for screens rather than hedges, except for such species as *Salix alba* 'Chermesina' (syn. *S.* 'Britzensis') and *S.a.* 'Vitellina', as informal hedges or screens. Willows have two great merits; they thrive in damp situations, and are fast growers. They do best on acid, loamy, or clay soils. They mostly have green, greyish-green or silvery leaves, and many have coloured stems which make them particularly attractive in the winter months; their catkins are equally beautiful. Most of us know the yellow pussy willow (botanically *S. discolor*), though the willow which is usually called pussy willow or palm is *S. caprea*, the goat willow or common sallow. Pollarded willows by streams and canal banks are a familiar sight, especially in the Fens, and in a winter sun when their branches are bare they look singularly attractive. Plant from October to March, planting sizes vary from 4–5 ft. high and distances from 2–12 ft. apart. Trim at the end of March or early in April, whether pollarding large trees or cutting back stool-like bushes, as in the case of *S. alba* 'Chermesina' and *S.a.* 'Vitellina'. Propagate by hard-wood cuttings in late autumn or winter. Species and varieties are many, but the following are worth growing.

S. alba (White Willow or Huntingdon Willow)

This makes a fine fast growing, pyramidal screen tree having grey-green foliage, useful for coastal and riverside planting. Plant at 12 ft. apart and pollarded at 7 ft. high, at the time of planting. Planted as a free-growing screen. Height up to 70 ft.
S.a. 'Chermesina' (syn. *S.* 'Britzensis'). The bark of young shoots is a brilliant orange-scarlet. To obtain the brilliantly coloured stems the bushes should be cut hard back to within a bud or two of the old stools each year at the end of March or early April. Plant 3–6 ft. apart. As a screen tree. Height up to 50 ft.
S.a. 'Vitellina' (Golden Willow). Although this willow will make a tall tree it can be used for stooling like *S.a.* 'Chermesina'. Plant 3–6 ft. apart. Height up to 50 ft.

S. caprea (Palm, Goat Willow or Common Sallow)

Its yellow male catkins, which bloom during March and April, are well

274

known as a decoration on Palm Sunday. It will grow excellently by the seaside and in exposed places, where it makes a first-class windbreak. It does best in damp soil. Plant 4–5 ft. apart. Trim after flowers fade in April. Height 15–20 ft.

S. 'Caerulea' (Cricket-bat Willow). A useful fast-growing willow, rather pyramidal in growth; it thrives on stiff, moist clay, but not a soil that is waterlogged. Plant 12–15 ft. apart. Makes a first-class screen tree. Height up to 60 ft.

S. daphnoides (Violet Willow)

This is so called on account of its conspicuous bark, which is violet or plum coloured with a bluish-white bloom. It also has striking yellow catkins in March like the goat willow. It is erect and vigorous in habit. There are several varieties of this species with bark of similar colour. Plant 12–15 ft. apart. Height up to 40 ft.

SALLOW, *see Salix caprea*

SAMBUCUS

S. nigra (Common Elder)

A hardy, deciduous shrub, which will grow in town or country and by the coast, provided it has some shelter. Excellent for industrial areas and for growing under trees and in other shady sites where other shrubs will fail to thrive. It is chiefly used as a screen tree but it also makes a useful hedge or it can be planted in a mixed country hedge. It has long pinnate leaves composed of three, five or seven leaflets, with rough grey-white grooved stems. In June it produces flat umbels 5–8 in. wide, of yellowish or dull white flowers with a strong and rather sickly odour, followed by shining black berries in September, which make excellent wine, as does the blossom. Sambucus will grow well in any type of soil. Best planting size is 3 ft. high, spaced 2–3 ft. apart in October to March. Trim in late summer or cut hard back in early March. Propagate by seed sown in spring or hard-wood cuttings in late December to February. Height 15–20 ft.

S.n. 'Aurea' (Golden Elder). At first the foliage is palish yellow-gold which deepens as it grows older. It makes a vigorous hardy, quick-growing summer screen. Other remarks as for *S. nigra*. Height 12–15 ft.

275

SANTOLINA

S. chamaecyparissus (syn. *S. incana*) (Lavender Cotton or Cotton Lavender)

This attractive hardy evergreen shrub, with silvery-grey filigree-cut foliage is, as W. J. Bean says, 'probably the whitest of all hardy shrubs'. The leaves are entirely covered with a white felt. In July and August it produces an abundance of button-like yellow flower heads, borne singly on wiry stalks 4–6 in. long. When lightly rubbed the plant gives off quite an agreeable odour, but when crushed it is not so pleasant. It makes an ideal dwarf hedge. Best planting size is 6–9 in. high; young plants are usually grown in pots. Plant 1 ft. apart from September to April. It will grow in any good garden soil, but is especially happy in light well-drained soils. Trim off old flower heads, when faded, with shears, and clip the hedge itself in April, cutting back just above the base of the previous year's growth. Propagate by half-ripened wood cuttings with or without a heel in July or August. Height 1½–2 ft.

S. neapolitana (syn. *S. rosmarinifolia*)

In most respects this species is similar to *S. chamaecyparissus*. Its bright yellow cushion-like flowers are borne in clusters of six to twelve, near the end of each shoot. It does best in a poor soil rather than a rich one. Height 2–2½ ft.

S. virens (syn. *S. viridis*)

Deep green leaves, strongly scented, its odour being emitted at the slightest touch. Yellow flower heads, borne singly at the end of slender erect stalks 6–10 in. long. Other remarks as for *S. chamaecyparissus*— not such a good plant as the other two. Height 1½–2 ft.

SARCOCOCCA

S. hookerana

Hardy evergreen shrub, narrow bright green leaves, small fragrant white flowers in autumn, with an almond blossom scent, followed by egg-shaped blue-black fruits. It makes an informal hedge; one of its assets is that it grows in semi-shade. Plant 1 ft. apart in October to March. It grows best in a moist soil. It is closely allied to the box (Buxus) family. Prune when necessary in April. Propagate by division in spring. Height 4–5 ft.

S.h. digyna. Similar in most respects to *S. hookerana*, though its leaves are a little more pointed and its shoots are often purplish-red. The scented flowers are flesh coloured with pink stamens and borne in February. These are followed by black egg-shaped fruits, which are larger than those of *S. hookerana.* Height 4–5 ft.

SCHISANDRA

A genus of deciduous climbing or twining shrubs, all having unisexual flowers. They prefer a rich, loamy or acid soil and are best planted in a semi-shady position rather than in full sun, in fact they grow well on a north or east wall or on a pergola.

S. grandiflora rubriflora

A deciduous climber or twiner, having solitary crimson flowers in the axiles of the leaves, in April–May, followed by closely packed spikes of round red berries. Other remarks as for *S. sphenanthera.* Height 16–20 ft.

S. propinqua sinensis

This deciduous climber or twiner has pale rose flowers, fragrant, produced in twos or threes in April and May, followed by fig-shaped to roundish fruits, on 4–6 in. long stalks. Other remarks as for *S. sphenanthera.* Height 20–30 ft.

S. sphenanthera

A deciduous climber or twiner. The shoots are very warted, and the leaves are glaucous beneath. The orange flowers are borne on slender 2 in. long stalks in April and May, these are followed by scarlet fruits in spikes 2–4 in. long. Plant in September to October, or April. Propagate by half-ripened cuttings in July–August in a propagating frame with gentle bottom heat, or by seed sown in March. Prune by cutting back any shoots that have become too long, and cut out worn-out growths during the winter. Height 20 ft.

SCHIZOPHRAGMA

This handsome genus which closely resembles the climbing hydrangea, *H. petiolaris*, has two species, both of which are self-clinging. Their chief difference is that the bract-like flower heads are larger and, therefore, more showy than *H. petiolaris*. They are ideal for clothing walls in any aspect, or for clambering up trees. It is not particular with regard to soil. Plant any time from October to March, pot-grown plants. No pruning required. Propagate by half-ripened cuttings inserted in sandy soil in a closed frame in August.

S. hydrangioides

A deciduous, vigorous, self-clinging climber, with larger ovate leaves 4–6 in. long and 4 in. wide, and coarsely toothed, deep green above, slightly glaucous beneath. The large inflorescences, made up of pale yellow bracts which surround the small, yellow flowers, are slightly scented, and 8–10 in. across, produced July to October. Height up to 40 ft.

S. integrifolium

Similar in most respects to *S. hydrangeoides* except that the leaves are a little larger, smaller teeth on the edges and downy on the veins. The inflorescences consist of creamy-white bracts, each being 3–3½ in. across, and are produced from July to September. It does best in a shady to semi-shady position. Height 30–40 ft.

S. viburnoides, *see Pileostegia viburnoides*

SCHIZOPHRAGMA, EVERGREEN, *see* PILEOSTEGIA

SEA BUCKTHORN, *see* HIPPOPHAE

SENECIO

S. greyi

An evergreen shrub, with silvery-grey foliage. The leathery leaves are up to 2¾ in. long and 1¼ in. wide; when young they have a grey cobweb-like covering above, later become smooth, and the under surface is covered with a white felt. In June and July they produce upright panicles of golden-yellow daisy-like flowers. This species is more often than not erroneously sent out from nurseries as *S. laxifolius* which in fact is a very rare plant. This is not the shrub for a formal hedge, but is excellent as an informal one, especially at the top of a low bank. It is of bushy habit. It does well by the sea. It is often considered a not too hardy plant, but I have thought differently since I saw it flourishing in a garden at Dudley, near Birmingham. They thrive in any type of soil. Best planting size is 12–15 in. high. Space plants 15–18 in. apart. Plant October to March. Trim in April by cutting hedges back fairly hard. This will then keep a moderately tidy hedge. Propagate by half-ripened wood cuttings in August or early September. Height 3–4 ft.

S. reinoldii (syn. *S. rotundifolius*)

An evergreen shrub with roundish leaves, dark shining green above, yellowish-white and downy beneath. The leaves vary in size from 2–5 in. long and nearly as much wide. This is a shrub to plant as a first line of defence in a maritime garden, and W. J. Bean quotes it as having stood up to an exposed position in Edinburgh. It makes a broad bush or shrub and is best planted as a windbreak rather than as a hedge. Best planting size 12–15 in. high, spacing the plants 15–18 in. apart. Plant October to March. Trim in April when necessary. Propagate by half-ripened cuttings in August or September. Height 6 ft. but will grow taller.

S. scandens

This semi-woody, herbaceous, rampant climber of the groundsel family dies down to the ground each winter. It requires a sunny position on a wall, or fence or it can scramble up a tree or through a large shrub. When grown against a wall it will need something to cling against. It has narrowly triangular, pointed leaves, toothed and 2–4 in. long. The small, bright-yellow daisy-like flowers are freely produced in terminal, compound panicles from July to October. Plant in spring. Prune by cutting back dead growth in early spring. Propagate by seeds sown in March or half-ripened cuttings inserted in sandy soil in a closed frame in July–August. Height 15–20 ft.

SHRUBBY CINQUEFOIL, *see* POTENTILLA

SHRUBBY GERMANDER, *see* TEUCRIUM

SILK VINE, *see* PERIPLOCA

SINOFRANCHETIA

S. chinensis

A hardy, deciduous, vigorous twining climber, its three-foliate leaves—similar to those of the scarlet runner bean, but glaucous beneath—have a 6–9 in. purplish coloured stalk. The white flowers which are borne on drooping racemes, in May, are of little consequence, though the blue-purple grape-like berries which follow are interesting. It will grow in any good garden soil. Plant in spring. No pruning required. Propagate by seeds, when available, which should be sown as soon as ripe, in pots filled with well-drained soil and placed in a frame or greenhouse. Also by layering ripened growths in the autumn Height 20–30 ft.

SIPHONOSMANTHUS, *see Osmanthus delavayi*

SKIMMIA

S. japonica

Hardy, evergreen, flowering and berrying shrub. I have seen a hedge doing very well in Yorkshire. This is a first-rate evergreen for a smoky district. It makes a dense bush or a good low semi-formal hedge. One of its merits is that it thrives in shade, but it does equally well in sun. Its sweetly-scented white flowers, in terminal panicles, are produced in March and April. The leaves when crushed are strongly aromatic. Plants are dioecious; therefore, where berries are wanted male and female bushes must be planted. It has scarlet fruits in autumn. It is a slow grower and does best in a moist soil, but it does not like chalk soils. Best planting size is 1–1½ ft. high. Space 15 in. apart, plant September to October, or March to April. Propagate by seed. Height 4–5 ft.

SLOE, *see Prunus spinosa*

SMILAX

S. discotis (Horse Brier)

This deciduous to semi-evergreen lilaceous hardy climber, has curiously angled stems which are armed with spines. The broadly heart-shaped leaves are glossy green. It needs good soil, but dislikes chalk soils. It is useful to grow over tree stumps or arbours. It dislikes draughts or cold winds so choose a protected position. The greenish-yellow flowers in June are followed by roundish, blue-black fruits. Plant in spring. No pruning required. Propagate by division of the roots in spring. Height 10–20 ft.

SOLANUM

These members of the potato family are not true climbers, though they make extremely attractive wall shrubs. They need a sheltered wall or fence, south or west where they will receive full sun. They must have support to which they can be trained and tied. However, I remember seeing a flourishing, unsupported plant of *S. crispum* 'Glasnevin variety' flowering freely, not against a wall, a few years ago at Harrogate in the centre of the town. The solanums are vigorous plants and are best in not too rich soil, but not chalk soil. Plant pot-grown plants in spring. Prune in spring by spurring them back fairly hard, as the flowers are produced on the new shoots. Propagate by half-ripe cuttings inserted in sandy soil beneath a large glass jar or frame.

281

S. crispum (Chilean Potato Tree)

Semi-evergreen wall shrub which is grown as a climber. The rich purple flowers have centres of rich yellow stamens. The flowers are freely produced from June to August. Height 15 ft. or more.

S.c. 'Glasnevin' (syn. *S.c.* 'Autumnale'). Hardier than the species, more or less evergreen, deeper coloured and flowers more freely from June to September. Height 12–14 ft.

S. jasminoides (Potato Vine)

This more or less rambling climber is less hardy than *S. crispum* and *S.c.* 'Glasnevin'. It is a vigorous plant and requires the protection of a wall and full sun. The slaty-blue flowers are freely produced from July to October. It is as well to prune it fairly hard each spring. Height 20 ft.

S.j. 'Album'. Similar in all respects except that it has white flowers.

SOPHORA

S. tetraptera (Kowhai)

Although evergreen in its native land, New Zealand, when grown out of doors in this country, it is deciduous. And what is more, it is usually thought of as a shrub or small tree, but to grow it successfully it does require the protection of a warm south or south-west wall. Its pinnate leaves, 3–6 in. long, are composed of as many as 13 to 50 leaflets. The strangely tubular-shaped golden-yellow flowers, four to eight in a raceme, are produced in May and June. These are followed by pea-shaped pods 2–8 in. long. I shall never forget the specimen I saw at Christopher Lloyd's garden, Great Dixter, on a wall which was a picture. It was 20 ft. high. It will thrive in all types of soil. Plant in spring. No pruning required. Propagate by grafting in August on to stocks of *S. japonica* in a close case in heat. Height 15–40 ft.

SNOWBALL TREE, *see Viburnum opulus* 'Sterile'

SNOWBERRY, *see* SYMPHORICARPOS

SORBUS

S. aria (syn. *Pyrus aria*) (Whitebeam)

This hardy, deciduous tree is a native of the chalk downs, but grows equally well in all other soils. It makes a useful screen tree, is especially good for exposed positions, and flourishes by the sea coast. I have not seen it used as a hedge shrub, but there is no reason why it should not be. The bright green, handsome leaves are covered with a white felt beneath. It bears heavily-scented dull white flowers in May, followed by scarlet-red fruits speckled with brownish dots. Best planting size is 6–8 ft. or 10–12 ft. high, spaced 8–9 ft. apart or 16–20 ft. according to requirements. For hedge planting, space bushes 2–3 ft. apart. Trim in late winter or early spring. Height 30–45 ft.

S. aucuparia (Mountain Ash or Rowan)

A hardy, deciduous tree, a native of Britain. It has dark green, pinnate leaves, and white flowers in May, followed by scarlet berries in September, which are beloved by the birds. An ideal town tree. Unlike *S. aria*, the mountain ash or rowan likes a moist cool soil in which to grow but, it also stands exposure well, which makes it a useful screen tree. It could no doubt be used as a hedge shrub. Best planting size is 6–8 ft. or 10–12 ft. high, spaced at 8–9 ft. apart or 16–20 ft., according to requirements. For hedge planting space bushes 2–3 ft. apart. Trim in late winter or early spring. Propagate by seed. Height 30–50 ft.

S. intermedia (Swedish Whitebeam)

This deciduous tree is just as hardy as the previous two. It has large, oval tapering leaves 2–4½ in. long and 1–3 in. wide, with lobed margins and jagged teeth near the apex; above they are dark polished green, below covered in close grey felt. It has dull white flowers in May, and red fruits in autumn. It is an excellent screen tree and on account of its bushiness I understand it is used freely in Sweden as a hedge shrub. Best planting size is 6–8 ft. high, spaced at 8–9 ft. apart or 16–20 ft. according to requirements. For hedge planting, space bushes 2–3 ft. apart. Trim in late winter or early spring. Propagate by seed. Height 20–40 ft.

SOUTHERNWOOD, *see* ARTEMISIA

SPANISH BROOM, *see* SPARTIUM

SPARTIUM

S. junceum (Spanish Broom)

A deciduous shrub, having an inverted spoke-like appearance; its dark green, smooth rush-like stems, have few leaves. Nevertheless its 1–1½ ft. spikes of glowing golden-yellow fragrant pea-shaped, flowers—from June to September—are a compensation for its rather gaunt habit. It is excellent for the top of a dry bank and flourishes in coastal areas. It enjoys hot dry summers. Not fastidious over soils. Best planting size 1–1½ ft. high, pot grown and planted at 1½–2 ft. apart. Plant in October or March. Trim in March. Propagate by seed, sow under glass in February or March. Height 8–12 ft.

SPINDLE-TREE, *see* EUONYMUS

SPIRAEA

This is a family of hardy deciduous flowering shrubs—many also having good autumn foliage. They are easily cultivated and will grow in any soil and under almost any conditions. All make good informal hedges. There are tall and short kinds. Best planting size is 1–3 ft., spacing them from 1–2 ft. apart. Spiraeas will grow in any type of soil. Plant any time from October to March. Trim spring-flowering kinds after flowers have faded. Trim summer and autumn flowering ones in February or March. When hard pruning is needed it may also be carried out in February or March. Propagate by hard-wood cuttings, by division or by suckers.

S. × arguta (Bridal Wreath)

This spiraea, as its common name implies, is festooned with dainty

284

white flowers. It blooms in late April and early May. Trim after flowering. Space plants 1½–2 ft. apart. Height 4–5 ft.

S. × billardii 'Triumphans'

This is a first-class deciduous shrub where a tall screen or semi-formal hedge is needed. Its stiff light brown stems produce narrow, bottle-brush, purple-rose terminal flowers from June to the end of September. It suckers freely and is easily propagated by division in autumn or spring, and also by hard-wood cuttings taken in autumn or winter. I have often rooted prunings used to mark seed rows. Best planting size, 2–3 ft. Space 2 ft. apart. Trim in winter or spring. A useful hedge for a dry site. Height 4–6 ft.

S. × bumalda

This species and its varieties are all useful, although undoubtedly the most popular variety is 'Anthony Waterer', which has deep carmine flowers from July to September. Space 1½ ft. apart. Trim in February or March by cutting back all old flowering wood. Young foliage looks pink and tender like new rose shoots. Height 3–4 ft.
S. × b. 'Froebelii'. Purplish-red flowers in July to August, a little more vigorous in habit than the species, and its its foliage turning red in autumn. Space 1½ ft. apart. Height 5–6 ft.

S. japonica 'Bullata' (syns. *S. crispifolia* and *S. bullata*)

An excellent shrub for a low hedge, it is dwarf, compact and rounded in habit. It has attractive, dark green puckered foliage and rosy-red flowers at the end of July, when the bushes will be smothered. Trim by removing dead flower heads in late summer. Space plants 1 ft. apart. Height 1½ ft.

S. thunbergii

This is one of our beauties among the spring-flowering shrubs. It has bright green foliage, and in mid-March to mid-April sprays of dainty white star-like flowers are produced in abundance, on masses of twiggy growths. Trim after flowering. Space the plants 1½–2 ft. apart. Propagate from hard-wood cuttings. Height 4–5 ft.

285

S. × vanhouttei

Another lovely spiraea, having arching branches which are grey-green. Space 1½–2 ft. apart. Trim after flowering. Propagate from hard-wood cuttings. Height 5–6 ft.

SPRUCE, *see* PICEA

SPRUCE, NORWAY, *see Picea abies*

ST. JOHN'S WORT, *see* HYPERICUM

STAUNTONIA

S. hexaphylla

An evergreen, twining climber, very vigorous. The 3–5 in. long leaves consist of three to seven separate leaflets each on 1–2 in. long stalks. The unisexual flowers are white, tinged violet and fragrant, appearing in spring. It is best planted beside a warm wall. The egg-shaped purplish fruits are seldom produced in this country. It does best in an acid, sandy loam. Plant in spring. Prune each winter by shortening back all long shoots. Propagate either by layering or by cuttings of half-ripened shoots, inserting them in a sandy soil in July. Height up to 30 ft.

STRANVAESIA

S. davidiana

A hardy, evergreen shrub with glossy olive-green leaves 2½–3½ in. long and 1 in. wide. An added attraction is the red colouring at the base of each leaf-stalk. Older leaves often turn or are tinted red in autumn, and the white flowers in May are followed by clusters of scarlet hawthorn-like berries in autumn and winter. It is a strong grower, and I have seen old 12–15 ft. bushes cut hard back and afterwards make as much as 2½ ft. growth in a summer. It grows well in heavy soils, but does not object to chalk soils. Makes an ideal, semi-formal hedge, screen or windbreak. Best planting size 2–3 ft. high, spaced at 2–3 ft. apart and planted in September or early November, or March–April. Trim in late August, or April, when hard pruning can also be undertaken. Propagate by seed or layers. Height 10–18 ft.

STRAWBERRY TREE, *see* ARBUTUS

SWEET BAY, *see* LAURUS

SWEET PEA, *see Lathyrus odoratus*

SWEET-SCENTED VERBENA, *see* LIPPIA

SYCAMORE, *see Acer pseudoplatanus*

SYMPHORICARPOS (Snowberry)

S. rivularis (syn. *S. albus laevigatus*)

Hardy, deciduous free-berrying shrub. At one time the common snowberry was much planted in cottage gardens. It has roundish, grey-green leaves and coral-pink bell-shaped flowers of little significance, in June and July, which are followed by pure white, mothball-like berries from October onwards. Not fastidious as to soil; does well in shade and is quite a town dweller. A useful shrub for a mixed informal hedge, where beauty of berry is more important than neatness. Best planting size, 1½–2 ft. and spaced 1–1½ ft. apart. Snowberries will grow in any type of soil. Plant from October to March. Trim in February, when berries start to brown. Propagate by suckers, hard-wood cuttings in winter or seed sown in spring. Height 3–6 ft.

S. × chenaultii

Deciduous, with dainty oval fresh green leaves, pink bell-shaped

287

flowers, followed by rosy-purple berries. Best planting size 1½–2 ft., spaced at 1–1½ ft. apart and planted from October to March. Trim in February. Propagate as for *S. rivularis*. Height up to 6 ft.

SYRINGA (Lilac)

S. vulgaris (Common Lilac)

A hardy deciduous shrub, and one that is usually considered for its sweetly-scented blooms. But for a spring and summer hedge of green it is as useful and accommodating as privet. The finest hedge I have seen was 5–6 ft. high in a Crawley garden. Common lilac will grow in nearly any soil, on chalk, clay or sand, though it is best on the heavier soils. It can be used as a formal hedge or as an informal one, if flower is wanted. It suckers, however, so it must be controlled. Best planting size is 2½–3 ft. spaced at 2½–3 ft. apart and planted from October to March. Trim after flowering or in early April, and always remove old flower heads, as soon as blooms fade, from informal hedges. Propagate by division of suckers, or by layers. There are many varieties in varying shades of lilac, blue, purple, red and pink, also white, rather expensive for a close hedge, but ideal where an informal screen is needed. Height 15–18 ft. Hedges 5–10 ft. Some species, other than *S. vulgaris*, can be used with equal success, especially as screens.

S. × chinensis (Rouen Lilac)

A graceful shrub of rounded habit with twiggy growth, which produces dainty sprays of common lilac-coloured, scented flowers in May. Height 6–10 ft.
S. × c. 'Saugeana' (syn. *S.c.* 'Rubra'). This is similar in habit to *S. chinensis*, but has purplish-red scented flowers in May. Height 9–12 ft.

S. × persica (Persian Lilac)

This species is smaller in stature than *S. × chinensis*, though equally attractive. It bears panicles of lilac-coloured scented flowers in May. One outstanding difference is its lance-shaped leaves. Space plants 2–2½ ft. apart. Height 4–6 ft.
S. × p. 'Alba'. White flowers. Height 5–7 ft.

Atriplex halimus provides a useful shelter from the sea at St. Ouen, Jersey

Another evergreen for coastal or inland areas is *Olearia haastii*

A lavender hedge has a pleasing fragrance

ABOVE LEFT: the field maple, *Acer campestre*, is colourful in spring and autumn
ABOVE RIGHT: *Cornus alba* 'Elegantissima' has attractive variegated foliage and crimson stems
BELOW LEFT: sea buckthorn, *Hippophae rhamnoides*, is tough and thorny
BELOW RIGHT: the red flowers of *Ribes sanguineum* make it an attractive hedge in spring

TAMARISK, *see* TAMARIX

TAMARIX (Tamarisk)

Mostly a deciduous maritime shrub, though the naturalized species, *T. gallica*, is evergreen. There is probably no more popular shrub, grown on the south coast, at least, than tamarisk. It stands up to the salt spray, winds and buffetings better than almost any shrub I know. Tamarix will thrive in poor sandy soil and does not mind lime. Best planting size is 1½–2 ft. spaced 1½ ft. apart. Plant October to March. Trim in late February or March. Propagate by hard-wood cuttings in the autumn.

T. gallica (syn. *T. angalica*) (Common Tamarisk)

An evergreen or deciduous shrub. It is erect in habit, with purplish-coloured branches bearing slender racemes of pink flowers in late summer and early autumn. Trim in February or March. Height 10–12 ft., or higher in very favoured localities.

T. pentandra

A deciduous shrub bearing long, graceful plumes of rosy-pink flowers in late July and August. Trim in April. Height 12–15 ft.

T. tetrandra

A deciduous shrub with smooth dark branches and thin, twiggy side branchlets which bear small reddish-pink flowers in May, produced on the previous year's growth. Trim after flowering. Height 10–15 ft.

TASSEL BUSH, *see* GARRYA

TAXUS

T. baccata (Common Yew)

Yew makes a first-class hedge (Plate 17) or screen and is invaluable

T   289

where topiary is needed in formal gardens—a cult which has regrettably diminished since the Second World War. Looking back on my early days at Cheal's nursery in Crawley, Sussex, I can well remember seeing ships, peacocks, crocodiles, bears, armchairs, balls, cones and many other shapes sold for as much as £40 or £50 apiece. At Hever castle in Kent there is a fine set of chessmen in yew which came from that nursery. They were cut out and trained between 1900 and 1903, by Peter Breden of Tushmore, Crawley, who died in 1955, and today these pieces of topiary are still in good condition.

It is often thought that yew is slow-growing, but this is far from the truth, for a young hedge once established will put on as much as $1-1\frac{1}{2}$ ft. of growth in one season. When planting yews one must be prepared to be patient and should always plant small, young bushes, as these will make the best hedge. Yews require good drainage above all; this is evident when one considers how well they flourish on the chalk downs near Box Hill, Surrey. They also require humus in the soil and well-dug ground. Bastard trenching or double digging is best, as described in Chapter 2, page 24. At the time of digging, work in well-rotted farmyard manure in the second spit. If farmyard manure is not available, use hop manure, peat or leaf soil plus blood and bonemeal, 50 per cent of each, at the rate of 6 oz. per sq. yd. for old established trees, and 3–4 oz. per oz. per sq. yd. for young trees. As a spring tonic the late Hon. Vicary Gibbs recommended a small handful of nitrate of soda per plant.

To obtain the best hedge one should clip yew so that it tapers towards the top. The yew will grow in any good soil—chalk or clay, light or medium loam—but not on waterlogged ground. Although very hardy, it does need some shelter when planted near the sea. Best planting size is from 1–3 ft., spaced at $1\frac{1}{2}$–2 ft. apart. Plant young trees in September to early October or late March to April; where there is time and labour for aftercare they can be planted in early May. However, whenever possible September or April are the best planting months. Trim in August to September. Care after planting is rather important with yews, and a thorough soaking followed by a mulch of leaf soil or similar material will be beneficial during the summer, as will a spraying with clear water in the evening after sunset, after very hot, drying days. It is as well to leave young and newly-planted yews for 12 months before the first clipping is made, apart from shortening back any extra long shoots that may unbalance the evenness of the hedge at the top. When hard pruning is needed on old and overgrown hedges, do this in April. Propagate by seed sown in spring, or cuttings taken in July and inserted in a sun frame; no doubt mist propagation will be useful, or later cuttings may be taken in September and inserted in a cold frame. Height 10–15 ft. for hedges, and up to 20–30 ft. for screens.

TECOMA, *see* CAMPSIS

TEUCRIUM

T. fruticans (Shrubby Germander)

A hardy evergreen, if wall protection is provided. The ovate leaves are 1–1½ in. long, greyish-green above and white-felted beneath, with a mist-like fragrance. The stems are also covered with felt. The rosemary-like lavender-blue flowers are borne in racemes, 3–4 in. long and produced during summer and autumn. It is wind hardy and does best in a lightish soil; if not too rich it will flower freely. It does well on chalk soils. Plant pot-grown plants in spring. Prune by shortening the secondary branches each March in order to keep the bush neat and tidy. Propagate by cuttings of half-ripened side shoots, inserted in sandy soil in a closed frame any time from June to August. Height 7–8 ft.

THORN, *see* CRATAEGUS

THUJA (Arbor-vitae)

This handsome and useful conifer, commonly known as arbor-vitae, has a slight similarity in looks to the Lawson cypress; its difference is that it has thicker foliage and a strong cedar-like aroma when the wood is bruised or broken. Thujas are best planted on moist, loamy soils, but I have seen them thrive in Sussex clay soils; they will also grow satisfactorily in chalk soils.

T. occidentalis (American Arbor-vitae)

This has greenish foliage in the summer, turning to a brown-rusty colour in the autumn and winter; it is not planted today so much as it used to be. This may be due to its brown-rusty appearance in winter, though to my mind this is pleasing. Best planting size is 2–3 ft. high, spaced at 1½–2 ft. apart, or for a screen spaced 5–10 ft. apart. Plant in late September to October, or March to April. Trim in late summer, and to obtain a thick hedge, trim plants in their early stages, but allow the top to reach its required height, as is done with *Chamaecyparis lawsoniana*. Propagation is by seed sown in March, or cuttings in September. Height 30–40 ft. as a screen, or as a hedge 5–12 ft.

T. plicata (syn. *T. lobbii*) (Giant Thuja, Western Red Cedar, Giant Cedar)

To call them cedars is wrong, to my way of thinking. This conifer was despised during the thirties on account of a fungus disease. But it is still planted, for when well grown and cared for, its dark, glossy green foliage makes a wonderful hedge or screen. It makes an excellent background for a tennis court. Best planting size is 1½–2 ft. high, spaced at 2–2½ ft. apart for a hedge, and 5–10 ft. apart for a screen. Trimming and propagation as for *T. occidentalis*. Height 50–60 ft. for a screen, 5–12 ft. for hedges.

T. p. atrovirens. Even though this cultivar of *T. plicata* has been known for at least 70 years, it has only recently appeared to become popular as a hedge plant: perhaps some of its popularity stems from a mention in *Amateur Gardening*, 27th March 1958. This conifer has also been known under the names of *T. stricta* and *T. pyramidalis*. The habit is upright but bushy; it is fairly rapid in growth and bright lustrous green. Best planting size is 1½–2 ft. high, spaced at 15–21 in. apart. Trimming and propagation as for *T. occidentalis*. Height 8–10 ft.

T.p. 'Zebrina'. The golden variegated form which requires the same treatment as *T. plicata*. Best planting size is 1½–2 ft. high, spaced 2–2½ ft. apart. Height 30–40 ft. for screens or 6–12 ft. for hedges.

THUJOPSIS

T. dolabrata (syn. *Thuja dolabrata*) (False Arbor-vitae)

This is a distinctive conifer, more suited as a screen tree or several specimen trees than as a hedge. It is pyramidal in habit; its branchlets are flattened and frond-like with dark, glossy green leaves above, and covered with a glaucous-white band beneath. It thrives in a good moist loamy soil. It does not like draughts and therefore it is not an ideal subject to plant by a windy corner. According to Mr. Williams of

Lanarth in Cornwall, *Thujopsis dolabrata* will grow under beech trees (quoted in *The Making of Lanarth*, by the late Bishop Hunkin of Truro, R.H.S. Journal, Vol. LXX, May 1954). Best planting size is 1½–3 ft. and spaced at 4–6 ft. apart. Plant in September to October, or March to April. Any trimming needed should be carried out in April. Propagate by seed in spring, or cuttings in September. Height 30–40 ft.

TILIA (Lime or Linden)

The lime or linden is a deciduous tree, perhaps best known for its sweetly-scented, yellowish-white blossoms during early July, which are much favoured by bees. Unfortunately the lime has a nasty habit of being attacked by aphids, and often trees will drop their sticky honey-dew. It also has attractive fruits which consist of five or more nutlets attached by a stalk to a papery bract. It is not normally used as a hedge shrub, but it makes a first-class screen or windbreak and is often used for pleaching. This is done by planting trees, usually lime trees, 8–12 ft. apart, their branches being trained horizontally along wires, bamboos or some similar form of support, to which the branches are tied. The trained trees need to be trimmed annually so that a hedge on stilts is created. This method of screening is particularly useful for small gardens, as it occupies little space laterally. A good example of a pleached screen planted and trained in recent years is one which surrounds a garden on three sides at the east end of St. Paul's Cathedral, London.

Limes are not fastidious as to soil; they will grow in chalk or non-chalk soils and thrive in towns, doing well in London and other smoky industrial cities.

Best planting size is young trees 6–8 ft. or 10–12 ft. high, spacing them 8–9 ft. apart or 16–20 ft. apart, according to requirements and how soon a screen is needed. Plant October to March. Trim during the winter as soon as the foliage is off the trees. Propagate by layers in late spring or early summer. Height varies from 40–80 ft.

T. cordata (The Small-leaved Lime)

This is slower growing than the rest and makes a useful screen tree. Height 40 ft.

293

T. × euchlora

This handsome tree is slightly pendulous in habit. Its rich glossy green leaves are paler beneath. Height seldom exceeds 50 ft.

T. × europaea (syn. *T. × vulgaris*) (Common Lime)

It has dark green foliage, pale beneath. Ideal for wind shelter or pleaching. Lime can make a useful hedge, and I understand that in Sweden it is not unusual to see lime hedges surrounding gardens. Plant from October to March, spacing them 1½ ft. apart. Trim in winter or early spring. Height, for a hedge, 10–15 ft. or more. Natural height 80 ft., but can easily be kept much smaller.

T. platyphyllos

This lime makes a large, handsome tree, having very large, dark green leaves, slightly downy above and very downy beneath. Yellowish-white blossoms in June. Height up to 100 ft.
T.p. 'Rubra' (syn. *T. corallina*) (Red-twigged Lime). The beauty of this lime is its brilliantly-coloured red branchlets in autumn and winter. Height 80 ft.

TRACHELOSPERMUM

T. asiaticum

An evergreen, and the hardiest of the trachelospermums. It is a vigorous and charming climbing shrub with oval leaves 1–2 in. long, which are a dark glossy green. The small, creamy-white fragrant flowers are similar in shape to those of vinca (periwinkle) which are freely produced on slender terminal cymes during July and August. It needs the protection of a south-west wall, also some form of support. It does best on an acid, clay or loamy soil. Plant from pots in spring. No pruning required. Propagate by cuttings of half-ripened shoots inserted in sandy soil in a warm propagating frame in July–August. Height 15 ft.

T. jasminoides (syn. *Rhyncospermum jasminoides*)

An evergreen, vigorous climbing shrub; though less hardy, again is satisfactory when grown against a south or west wall and support. The dark, glossy green, oval leathery leaves, tapering at each end, are $1\frac{1}{2}$–$3\frac{1}{2}$ in. long and $\frac{1}{2}$–1 in. wide and produced on slender stalked cymes on short lateral twigs. It enjoys a peaty soil. Stands up to salt spray. Other remarks as for *T. asiaticum*. Height 10–15 ft.

TRAVELLER'S JOY, *see Clematis vitalba*

TREE PURSLANE, *see* ATRIPLEX

TROPAEOLUM

T. majus (Common Nasturtium)

This half-hardy annual climber or ground cover plant, is almost too well known to need any description. The flowers are shaped like the miniature loud speakers of the early days of radio, each flower having a long rounded spur coming to a point. Their colours vary from yellow, orange, orange-scarlet, and scarlet to rich mahogany-red. Where a quick climber is needed this is the answer. Plant young seedlings out of doors in late May or early June. Propagate either by sowing seed under glass in March or later out of doors in April, where the plants are to flower.

T. speciosum (Flame Flower or Scotch Flame Flower)

This attractive hardy perennial, deciduous, climber or twiner, has five to six-lobed bright green leaves. The small, scarlet nasturtium flowers have an abruptly clawed spur. The plants have white fleshy roots, which look like those of bellbine—the white convolvulus—and they enjoy a cool leafy soil and a site where they can clamber through an old evergreen, such as yew, holly or a box tree. However, it is sometimes difficult to get plants started, but once the roots are established their long wiry shoots will clamber through the bush and produce the scarlet flowers in the sun. It does well on a north or east wall, where it can be trained on a trellis or wire netting. Plant in March or April. Propagate by division of the roots in April or by seed sown in March.

TSUGA (Hemlock Firs)

The hemlock firs are some of the most elegant conifers. In outline they are pyramidal, yet they have a sweeping or weeping habit, their slender branches being draped with small, fine leaves, which are dark green above and grey-green to glaucous-white beneath. I cannot remember ever having seen a tsuga hedge, but it is successful as such and, according to the late J. Coutts, is used extensively in Canada. Tsugas certainly make excellent hedges and screens, and the illustration (plate 27) shows a fine example of *T. heterophylla* in the far north of Scotland, where it is subjected to severe winds so Mr. Alan Mitchell tells me. They are best suited to moist, well-drained soils, and localities where the atmosphere is moist. Dry hungry soils are not suitable. As the hemlock dislikes hungry soils, it is as well to prepare the ground thoroughly before planting. Work in rotted manure or leafmould, and bonemeal at the rate of 4 oz. per sq. yd. In very dry weather a good watering followed by a mulch will be advantageous. *T. albertiana, see T. heterophylla.*

T. canadensis (Eastern Hemlock)

The foliage is green above, but its undersides give it a silvery appearance. This will grow on chalky soils. Other remarks as for *T. heterophylla.*

T. heterophylla (syn. *T. albertiana*) (Western Hemlock)

The leaves are dark green above, white-lined beneath. This is the best species for growing on chalky soils. Best planting size is $1\frac{1}{2}$–2 ft. high, spaced at $1\frac{1}{2}$ ft. apart for hedges. For screens the best size is 2–3 ft. and spaced 2–3 ft. apart, later thinned to 6–9 ft. apart. Little trimming is needed during the first two years, except to restrict straggly top or side growths. Until the hedge is fully established trim with a pair of secateurs, normally in April. Later on, a hedge may require clipping three times a year, in spring and early and late summer. Propagation is by seed in spring or cuttings in July in a hand sun frame, or cuttings in September, but these do not root so readily as the July ones. Height 70 ft.

ULEX

U. europaeus (Gorse or Furze)

Gorse is closely allied to the broom family. The spine-tipped shoots and foliage, which are dark green and more or less persistent, make gorse almost evergreen, and the golden-yellow flowers can be seen on bushes at almost any time of the year. No other shrub can make a better windbreak, for it will grow in the bleakest of localities, though it can be badly frosted in inland districts. Best planting size is young seedling plants, or older pot-grown plants. Space 15–21 in. apart, plant in autumn or spring. Trim after flowering. Propagation by seed sown out of doors in spring. Height 2–5 ft.

U.e. 'Plenus' (Double-flowered Gorse). This variety is more bushy in habit than the species, and makes a blaze of colour with its double, golden-yellow flowers from April to May. Unfortunately it does not produce seed; therefore it must be propagated by cuttings of the current year's growth in July and August. Insert cuttings in very sandy soil, or sand alone if time is no object, the reason being that they need what is known as a Paris frame, which necessitates spraying them several times throughout the day, especially during hot sunny days. No shading is given. Today, however, the propagator has the advantage of mist propagation. Height 4–5 ft.

U. minor (syn. *U. nanus*) (Dwarf Gorse)

This is an erect and compact growing shrub of dense, close habit. Its golden flowers are freely produced in September. It is ideal for a dwarf hedge or edging and can be used in a similar way to lavender. Its general treatment is the same as for other species and varieties of gorse. To keep it dwarf it needs to be grown in poor soils, when it will reach 1–2 ft.

ULMUS (Elm)

U. procera (syn. *U. campestris*) (English Elm)

This tree is perhaps too well known as part of the English countryside to require any description. It is deciduous and makes a very tall tree, up to 100 ft. high. It makes a good screen tree, especially for coastal shelter-belts, planted at 10 ft. apart. One does not see it used as a hedge nearly as much as it deserves. My first recollection of seeing it as a hedge was near my home at Lingfield in Surrey. Several hedges had arisen from the suckers at the base of tall trees. Here it was clipped regularly and formed a real thicket of a hedge. But the finest elm hedge I ever saw was near Chichester, Sussex. Elm, however, does not seem to mind how often or how severely it is trimmed, or when. It is not fussy with regard to soils. The planting size is 1½–2 ft. high, spaced 1–1¼ ft. apart and planted any time from October to March. Trim elms at any time of the year. Propagate either by seed sown out of doors in open beds or by suckers. Height 4–10 ft. as a hedge, screens 80 ft. or more.

It would be wrong of me not to mention the disastrous epidemic that has befallen our elms in the early 1970s. However, the Dutch breeders and nurserymen are endeavouring to breed and propagate disease-resistant clones, two of which are Bea Schwarz and Christine Buisman.

U. × sarniensis (syn. *U. carpinifolia sarniensis*, *U. wheatleyi*) (Guernsey or Jersey Elm)

A tree of stiff erect habit. Ideal as a screen, but not as a hedge. Best size for planting is young standards or feathered trees 10–12 ft. high, spaced 8–10 ft. apart. Plant from October to March. Propagate by grafting on to stocks of *U. glabra*. Height up to 80 ft.

VERBENA, LEMON, *see* **LIPPIA**

VERONICA, *see* **HEBE**

VIBURNUM

This is a large genus, with some evergreen but mostly deciduous shrubs. Most viburnums are grown as ornamental shrubs, though some are particularly useful as hedge or screen shrubs, and when grown in this way their flowers and fruits are pleasing. They are most suitable as informal hedges. Many of them enjoy a rich loamy soil, but they do equally well in a chalk soil. Two of them make excellent wall shrubs, *V. × burkwoodii* and *V. macrocephalum*.

V. × burkwoodii

A fairly vigorous evergreen, or almost evergreen, hybrid, being a cross between *V. carlesii* and *V. utile*. The oval foliage is dark green and glossy. It does not appear fussy in regard to soil and I have grown it against a fence in Sussex clay, where it has bloomed freely producing its

2½–3½ in. wide, sweetly scented flowers, which are pink in bud, opening white. Plant from October to March, preferably pot-grown plants. Prune after flowering as and when necessary, so as to keep the plant neat and tidy. Propagate by layers during the summer or by cuttings of half-ripened shoots inserted in sandy soil in a propagating frame in July–August. Height 8–10 ft.

V. farreri (syn. *V. fragrans*)

This makes an excellent hedge, so Frances Perry once told me, and a fine example of one grew at Enfield, Middlesex. The white and pink flowers are richly fragrant, having an almond-like scent, and it blooms from autumn and throughout the winter. Plant young bushes 15–18 in. apart, from October to March. Trim when necessary after flowering. Propagate by layering in the spring. Height 3–4 ft. for a hedge, 9–12 ft. for a screen.

V. lantana (Wayfaring Tree)

A deciduous shrub with rather rough, deep green leaves, oblong in shape. White flowers in May and June, followed by red fruit in autumn which eventually turns black. As this is a vigorously growing shrub it is ideal as a screen, though it can be used as a semi-formal hedge. Best planting size is about 3 ft. spaced 2–3 ft. apart. Plant from October to March. Trim during the winter. Propagate by seed sown in spring, or hard-wood cuttings in late autumn. Height up to 8 ft.

V. macrocephalum (Chinese Snowball Tree)

This is a semi-evergreen, a most handsome wall shrub, which I can well remember admiring on the inside wall of the alpine yard at the Royal Botanic Garden, Kew, during my student days. It has large dull green leaves 2–4 in. long and 1¼–2 in. wide. The hydrangea-like sterile flowers are in the form of an enormous globular truss 3–6 in. wide, in May. The individual sterile flowers are 1–1¾ in. wide. Plant in spring. Prune after flowering when any unwanted or worn-out shoots can be cut back. Propagate by half-ripe cuttings in June–July, inserted in sandy-peaty soil in a propagating frame. Height 12–20 ft.

V. opulus (Guelder Rose)

A hardy, deciduous shrub, well known for its flat bract-like white

299

flowers in early June, and bright red berries and attractive foliage in autumn. Even when bare of leaves its grey stems are a pleasing sight during the winter months. One sees *V. opulus* flourishing in moist clay soils as well as on the chalk downs. Best planting size is 3 ft., spaced 2–3 ft. apart. Plant October to March. Trim during the winter. Propagate by hard-wood cuttings of current year's growth in late autumn or winter. Height 8–10 ft. for a hedge, 10–15 ft. for a screen.

V.o. 'Sterile' (Snowball Tree). Hardy, deciduous flowering shrub, bearing white snowball-like blooms in June. There is a particularly fine planting of this viburnum on the Crawley by-pass in Sussex which makes a bank of white in June. Treat as *V. opulus*. Height 8–10 ft. for a hedge, 10–15 ft. for a screen.

V. rhytidophyllum

An evergreen flowering and berrying shrub. The dull yellowish-white flowers are produced in May or June, followed by red berries in autumn, which eventually turn black. It might well be called the elephant-leaved viburnum on account of its large, dark green, felted leaves. It is not a hedge shrub, but is excellent for a screen or windbreak. It thrives in heavy or light soils. Best planting size about 3 ft., spaced 3–4 ft. apart. Plant from October to March. Propagate by seed or by layering in spring. Height 10–20 ft.

V. tinus (Laurustinus)

This evergreen shrub is probably the best known of the viburnums, apart from the guelder rose. Its leaves are dark glossy green above, paler beneath. It has white flowers and pink stamens, which are produced throughout the winter and spring. In autumn there are deep blue fruits, which finally turn to black. It does well on chalk, or non-chalk soils, and makes an ideal seaside hedge, though it flourishes equally well inland. In Bournemouth and the surrounding district one sees laurustinus hedges and shrubs in many gardens. Best planting size is 1–1½ ft. high, spaced 1½ ft. apart. Plant in early autumn or spring. Trim in April. Propagate by cuttings in September, or layer in spring. Height 6–10 ft.

VINE, CROSS, *see* BIGNONIA

VINE, RUSSIAN, *see* POLYGONUM

VINE, SILK, *see* PERIPLOCA

VINE, TRUMPET, *see* CAMPSIS

VIRGINIA CREEPER, *see* PARTHENOCISSUS

VITIS (Vine)

The beauty of the ornamental vines is in their variety of foliage and in particular their brilliant colourings in autumn. Some of them, however, also bear pleasant edible fruits. All are excellent for covering walls, arbours, pergolas or for clambering over trees or outsize shrubs. Any good garden soil will suit vines, but they succeed best in a moderately rich, cool, loamy soil and one that has good drainage. The latter will certainly help good colouring in autumn which these vines are noted for. Poor soil should be enriched with well-rotted farmyard manure, or the best possible equivalent, such as well-rotted compost, plus bonemeal or a well balanced fertilizer. Rotted turf is also good, in fact anything that will help give a loamy effect. Plant pot-grown plants from November to March. Where plants are clambering over trees or over arbours, no pruning will be necessary, but if trained up poles or in a restricted area, young growths of the previous summer should be close pruned in early winter. During the growing season the ends of the shoots should be stopped two or three times.

Propagation is by 'eye' cuttings, inserted singly in small pots filled with a sandy compost and placed in a warm propagating case in early spring; or by half-ripened cuttings, 6–9 in. long, taken in early autumn and, again, inserted singly in pots and placed in a propagating case. Propagation is also by seed sown under glass in February or March, in a temperature of 50°–60° F. (10°–16° C.); or by layering the half-ripened growth during the summer months.

V. brevipedunculata, *see Ampelopsis brevipedunculata*

V. coignetiae

A most handsome and luxuriant deciduous, hardy climber introduced from Japan to France by Madame Coignet as long ago as 1875. This ornamental vine clings on by tendrils of which there is one at every third joint. The enormous three to five-lobed leaves are quite often 12 in. long and 10 in. wide, deeply heart-shaped at the base and narrowing at the apex. During the summer they are dark green above with a rusty brown felt beneath. This vine's glory is, however, in the autumn when the leaves are a rich warm crimson; as I write I have a pressed leaf in front of me which I keep in my set of Bean's *Trees and Shrubs Hardy in the British Isles*. The berries are black with a purple bloom and ½ in. wide. Height 60 ft. or more.

V. henryana, *see Parthenocissus henryana*

V. heterophylla, *see Ampelopsis brevipedunculata*

V. inconstans, *see Parthenocissus tricuspidata*

V. labrusca (Northern Fox Grape or Skunk Grape)

This vigorous, deciduous climber has thick-textured leaves, not as large as *V. coignetiae*, usually three-lobed and 3–7 in. wide and as long, being round or heart-shaped, dark green above, beneath at first whitish felt, later rusty-brown. There is a tendril at each joint. The flowers are sweetly scented, and are followed by purple or amber coloured berries with a foxy or musky aroma. Height 12–15 ft.

V. quinquefolia, *see Parthenocissus quinquefolia*

V. riparia (syns. *V. odoratissima* and *V. vulpina*) (Riverbank Grape)

A hardy, vigorous, deciduous climber, having thin leaves, three-lobed, 3–8 in. wide, glossy green on both surface. But what is so charming about this vine is the sweet, mignonette scented flowers during May and June, which are followed by purple-black berries, covered with blue bloom. Height 10–12 ft.

V. striata, *see Cissus striata*

V. thomsonii, *see Parthenocissus thomsonii*

V. vinifera 'Brandt'

A hardy, vigorous, deciduous vine—a variety of the common grape vine
—with large, green-lobed foliage which in autumn changes to brilliant
tints varying from yellow to orange through to rosy-crimson and
scarlet. Also blue-black berries of good flavour. Height 12 ft. or more in
Devon and Cornwall.

V.v. 'Purpurea' (Teinturier Grape, or Purple-leaved grape or the
Claret-vine). A hardy, deciduous climber. Its leaves, which are at first
claret-red, deepen later to a beautiful vinous-red, and finally turn to a
deep purple before falling. When planted on a warm, sunny wall, the
black berries will ripen.

WATTAKAKA

W. sinensis (syn. *Dregea sinensis*)

This climbing, deciduous shrub, which is not 100 per cent hardy, is included because it is very similar to hoya, and I therefore feel that where
a west wall is available it is well worth the room on account of its richly
scented flowers, 2–3 in. across, which are creamy-white with pinkish-red
spots, blooming in June and July. The first time I saw this climber was
at Wye College, Kent, in 1971. It is not worth risking growing it in unfavourable localities. This lovely climber does not appear to be fussy
over soils. Plant from pots in spring. Propagate by seed. Prune when
necessary after flowering. This usually consists of the removal of old
flower heads and thinning out unwanted shoots; this will help new
growth to develop for next year's flowering. Height 10 ft.

WAYFARING TREE, *see Viburnum lantana*

WEIGELA (syn. 'Diervilla')

An attractive deciduous, hardy flowering shrub, suitable for making an
informal hedge. Most weigelas (or diervillas, as they used to be called)

have fairly arching branches, with darkish green foliage, oval to oval-lanceolate in shape and pointed. The honeysuckle, trumpet-like flowers are freely produced from May to August. Weigelas thrive best in moist, loamy soils, though they will grow in almost any soil or situation, and are satisfactory in either sandy or chalk soils. The best planting size is 2–3 ft. in height, spaced at 2–3 ft. apart. Plant from October to March. Trim after flowering. Propagation is by cuttings of half-ripened wood in June to July or hard-wood cuttings in October. Height 6–9 ft.

W. florida

Deep rose flowers, May to June. Height 6–7 ft.

W.f. 'Variegata'. Silver variegated foliage, with strawberry-ice-pink flowers, May to June. Height 6–8 ft.

W. 'Abel Carrière. Carmine-rose flowers, ageing to red. May to June. Height 6–8 ft.

W. 'Bristol Ruby'. Free-flowering, bushy habit, red flowers, May to June. Height 6–8 ft.

W. 'Eva Rathke'. Deep crimson flowers, May to August. At first a rather slow grower, needs a heavy moist soil. Height 4–5 ft.

W. 'Styriaca'. Red in bud with deep rose-coloured blooms later, free-flowering, May to June. Height 6–8 ft.

W. 'Vanhouttei'. It makes a vigorous bush with arching branches, clear pink flowers, very free-flowering. May to June. Height 7–9 ft.

WHITEBEAM, *see* SORBUS

WILLOW, *see* SALIX

WINTER SWEET, *see* CHIMONANTHUS

WISTERIA

One of our most beautiful climbers. It is a vigorous deciduous climber introduced in 1816 and according to J. C. Loudon in *An Encyclopaedia of Trees and Shrubs* published in 1842, states that, 'A plant (at that time) in the Hort. Soc. Garden, against a wall, extends its branches above 100

ABOVE LEFT: an effective screen of *Stranvaesia davidiana*
ABOVE RIGHT: a bamboo screen or wind break of *Arundinaria nitida*
BELOW LEFT: Beech, *Fagus sylvatica*, has smooth, green leaves, which turn brown in autumn
BELOW RIGHT: Hornbeam, *Carpinus betulus*, has rougher foliage

Planting a hedge of the free-berrying holly, *Ilex* × *altaclarensis* 'J. C. van Tol'
ABOVE LEFT: correct planting depth and spacing
ABOVE RIGHT: filling in after planting
BELOW LEFT: forking up bottom of trench
BELOW RIGHT: firming after planting

ft. on each side of the main stem; one at Coughton Hall covers 905 superficial feet of walling.' He does, however, refer to it as wistaria, and it was indeed named after Dr. Wistar, but first incorrectly spelt wisteria, and therefore in accordance with botanical nomenclature must remain so. Since its introduction the wisteria has always been popular as a wall climber, also for pergolas and often to cover rustic bridges and fences beside water where its pendulous racemes can be reflected, such as can be seen at the Royal Horticultural Society's Garden, Wisley. It will grow freely in almost any aspect, though a south or west wall will encourage better ripening of the wood and help the next year's flowering wood. However, it should be remembered that the wisteria enjoys its share of moisture and appreciates a good rich loamy soil, though it will grow satisfactorily in other soils. It is a twiner and, on my neighbour's house, a specimen planted about 1908 has securely wound itself around the pillar of the front porch from whence my share of the climber comes; our houses face north. Beware of plants raised from seed as they take a long time to flower, anything from 10 to 15 years; so always buy a vegetatively propagated plant. The foliage is pinnate and varies from five to thirteen pairs of leaflets. The flowers are pea-shaped and vary from mauve, lilac, purplish-blue to violet and white, single and double. The seed pods are similar to those of the kidney bean, with a velvety covering, from 3–6 in. long. The wisteria, as I have said, likes good living, so before planting see that the ground is well prepared by incorporating some well-rotted manure or compost and bonemeal at 4 oz. per sq. yd. Plant from October to March ex pots. Some form of support will be needed around which the plant can twine. Prune in summer by pinching out the tips of all laterals or young shoots when they have made four to five leaves; this should be done at least four to five times throughout the summer. Then in winter when all foliage is off, prune back all side shoots to within two or three buds, leaving, of course, any shoots which are required to extend the plant further. If this is done annually plenty of flowers should be the result. Obviously where a plant is clambering through a tree this type of pruning will not be possible or practicable. Propagate by grafting named varieties on to the roots of *W. sinensis*, in March, in a heated propagating frame, or by half-ripened cuttings in August inserted in a propagating frame, or by layering out of doors in July. Seed can be sown in March. Height up to 100 ft.

W. floribunda (Japanese Wisteria)

A twining climber, heaving leaves 10–15 in. long; the dark purplish-

U   305

blue flowers appear in May and June and are borne in 3–5 in. long racemes on the previous year's wood.

W.f. 'Alba'. White flowers borne in racemes 1½–2 ft. long. May to June.

W.f. 'Macrobotrys' (syn. *W. multijuga*). This form is far superior to the species, having lilac flowers, tinged with bluish-purple, in May to June on racemes as much as 2–3 ft. long. On account of this it makes an ideal climber to grow on a trellis or bridge where its beautiful flowers can be reflected in the water.

W.f. 'Rosea'. The pale pink blossoms are lightly tipped with purple. May to June.

W.f. 'Violacea Plena'. This double flowered form has violet-blue flowers. May to June.

W. × formosa

This hybrid from America has pale violet-pink flowers on much shorter racemes, about 10 in. long.

W. sinensis (Chinese Wisteria)

This is the wisteria seen most frequently in gardens, trained on walls or over porches. The pleasantly fragrant flowers are deep mauve to heliotrope and borne on 6–12 in. long racemes, in May and June.

W.s. 'Alba'. White flowers May to June.

W.s. 'Plena'. Double mauve flowers in May to June.

W. venusta

Has pleasantly fragrant pure white flowers, longer than those of *W. sinensis* in May to June.

W.v. violacea. Has violet coloured flowers in May to June.

WOODBINE, *see* LONICERA

YEW, *see* TAXUS

8

Climbing and Screening Plants
at a Glance

Name	Dry or Sandy Soils	Clay or Damp Soils	Chalk Soils	Acid or Loamy Soils	Wind Hardy	Coastal Areas	Screening	Hedge	Wall or Fence	Climbing and Twining	Autumn Colour	Fruiting	Flowering	Semi-evergreen	Evergreen	Deciduous
Abelia floribunda	×		×						×				×	×		
A. grandiflora	×		×			×			×				×	×		
A. schumannii	×		×						×				×			×
Abeliophyllum distichum	×	×	×						×				×			×
Abutilon megapotamicum	×		×	×					×				×			×
A. vitifolium	×		×	×					×				×			×
Acer campestre	×	×	×	×		×	×	×			×	×	×			×
A. platanoides and varieties	×	×	×				×				×	×	×			×
A. pseudoplatanus and varieties	×	×	×		×	×	×				×	×	×			×
Actinidia arguta	×	×	×	×					×	×		×	×			×
A. chinensis	×	×	×	×					×	×		×	×			×
A. kolomikta	×	×	×	×					×	×						×
Akebia quinata				×					×	×		×	×	×		
A. trifoliata				×					×	×		×	×	×		
Alnus glutinosa		×			×		×	×			×		×			×
Ampelopsis brevipedunculata				×						×		×				×
A. sempervirens	×	×	×	×					×	×					×	
Arbutus unedo	×	×	×	×	×	×	×	×				×	×		×	
Aristolochia durior	×	×	×	×						×			×			×

Artemisia abrotanum

Arundinaria, see Bamboo

Asteranthera ovata

Atriplex halimus

Aucuba japonica

Azara serrata

Bamboo

Berberidopsis corallina

Berberis, species and varieties

Berchemia racemosa

Betula pendula

Bignonia capreolata

Buddleia davidii

B. d. nanhoensis

Bupleurum fruticosum

Buxus sempervirens

B. s. 'Suffruticosa'

Calluna vulgaris

Camellia japonica varieties

Campsis (all)

Caragana arborescens

Carpenteria californica

Carpinus betulus

Cassinia fulvida

Castanea sativa

Ceanothus delilianus and varieties

All other ceanothus

Celastrus orbiculatus

Table of shrubs and climbers (C. scandens – C. a. purpurea), cross‑referenced by Soils, Uses and Virtues. (× = applicable)

Name	Deciduous	Evergreen	Semi‑evergreen	Flowering	Fruiting	Autumn Colour	Climbing and Twining	Wall or Fence	Hedge	Screening	Coastal Areas	Wind Hardy	Acid or Loamy Soils	Chalk Soils	Clay or Damp Soils	Dry or Sandy Soils
C. scandens	×			×	×	×	×	×					×	×	×	×
Ceratostigma willmottianum	×			×		×			×		×			×	×	×
Chaenomeles (all)	×			×	×	×		×	×	×			×	×	×	×
Chamaecyparis (all)		×							×	×	×		×	×	×	
Chimonanthus praecox	×			×				×						×	×	×
Choisya ternata		×		×				×	×		×			×	×	×
Cissus		×												×	×	×
Cistus (all)		×		×				×	×		×		×	×		×
Clematis armandii varieties				×			×							×	×	
C. flammula, montana and *tangutica*							×	×								
Other species	×			×	×		×	×		×	×			×	×	
Clianthus puniceus	×		×	×	×		×	×		×				×	×	×
Cobaea scandens				×			×	×						×		
Cornus (all)	×			×	×	×			×	×	×		×	×	×	×
Corokia virgata		×		×	×				×				×	×	×	×
Coronilla glauca		×		×	×			×			×		×	×	×	×
Corylus avellana	×			×		×			×	×	×		×	×	×	×
C. a. purpurea	×			×		×			×	×			×	×	×	×

Plant												
Cotoneaster, some	x		x		x	x	x	x	x	x	x	x
Cotoneaster, others		x	x	x	x	x	x	x	x	x	x	x
Crataegus oxyacantha	x	x	x	x	x	x	x	x	x	x	x	x
Cryptomeria japonica elegans		x	x	x		x	x	x	x	x	x	x
Cucurbita (gourds), annuals	x	x	x	x								
Cupressocyparis leylandii		x	x	x		x	x	x	x	x	x	x
Cupressus macrocarpa and C. m. lutea		x	x	x		x	x	x	x	x	x	x
Cytisus (all)	x	x			x	x	x		x	x	x	x
Decumaria barbara	x	x	x	x	x	x	x	x	x	x	x	x
D. sinensis		x	x	x	x	x	x	x	x	x	x	x
Dendromecon rigida	x		x	x	x	x	x	x	x	x	x	x
Deutzia scabra	x		x	x	x	x	x	x	x	x	x	x
Eccremocarpus scaber		x	x		x	x	x	x	x	x	x	x
Ercilla volubilis		x	x	x	x	x	x	x	x	x	x	x
Erica arborea		x	x		x	x	x	x	x	x	x	x
E. carnea		x	x		x	x	x	x	x	x	x	x
E. mediterranea		x	x		x	x	x	x	x	x	x	x
E. terminalis		x	x		x	x	x	x	x	x	x	x
E. vagans		x	x		x	x	x	x	x	x	x	x
Eriobotrya japonica		x	x		x	x	x	x	x	x	x	x
Escallonia (all)		x	x		x	x	x	x	x	x	x	x
Eucalyptus (all)		x	x		x	x	x	x	x	x	x	x
Euonymus europaeus	x		x	x	x		x	x	x	x	x	x
E. fortunei	x	x	x	x	x	x	x	x	x	x	x	x
E. japonicus and varieties	x	x	x	x	x	x	x	x	x	x	x	x
Fagus sylvatica	x		x	x	x	x	x	x	x	x	x	x

Comparison chart of climbers, wall shrubs and related plants, showing their virtues, uses and soil preferences. (Plant names as row labels; attribute categories as column headings.)

Name	Virtues						Uses						Soils			
	Deciduous	Evergreen	Semi-evergreen	Flowering	Fruiting	Autumn Colour	Climbing and Twining	Wall or Fence	Hedge	Screening	Coastal Areas	Wind Hardy	Acid or Loamy Soils	Chalk Soils	Clay or Damp Soils	Dry or Sandy Soils
Feijoa sellowiana		×		×				×					×		×	×
Ficus pumila		×					×	×					×		×	×
Forsythia intermedia and varieties	×			×		×		×	×	×	×		×	×	×	×
F. suspensa and varieties	×			×				×		×	×		×	×	×	×
Fraxinus excelsior	×					×				×	×		×	×	×	
Fremontodendron californicum			×	×				×			×	×		×		×
Fuchsia (all)	×			×					×	×	×		×	×	×	×
Garrya elliptica		×						×				×				
Griselinia littoralis		×		×	×				×	×	×		×	×	×	×
Hebe (shrubby veronicas)		×		×					×	×	×		×	×	×	×
Hedera (all)		×					×	×	×	×		×				
Hibiscus syriacus and varieties	×			×					×	×	×		×	×	×	×
Hippophae rhamnoides	×			×	×				×	×	×	×	×	×	×	×
Holboellia coriacea		×		×	×		×	×			×		×	×	×	×
H. latifolia		×		×	×		×	×			×		×	×	×	×
Humulus japonicus	×			×	×		×						×	×	×	×
H. lupulus	×			×	×		×						×	×	×	×

Table continued (column headers appear on the facing page). Plant entries with presence marks (×):

Plant	1	2	3	4	5	6	7	8	9	10	11	12	13	14	15	16	17
Hydrangea anomala	×	×	×	×				×					×	×	×	×	×
H. macrophylla	×	×	×	×				×				×		×	×	×	×
H. petiolaris	×	×	×	×				×				×		×	×	×	×
Hypericum	×		×	×	×			×	×					×	×	×	×
Hyssopus officinalis				×			×	×							×	×	×
Ilex (all)	×			×				×		×			×	×	×	×	×
Itea ilicifolia	×			×					×				×	×	×	×	×
Jasminum beesianum	×		×	×	×	×		×	×	×			×	×	×	×	×
J. nudiflorum	×			×	×	×		×	×	×			×	×	×	×	×
J. officinale		×	×	×		×		×	×	×			×	×	×	×	×
J. polyanthum	×	×	×	×		×		×	×	×			×	×	×	×	×
J. primulinum	×	×	×	×		×		×	×	×			×	×	×	×	×
J. stephanense	×		×	×				×	×	×			×	×	×	×	×
Juniperus (all)		×							×	×	×	×		×	×	×	×
Kadsura japonica	×		×	×	×	×		×	×	×			×	×	×	×	×
Kerria japonica	×			×	×				×	×	×		×	×	×	×	×
K. j. pleniflora	×			×	×				×	×	×		×	×	×	×	×
Laburnum	×			×				×	×	×	×		×	×	×	×	×
Lapageria rosea	×	×		×	×			×	×	×	×		×		×	×	×
Lardizabala biternata	×	×	×	×	×			×	×	×	×		×		×	×	×
Larix decidua	×		×	×		×		×	×	×	×		×	×	×	×	×
Lathyrus (all)	×		×	×					×				×	×	×	×	×
Laurus nobilis	×	×		×	×	×			×	×	×	×	×		×	×	×
Lavandula (all)		×		×					×	×	×		×		×	×	×
Leycesteria formosa	×	×	×	×	×	×			×	×	×		×		×	×	×
Ligustrum delavayanum	×			×	×	×		×							×	×	×

Name	Dry or Sandy Soils	Clay or Damp Soils	Chalk Soils	Acid or Loamy Soils	Wind Hardy	Coastal Areas	Screening	Hedge	Wall or Fence	Climbing and Twining	Autumn Colour	Fruiting	Flowering	Semi-evergreen	Evergreen	Deciduous
		Soils					Uses						Virtues			
L. ovalifolium	×	×	×	×	×	×	×	×				×	×	×		
L. vulgare	×	×	×	×	×	×	×	×			×	×	×			×
Lippia citriodora	×		×	×					×							×
Lonicera, climbing forms	×	×	×	×		×			×	×		×	×			×
L. nitida and its varieties	×	×	×	×	×	×	×	×							×	
Lycium chinense	×	×	×	×		×	×	×	×	×		×	×			×
Magnolia grandiflora	×	×		×			×		×				×		×	
M. soulangeana	×	×	×	×			×	×					×			×
Mahonia aquifolium	×	×	×	×			×	×	×		×	×	×		×	
M. pinnata	×	×	×	×			×	×	×		×	×	×		×	
Mandevilla suaveolens				×					×	×		×	×			×
Menispermum canadense		×							×	×			×			×
Metasequoia glyptostroboides		×		×			×				×					×
Muehlenbeckia complexa	×	×	×	×					×	×			×			×
Mutisia (all)	×	×		×		×	×	×		×			×		×	
Myrtus (all)	×	×	×	×		×	×	×					×		×	
Nothofagus obliqua		×	×	×			×	×			×					×

Species	1	2	3	4	5	6	7	8	9	10	11	12	13	14	15	16
Olearia (all)	x	x	x	x				x	x	x	x		x	x	x	x
Osmanthus delavayi	x	x	x	x				x	x	x	x	x	x	x	x	x
O. heterophyllus	x	x	x	x				x	x	x		x	x	x	x	x
Osmarea burkwoodii	x	x	x	x				x	x			x	x	x	x	x
Osmoronia cerasiformis	x			x	x			x				x	x		x	x
Parthenocissus (all)	x	x	x		x		x	x		x	x		x	x	x	x
Passiflora caerulea	x	x	x	x		x	x	x		x	x	x	x	x	x	x
Periploca graeca	x	x	x	x		x	x	x				x	x	x	x	x
Pernettya mucronata	x		x	x				x	x		x		x	x	x	x
Perovskia atriplicifolia	x		x	x				x	x		x		x	x	x	x
Pharbitis purpurea	x			x			x						x		x	x
Philadelphus (all)	x			x				x	x	x		x	x	x	x	x
Phillyrea angustifolia	x	x		x			x	x	x	x	x	x	x	x	x	x
Phyllostachys, see Bamboo																
Picea abies	x	x					x	x	x				x	x	x	x
P. omorika, P. sitchensis	x	x					x	x	x		x		x	x	x	x
Pileostegia viburnoides	x	x		x		x	x			x		x	x	x	x	x
Pinus (all)	x	x					x	x	x		x		x	x	x	x
Piptanthus laburnifolius	x	x	x	x			x	x	x	x			x	x	x	x
Pittosporum (all)	x	x						x	x	x	x		x	x	x	x
Podocarpus andinus	x	x						x	x	x	x		x	x	x	x
Polygonum baldschuanicum	x	x	x		x		x	x	x			x	x	x	x	x
Poncirus trifoliata	x	x		x				x		x			x	x	x	x
Populus (all)	x	x	x	x				x	x		x		x	x	x	x
Potentilla fruticosa and varieties	x	x	x	x				x	x	x	x	x	x	x	x	x
Prunus	x	x	x	x				x	x	x		x	x	x	x	x
P. laurocerasus	x	x	x	x				x	x	x	x		x	x	x	x
P. lusitanica	x	x	x					x	x	x			x	x	x	x
Pseudotsuga menziesii	x	x						x	x	x	x		x	x	x	x

Group		Punica granatum	Pyracantha (all)	Quercus cerris	Q. ilex	Q. robur	Rhododendron luteum	R. ponticum	R. praecox	Ribes aureum	R. laurifolium	R. sanguineum	R. speciosum	Rosa	Rosmarinus officinalis	Rubus flagelliflorus	R. henryi	R. h. bambusarum
Soils	Dry or Sandy Soils	×	×	×	×	×	×	×	×	×	×	×	×	×	×	×	×	×
	Clay or Damp Soils	×	×	×	×	×	×	×	×	×	×	×	×	×	×	×	×	×
	Chalk Soils		×	×	×						×	×	×	×	×	×	×	×
	Acid or Loamy Soils	×	×	×	×	×	×	×	×	×	×	×			×	×	×	×
Uses	Wind Hardy				×			×				×						
	Coastal Areas		×	×	×			×			×			×	×			
	Screening		×	×	×	×	×	×	×		×			×				
	Hedge		×	×	×	×	×	×	×	×	×			×	×			
	Wall or Fence	×	×								×		×	×		×	×	×
	Climbing and Twining												×			×	×	×
Virtues	Autumn Colour						×			×		×						
	Fruiting	×	×									×		×		×	×	
	Flowering	×	×				×	×	×	×	×	×	×	×	×	×	×	×
	Semi-evergreen								×				×					×
	Evergreen		×		×			×			×				×	×	×	
	Deciduous	×		×		×	×			×		×		×				

Species														
R. lambertianus	x					x	x					x	x	x x x x x
R. phoenicolasius		x x			x x						x x	x x x x x
R. tricolor			x			x							x	x x x x x
Ruscus aculeatus	x x		x		x					x		x x	x x x x x
Ruta graveolens	x x		x			x					x	x x	x x x x x
Salix (all)	x x			x	x	x		x	x	x	x	x x	x x x x
Sambucus nigra	x x		x	x		x	x x	x x		x	x	x x	x x x x x
Santolina chamaecyparissus		x	x		x		x		x		x x	x x x x x
S. virens		x	x		x		x	x			x	x x	x x x x x
Sarcococca hookerana	x	x		x	x						x	x x	x x x
Schisandra (all)	x		x	x	x	x x				x	x	x x	x x x x x
Schizophragma hydrangioides	x		x	x	x	x x	x	x		x x	x x	x x x x x
S. integrifolium	x		x	x		x	x			x x	x x	x x x x x
Senecio greyi	x		x	x	x		x	x		x	x x	x x x x x
S. rotundifolius	x		x	x x	x		x			x	x x	x x x x x
S. scandens	x		x		x	x				x	x x	x x x x x
Sinofranchetia chinensis	x	x	x		x x			x		x	x x	x x x x x
Skimmia japonica	x		x x	x	x x	x			x	x	x x	x x x x x
Smilax rotundifolia	x	x x	x	x	x x	x				x x	x x	x x x x x
Solanum (all)		x	x		x		x x		x		x	x x	x x x x x
Sophora tetraptera	x		x	x	x			x		x	x	x x	x x x x x
Sorbus (most)	x		x	x	x			x x	x x		x x	x x	x x x x x
Spartium junceum	x		x		x		x			x	x x	x x x x x
Spiraea	x		x	x	x	x				x	x x	x x x x x
Stauntonia hexaphylla		x	x		x	x		x			x x	x x x x x
Stranvaesia davidiana	x x	x	x	x x	x					x	x x	x x x x x
Symphoricarpos (all)	x		x	x x	x		x			x	x x	x x x x x
Syringa (all)	x		x	x	x		x	x		x	x x	x x x x x

Category	Characteristic	Tamarix gallica	T. pentandra	T. tetrandra	Taxus baccata	Teucrium fruticans	Thuja occidentalis	T. plicata	Thujopsis dolobrata	Tilia (all)	Trachelospermum asiaticum	Tropaeolum	Tsuga canadensis	T. heterophylla	Ulex europaeus	Ulmus (all)	Viburnum burkwoodii	V. lantana
Soils	Dry or Sandy Soils	×	×	×	×	×	×	×		×	×	×	×	×	×	×	×	×
Soils	Clay or Damp Soils	×	×	×	×		×	×	×	×	×	×	×		×	×	×	×
Soils	Chalk Soils	×	×	×	×	×	×	×		×				×	×	×	×	×
Soils	Acid or Loamy Soils	×	×	×	×		×	×	×	×	×	×	×		×	×	×	×
Uses	Wind Hardy	×	×	×	×										×	×		
Uses	Coastal Areas	×	×	×	×	×						×			×	×		
Uses	Screening	×	×	×	×		×	×	×	×			×	×	×	×		×
Uses	Hedge	×	×	×	×	×	×	×	×				×	×	×	×		×
Uses	Wall or Fence					×					×						×	
Uses	Climbing and Twining										×	×						
Virtues	Autumn Colour									×						×		×
Virtues	Fruiting									×						×		×
Virtues	Flowering	×	×	×		×				×	×	×			×	×	×	×
Virtues	Semi-evergreen																×	
Virtues	Evergreen				×	×	×	×	×		×		×	×	×		×	
Virtues	Deciduous	×	×	×						×		×				×		×

	1	2	3	4	5	6	7	8	9	10	11	12	13	14
V. macrocephalum	×	×	×	×	×				×					×
V. opulus	×	×	×	×		×		×		×	×	×		
V. rhytidophyllum	×	×	×	×			×				×	×		
V. tinus	×	×	×	×		×	×	×		×		×		
Vitis coignetiae	×	×	×	×					×					×
V. labrusca	×	×	×	×					×	×	×	×		×
V. riparia	×	×	×	×					×	×	×	×		×
V. vinifera Brandt	×	×	×	×					×	×	×			×
V. v. 'Purpurea'	×	×	×	×		×			×	×	×			×
Wattakaka sinensis	×	×	×	×					×	×				×
Weigela (all)	×	×	×	×							×	×		×
Wisteria (all)	×	×	×	×					×	×				×

Varieties of Climbing and Rambling Roses	Arches and Pergolas	Fences, Open	Pillars	Walls and Close Fences	Walls and S.E. East N.N. East	Walls South or West	Repeat Flowering
Albéric Barbier	x	x					
Albertine	x	x	x	x			
Allen Chandler					x		
Aloha			x				
American Pillar	x	x					
Casino			x				x
Chaplin's Pink Climber	x	x	x				
Clair Martin		x	x				
Copenhagen			x				
Coral Dawn			x				
Crimson Conquest	x		x				
Crimson Shower	x						
Danse du Feu		x	x	x	x		x
Dorothy Perkins	x						
Dortmund			x				
Emily Gray	x	x		x		x	
Ena Harkness (Clg.)			x	x		x	
Etoile de Holland (Clg.)	x			x	x		
Excelsa	x		x				
François Juranville	x		x				
Golden Dawn (Clg.)						x	
Golden Showers			x				x
Goldilocks (Clg.)			x			x	
Grus an Teplitz					x		x
Guinée			x		x		
Handel			x	x			x
Hamburger Phoenix		x	x				
High Noon			x				x
Hugh Dickson	x			x	x		

Varieties of Climbing and Rambling Roses	Arches and Pergolas	Fences, Open	Pillars	Walls and Close Fences	Walls and S.E. East N.N. East	Walls South or West	Repeat Flowering
Lady Hillingdon (Clg.)						x	
Lady Sylvia (Clg.)						x	
Leverkeusen			x	x			x
Maigold			x	x	x		x
Meg	x	x	x				x
Mermaid				x		x	x
Minnehaha	x						
Mme Alfred Carrière				x	x		x
Mme Caroline Testout (Clg.)	x		x		x		
Mme Edouard Herriot (Clg.)			x			x	
Mme Grégoire Staechelin	x				x	x	
Mrs. Sam McGredy (Clg.)				x		x	x
New Dawn	x	x	x				x
Parade			x				x
Parkdirektor Riggers			x	x	x		x
Paul's Lemon Pillar			x	x	x		
Paul's Scarlet Climber	x	x	x				
Pink Perpetué	x		x	x			x
Purity	x		x				
Ritter von Barmstede			x				x
Royal Gold			x	x		x	x
Sander's White	x	x	x				
Shot Silk (Clg.)			x	x		x	x
Soldier Boy			x				x
Veilchenblau	x	x					
Violette	x	x					
Zéphirine Drouhin	x	x	x				x
Zweibrucken		x	x				x

Index

As the shrubs and trees suitable for climbing and screening plants are listed in alphabetical order in Chapter 7, pages 121–306, they have not been included in this index.